The Dream Warrior

The Dream Warrior

◆

A Viet Nam War Veteran's Memoir

Written by:

Anthony J. Chibbaro

iUniverse, Inc.
New York Bloomington Shanghai

The Dream Warrior
A Viet Nam War Veteran's Memoir

Copyright © 2008 by Anthony Joseph Chibbaro

All rights reserved. No part of this book may be used or reproduced by any means, graphic, electronic, or mechanical, including photocopying, recording, taping or by any information storage retrieval system without the written permission of the publisher except in the case of brief quotations embodied in critical articles and reviews.

iUniverse books may be ordered through booksellers or by contacting:

iUniverse
1663 Liberty Drive
Bloomington, IN 47403
www.iuniverse.com
1-800-Authors (1-800-288-4677)

Because of the dynamic nature of the Internet, any Web addresses or links contained in this book may have changed since publication and may no longer be valid.

The views expressed in this work are solely those of the author and do not necessarily reflect the views of the publisher, and the publisher hereby disclaims any responsibility for them.

ISBN: 978-0-595-51712-1 (pbk)
ISBN: 978-0-595-50569-2 (cloth)
ISBN: 978-0-595-62002-9 (ebk)

Printed in the United States of America

This is the story of a Navy Viet Nam War veteran's existence as a **"Warrior"** and as a **"Hero"** in "another dimension of time and space"—as **"The Dream Warrior"**. And it asks the question—"what are the thoughts and the feelings of other war veterans, and men in general, and how do they handle them?"

For my Son and for my Daughter whom I love more than they could ever imagine despite, at times, my appearing to be as harsh as 'Bull Durham' in 'The Great Santini.' I love them as high as the sky and deep as the ocean.

For my Granddaughter and very special Princess whom I love as high as the sky and deep as the ocean. She encouraged me to finally finish writing my book.

For my three Grandsons whom I love as high as the sky and deep as the ocean—may they <u>never</u> be 'warriors' and may they <u>never</u> experience the horrors of war—and for their Mother, my Daughter-in-Law whom I love just as much.

For the memory of Ron Tardio, the Navy pilot, who saved my life (he died), and for the memory of all of the 44 Officers and Sailors who lost their lives due to the tragic fire aboard the USS Oriskany CVA-34 (an attack aircraft carrier) that occurred off the coast of North Viet Nam on 26 October 1966.

For the memory of my Father—we shared too few years together.

"He has no home other than the memories of what his dreams might have meant if any of them had ever come true"—said of 'Ethan Edwards'—the John Wayne character in the movie—'The Searchers'—and it could possibly be said of our Warrior.

As I climbed onto the flight deck and looked back, all I could see were the flames and smoke that engulfed the ship. Fellow officers and sailors were scrambling around on the flight deck of the aircraft carrier, some manning hoses to assist in the fighting of the fire that endangered the ship. Others were simply walking about the flight deck dazed and numb and somewhat confused. None of us knew what had happened. All we knew is that the ship was on fire. All 3300 of us aboard the ship were now in very serious danger as was our ship.

I looked at the ships that surrounded us in the Gulf of Tonkin. The USS Constellation and the USS Franklin D. Roosevelt, the other two aircraft carriers in the Gulf were steaming close to us to assist us. The plane guard destroyers were steaming even closer to us. All flight operations were suspended. For one terrible and frightful morning the Navy's war against North Viet Nam had stopped.

Although I had heard the alarm "fire, fire", I had no idea where the fire was, how it had started—what I did know is that our ship was on fire and it looked to be extremely serious. I could see the flames shooting out from the starboard side of the ship but I had no idea what had caused the fire. We were on fire off the coast of North Viet Nam. I wondered if our 'enemy' was watching us in flames from the shore? What were they thinking as they watched us?

I could not believe that this was happening to us. My first thought was that I was going to die. The second thought that I had was maybe I should have taken the medical discharge that the Navy had offered to me in 1965. I became dazed and numb after that. What the heck had happened to us just minutes before we were to launch our first planes? Would we put the fire out? I wondered if we would have to abandon ship? Would the 'Mighty O', the USS Oriskany (CVA-34) have to be scuttled as had the USS Lexington was during WWII?

Like so many others on the flight deck, I grabbed onto to a hose and held it for the rest of the morning that it took the crew to extinguish the fire. The ship was saved—just barely! I had looked around for Ron and for the other junior officers from the junior officers' bunkroom, but I didn't see any of them on the flight deck. Since Ron had left the bunkroom long before me I had supposed that he was okay. I wondered why I didn't see him?

It was only later that afternoon while eating K-rations that all of us found out that 44 fellow officers and sailors had died in the fire. I was shocked to learn that

Ron had been one of the casualties. We lost four junior officers in the bunkroom. Four bodies of junior officers were found in the bunkroom. It could not be determined if they had left the bunkroom, or if they had sought refuge from the fire there?

The fire had started in a flare locker in the hangar deck and had swept forward through what was mostly officers' country—the staterooms of pilots and ship officers and the forward O-1 junior officers' bunkroom. That is why so many of the 44 who perished were officers. I knew most who died in the fire.

Sadly, the Oriskany was supposed to have been in Japan enjoying ten days of rest and relaxation the day that we caught fire. We had been extended on the line because the aircraft carrier that was due to relieve us out on the line had experienced mechanical problems. Instead of enjoying some 'R and R' we suffered death and destruction that day.

Why? Why did I not die in the fire aboard the USS Oriskany (CVA-34) that occurred on 26 October 1966 while the aircraft carrier was off the coast of North Viet Nam? Why did Ron, the A-4 pilot, who slept in the bunk below mine and who got me to get up, die in that fire while I was spared? The fire killed 44 of my fellow officers and sailors but not me? Why did they die and not me?

Why did I even turn down an offered medical discharge by the Navy for motion sickness in 1965 to remain in the Navy and to request duty aboard a West Coast aircraft carrier, which meant certain service in the Viet Nam War? Why did I make such a decision that very nearly cost me my life in that war?

Why am I the way that I am? What forces cause the way that I think, feel, act, and cause me to be the man that I am? Does a man have but one destiny? Do the stars—I am a Taurus—determine a man's life? Is a man dealt just one hand of cards for his life and is he forced to play that hand out no matter what?

How does a man handle his thoughts and feelings about the hand of cards for life that he is dealt? What survival mechanism does a man create for himself to escape the various tragic and challenging events of his life? This narrative memoir details my experiences as a young Naval Officer serving aboard the Oriskany in the Viet Nam War; surviving the fire; my vivid memories of that war experience and how those memories have haunted me for the past 41+ years.

As my survival mechanism I began escaping into a dream world in an attempt to avoid the painful memories of my war experiences. I developed the ability to shut down all of my emotions and feelings. I created the persona of a warrior. I began to exist in another dimension of time and space and in my dream world as a warrior and a hero. My night dreams and daydreams have increased in frequency and in intensity over the subsequent years. Have I lost the ability to distinguish between reality and my world of dreams? Was there a crossover from my dreams into my waking existence? What was happening to me? And so my story begins with the following vivid dream:

"NO ... DAMN ... no ... it can't be ... no!!" I cried out as I sat upright in my bed, dripping wet from perspiration, yet shaking from the icy chills that shook my body. I had turned the nightstand lamp on after feeling a wet gooey mess under my left arm, which had awakened me. It was more than the perspiration that soaked my bed sheets this night. It was red and it was blood. It was my blood from a deep gash on my left bicep. The blood had stained the bed sheets and the wound was still bleeding.

"No ... it just can't be." I repeated to myself as I wiped the blood from my arm. While not quite fully awake and still in a daze I somehow seemed to remember that it was a cut that I had received from my opponent's sword as it had glanced off my shield. I had blocked the thrust of my opponent's sword, but it did make contact with my left bicep, wounding me and leaving a deep gash. It had, wait, I couldn't remember anymore as to how I had suffered the injury and cut.

"Sword . . Shield . . No ... No." I cried out aloud to myself shattering the silence of the townhouse. My mind was in a muddled daze and I was very confused. Was it all just a dream? It did seem real and the memory of the dream was very vivid in my mind. I remembered it, didn't I? It had happened, didn't it? The gash in my left bicep was right where the sword had sliced at me. It was a deep gash and it was bleeding. And the blood that had soaked my bed sheets was indeed very real! Of course none of it made any sense to me. How could I suffer a real injury in a dream?

I looked at my alarm clock. It was 3:30 am. I felt really strange, really, really strange. Although my body was there in the bed, my mind was not quite there. I was trying to clear my mind while trying to make sense of the cut on my left arm. The sword and the shield had all been just a dream, hadn't they? This dream was not unlike other such dreams that I had been having for quite a few years now, although they were increasing in intensity over the past several months and they were becoming much more vivid than ever before. And now there was the cut on my arm and the blood. I had <u>not</u> ever awakened from such a dream to find that I was bleeding from an injury that I had suffered in that dream. It had to be some sort of coincidence—wasn't it?

"How the hell did I cut myself?" I asked out loud to myself as I was alone again this dark night. I was very irritated and frustrated over suffering a cut and not remembering how I had actually injured myself. It had to have happened during the night when I had gotten up to vomit—I told myself. I went to the bathroom, turned on the light, and opened a drawer looking for bandages to doctor my wound.

"Strange." I thought. There was no blood on the bathroom floor. I checked the sharp edges of the vanity. There was no evidence of blood there. I was certain that I had cut myself accidentally on the sharp bathroom vanity edges, perhaps as I had sunk to the floor to vomit. I'd had too much to drink the night before which was very rare for me. Although in my younger days I had the capacity for drinking large amounts of alcohol without showing any visible affect, now I was quite the infrequent and very moderate drinker of alcohol. The wine I drank last night did help to dull my emotional pain and my senses. But, wouldn't I have felt the sharp pain of such a deep cut? I'd had a lot to drink last night! It had made me sick to my stomach causing me to vomit during the night; that much I did remember.

"Hmmm." As my eyes and head cleared some, I realized that the toilet was to the left of the vanity with its sharp edges. If I had accidentally cut myself here, I would have a gash on my right arm and not on my left arm. And, there was no blood anywhere in the bathroom and none on the carpet leading to the bathroom. That was not the cause of my wound. At least I had not cut myself in this bathroom. I was even more confused, especially since I had gone to sleep in the back bedroom last night. I never slept in that bed. I was getting angry and very frustrated.

"Damn! It must have happened in the other bathroom." I said aloud to myself, although I wondered why I would have gone to the other bathroom to vomit when this one was closer to the bed in which I had slept last night? I wondered as I repeatedly asked of myself why I had even gone to bed in the back bedroom? Nothing made any sense to me.

I bandaged my left bicep the best that I could to stop the bleeding and then went to check out the other bathroom. I went to the front bedroom. Yes, the toilet in its bathroom was to the right of the vanity. Again I considered that I must have stumbled in the dark, and while falling to my knees to vomit, had cut my left bicep on the sharp edges of this vanity. But, there was no blood on the vanity or on the floor, no blood anywhere. The toilet bowl showed no indication that I had vomited in it. The bathroom even had a fresh clean smell—no odor of vomit. I had not vomited here nor had I cut myself in this bathroom. Turning around I looked at the bed—it had not been slept in, the bedspread had not been turned down, nor was it rumpled. I was in the front bedroom. And again there was no trail of blood on the carpet.

"Damn, what the hell is going on?" I shouted in frustration further stirring the stillness of my townhouse. I was getting quite angry and upset with myself. This was *my* bedroom. I always slept here because of the more comfortable queen size bed and because the only upstairs phone was in this front bedroom. Only when I had company did I sleep in the back bedroom with the double bed, a relic from my failed marriage. I looked down at the carpet—there was no blood on the carpet of either bedroom. The only blood was in the bed in which I had slept.

I quickly went to the other bedroom. I had indeed slept in the double bed in the back bedroom. It really made no sense to me at all, none of it! I had no idea of how I'd cut my arm or when? The cut was real. The blood was real. But that dream of being a gladiator in the area—wow—that could not be real, could it?

I washed my face as if it could clear my muddled mind and help me to remember what had happened. I rubbed my left bicep, as I softly patted the bandages I'd applied to the wound, wondering how did this happen?

"It was all just a dream, wasn't it?" I repeated to myself. The sword, the shield, my opponent's glancing blow, which cut my left arm—wasn't it just a dream? Yet the wound was real. And—as I tried to remember the dream—hadn't I been in training at the Gladiators' school? Hadn't I entered the arena along with my opponent, both of us bowed to the cheering crowd and then we faced each other to do battle. Hadn't I vanquished my opponent? No—it was just all a vivid dream—nothing more.

In the morning I'd remember how I had cut myself. For now I needed to get some rest and sleep. I closed all of the lights. I lay back in the double bed from which I had first gotten up, and the darkness enveloped me as I drifted off to a rare sound sleep. I sunk into the black darkness of my dream world—into that other dimension of time and space into which I often escaped. The year was 1992 yet my dream had taken me back to the time of the Roman Empire and to a time when gladiators met and fought in the arena. My dream had also allowed me to momentarily escape the painful memories of my experiences of having served in the Viet Nam War and of having nearly died in the Oriskany fire.

> **"A dream is an experience the soul has while we are asleep"**
> —Edgar Cayce

The arena; my sword; my shield; the glancing blow off the shield from my opponent's sword that slashed my left bicep; wasn't it just another dream? Something just seemed different about this dream—very, very different. I wasn't sure what it was and I was disturbed by it. Somehow this dream of being a gladiator in the arena had reached deeper into my subconscious, or, did it arise from my own mind? It was just a dream—wasn't it—just a dream? Had it arisen from one of my daydreams of being a gladiator? Of course I had never awakened from such a daydream or a night dream with a real injury. The gash on my left bicep was most real! The bloody sheet was real. Was there some connection between my daydreams and last night's dream? Yes, questions do get redundant when there are no answers to them! Again, that is why so many are repeated herein because I cannot find answers to them.

    I got out of bed. It was time for me to do some exercises, then to get out to jog and walk. One of the benefits—if there were any real benefit of being out of work—was that it allowed me the time to get myself into good physical shape and condition. While I am no health nut I do try to maintain myself in some semblance of physical conditioning by exercise, jogging, and walking most days.

    It had been at a meeting in Rochester in 1985 while I was still with Xerox that a manager and friend had remarked to me that I "was getting fat." I took that observation and comment to heart and when I returned home I bought a pair of running shoes and had been jogging/walking ever since. As of the writing of this memoir (it is now the year 2007) I've been at it on and off for 22 years and I hope to continue jogging/walking for the rest of my life. After all, wasn't Marv Levy the former head football coach of the Buffalo Bills now jogging three miles per day for five days per week at his age of 80! I am very thankful for the comment that had put me on the path of such exercise. Individuals like Levy give me something for which to strive, as I get older.

    The dream was still vivid in my mind, and, I had not answered the question of how I had injured my left bicep? I dismissed it all from my mind. It was time to exercise, then to jog and walk, and then later to concentrate on my job search, as I'd been unemployed since having been downsized from Xerox in May 1992. I worked up a sweat doing push-ups, sit-ups, then, went out to jog and walk. I needed the exercise to relieve my mind of the terrible stress of being out of work. The exercise was good for my body and even better for my mind, plus I really enjoyed it.

    I had always enjoyed running. I had been on the high school track team as a freshman in high school. While a sophomore playing on the high school junior varsity football team as a running back at 130 pounds. I was the fastest guy on the team. No one had ever beaten me in the end of practices 100-yard sprints! The coach use to kid me about running—that he'd have to find some other form of punishment for me when he made the team run laps—I enjoyed running too much as evidenced by the smile on my face when I ran. I had very strong legs. When I played baseball I was always the center fielder because of my speed and ability to cover lots of outfield territory.

This day I was very alone and I felt the loneliness. I certainly felt the loss of companionship and sexual intimacy that marriage brought. I had never been and was not now promiscuous. I had grown up in a different era in which it was desired that a man marry a virgin. I had also gone to parochial schools for twelve years graduating from high school in 1959. I remembered one of my college professors in a lecture class in 1963 making the comment: "now every man wants to have a virgin for a wife on his wedding night and every woman wants her husband to have experience—now how can every husband be experienced if every woman is to be a virgin?" That was at a secular state university in the early 1960's. It was also a conservative state university in the South. It was the other USC. The girls were all expected to wear skirts or dresses at all times everywhere on campus and there were no coed dorms in those days. It was another time in America. The times they had changed greatly since then and not for the better!

I remember a joke that one of my football player friends had told me. It went something like this: "an old couple who had been married for 50 years had been sitting in rocking chairs on the porch of their house when the woman got up out of her chair and smacked the heck out of the husband knocking him out of his chair. The husband got back into his chair, turned to his wife, and asked her why did she hit him. She responded because he had been such a lousy lover all of their years of marriage. He rocked for a while and thought it over then he got up and went over to her and smacked the heck out of her knocking her out of her chair. As she got up she asked him why did he hit her. He responded to her that's for knowing the difference."

I have always stated that I would rather be able to point to one good woman and proudly say that she was the only woman with whom I'd had sex and that I was the only man with whom she'd had sex than to brag about having had sex with many woman. I'd always believed that love and marriage were forever. I'd always believed that faithfulness to one's marriage vows was imperative and that they should never ever be broken. To cheat on one's mate was an indication of a total lack of morals. I did not, could not and would not ever cheat. I was a Taurus and for me love was forever. Morals, principles, ideals, honor, ethics, integrity, and self-respect were all too important to me. It is very sad that wedding vows do get broken and couples do divorce. As the Country and Western song goes: "what's forever for when no one stays together?" Wasn't it true that:

"An ethical man knows that it is wrong to cheat, on his wife. A moral man would <u>not</u> cheat on his wife"

The vast majority of the boys with whom I had gone to parochial school thought and felt as I did. Only bad girls had sex while still in high school and good boys had no interest in them. It wasn't much different in college in the early 1960's. I really wasn't interested in using women—I had too much respect for the opposite sex. I have often laughed about Wilt Chamberlain who claimed to have had sex with 20,000 women. I wonder how many of them had been pretty; how many of them had even liked Wilt; had any of them ever even felt love for him; how many were prostitutes; and anyway what was the point of such conquests? I had no interest in such conquests. It all seemed meaningless to me and was perhaps an indication that something was lacking within a man or a woman to be so sexually promiscuous?

I knew men who had cheated on their wives. Some even bragged about having had affairs. There were those who ended up getting divorced while several stayed together although in a not so loving relationship. I knew men who after their divorces went on a sexual binge bedding down woman after woman. Heck my ex-wife had done much the same thing as she went on a sexual binge immediately after our separation and then continued after our divorce bedding down man after man; and then getting married and divorced many times with some very brief marriages. One such husband, before their marriage, had bragged that she "was the wildest woman he'd ever been with." That marriage lasted barely six weeks before it ended. Isn't it interesting how even wild sex is not enough to keep a man and a woman together in marriage for very long? Marriages based on lust and sex rather than on mutual devotion just do not last very long.

The statistic that everyone hears is that fifty percent of all marriages in America end in divorce. The marriages of couples marrying for the first time actually end one third of the time in divorce. Second, third, fourth marriages all end up in divorce at extremely higher rates. And then there are the individuals who are on their fifth, sixth, seventh, and even eighth marriage whose rate of divorce is astronomical. With each subsequent marriage the divorce rate increases significantly. One must wonder if those who go through serial marriages have ever been happy in any marriage? What even drives them to marry so many times? Are they never happy? Do they fear being alone?

"The number of sexual partners correlates with marital unhappiness—as the number of partners increases so does unhappiness"

"Love and marriage go together like the horse and carriage"—is how the Frank Sinatra song went! Interestingly, when God is the third partner in the marriage and when the couple prays together those marriages have a divorce rate of only one in one thousand. Wow! Could it be that when there is a spiritual connection as well as an emotional and physical connection between a man and a woman it is indicative that true love is present and their marriage endures? Could it be that when a man and a woman share values and value that true love and faithfulness to one's marriage vows are present and then the marriage lasts? Isn't that much more satisfying than whoring around? I have always thought so! There is the saying: "IF you've ever loved someone you will always love that person." It does take true love for a marriage to last. As Lou Christie sang: "every boy wants a girl who he can trust to the very end." Doesn't a girl want the same in a boy? A relationship without trust was doomed to failure. And trust once broken was damn difficult to mend. It was sort of like breaking a vase—all of the pieces could be glued together and the vase could again hold water but the cracks in the vase would always be visible. In the end cheating always ends a relationship.

As to what other men thought and felt about sexual exploitation and pursuits, it never did really matter much to me. IF other men got satisfaction in bedding down many women so be it for them. I liked my core moral beliefs and I adhered to them. I got satisfaction in being true to myself. It was the source of my inner strength. I did not have the ability to let my hair down nor to act wild and crazy. That just was not me—I just could <u>not</u> be any other way than the way that I was and for better or for worse I am stuck with the way that I am. Although there were times when I wished that I could be different—I just do not have it within me to be any different from the way that I am. While I had hoped that I would have had a marriage that would have lasted because love, value, and values had been shared—it just was not to be. I realized that <u>all</u> twelve years of my marriage had been a terrible lie! That deeply saddened me and shook me to my core.

While walking, I thought of the dream in which I had been a gladiator, in the arena. For a moment I felt an incredible intensity, a surge of primitive power and strength. The sword was real in my right hand and I could feel the weight of the shield in my left hand. I could smell the dust of the arena floor kicked up by my movements and that of my opponent. I could even hear the crowd yelling and screaming as though it was some athletic event in which no one was to be vanquished.

That dream had been all too real. I still could not determine how my left bicep was injured? Something about this dream deeply disturbed me—it had been very real in the deep recesses of my subconscious mind. Had it arisen from my subconscious mind, or had the memory of the dream sunk into my subconscious mind? I thought about the dream and asked of myself—what was real, and what was just a dream, and what had been merely imagined? It was a redundant thought and question that I have asked time and time again. There seemed to be a merging of dreams with reality and that was something for which I could not find an explanation. Could the dream have merely reflected the memory of an actual event that had taken place in some other life? Was I the reincarnation of some Roman gladiator?

The feeling had existed within me ever since boyhood that I belonged to another time; that I should have been born in an earlier century, perhaps in the Old West of the nineteenth century? Then there were times when I felt as though I had been with Alexander's army as they conquered the ancient world. It was an odd feeling that surfaced from time to time within my consciousness. From whence did such thoughts and feelings arise within me? Were my night dreams and my daydreams a matter of déjà vu all over again? Had I once upon another time been there and done that? Was I merely remembering and reliving past lives?

To relieve stress, I often wrote in my daily journals; expressing my thoughts and feelings; writing to no one in particular. I wondered if anyone would ever get to read my journals, or would I destroy them all sometime before I died? If they were left behind after I died; and if they were read; what would the reader think of me? What would my children think of me if they read what I wrote? Since "time does not shout, it just runs out"—at what point would I destroy my journals? Death does indeed come as a thief in the night and when least expected! Do I really want anyone to read what I had written and expressed in my journals?

My writings often spoke of the mental imaging I have used within my mind in order to help me survive the stress of the adversity, failures, heartbreak, aloneness, and even unanswered prayers from which I suffered. I wrote about existing in another dimension of time and space in which I was a warrior. In this other dimension, I imagined myself to be a gladiator, a knight, a gunfighter, a fighter pilot—always a warrior in battle and always a hero. I often wondered if other men wrote journals? Did other men express their thoughts and feelings in private journals as I do? What did other men do? What did other men, especially war veterans, think and feel and how did they handle the thoughts about their lives that came to their minds? How did other men escape stress? How did other war veterans escape the demons that were surely in their minds?

What about all of the other Viet Nam War veterans—what had been their thoughts and feelings all of these years since the end of that war? What kind of lives had they lived? Were they happy about how things had turned out for them in their life all of these years? Had others had many disappointments? Had others suffered from adversity, failures, aloneness, heartbreak, and unanswered prayers? How had other war veterans handled their thoughts and feelings as they had passed from youth to mid-life to old age? How did other war veterans deal with the thoughts about those they knew who died in war? How did other war veterans deal with the question: had they earned it? Had they led lives that had earned their being spared death in war while others died? As all war veterans and men in general reach the September of their years—do they look back at their lives with regret or satisfaction? How do they look back at their lives? How do they answer so many questions? I cannot seem to answer these questions for myself and it is why I wonder if other men have found answers to them?

I had recently—June 2007—watched a PBS TV program about several veterans of the Normandy invasion; men who had served in the Armed Forces and who were at Normandy on that fateful day on 6 June 1944. The men all went back to Normandy to visit the sites where they had served; Omaha Beach, etc., and they visited the memorial graveyard in which 9000 Americans are buried. Upon remembering their comrades who lost their lives in that war, these old men came to tears. The repressed memories of their experiences in WWII came to the surface and were all too vivid in their minds! It was as though they had been at the Normandy invasion just yesterday! They could still see the dead bodies of comrades floating in the water; broken bodies on the sandy beach; and they could still hear the cries and groans of fallen soldiers. The war memories never fade and they remain with a man until he dies. It does not take much for the pain and the hurt to be felt by war veterans, and for the tears to flow! Sadly, 1000 veterans of World War II die every day and with their deaths go the memories of their sacrifices and the memories of their fallen comrades.

Since I was unmarried and not in any relationship it was in my journals that I expressed my thoughts and my feelings. I did not have a wife with whom to share them. I did not have a soul mate. Yet, what about those men who were married, did they express and share their thoughts and feelings with their wife? Are not men somewhat private beings? I certainly have always been a very private man and in so many ways not connected to anyone. Do not most men withhold many of their thoughts and feelings? Don't <u>all</u> war veterans repress and suppress their thoughts and feelings about their war experiences? How do they handle their thoughts and feelings? How can they express themselves to any other than another war veteran who can relate to such experiences? Why do so many war veterans never discuss their experiences?

I have an older Cousin through marriage who had been one of the replacement Marines in Korea for those who had been lost in the Chosin Reservoir Campaign. In the fifty plus years that we've knew each other, my Cousin had seldom ever mentioned his experiences in the Korean War. Then one summer day just a couple of years ago this Cousin talked extensively about his war experiences, even telling how he and another Marine found themselves late at night in an enemy foxhole in a forward position that had been booby trapped with hand grenades, which was something that they did not discover until the next morning. Had they disturbed the grenades that night my Cousin and the other Marine would most likely been killed. While I had not experienced ground combat, as had my Cousin, we were both war veterans and we had that in common! We could relate to each other as only war veterans can!

What about their fears—do men express or share their fears with anyone? Do men ever admit that they are afraid of anything to anyone? Would a man ever admit to another man or to a woman, even to his wife, that he was afraid of anything? Sadly it seems that in their attempts at being fearless men sure do cut themselves off from all others and withdraw into themselves. Would a son ever express to his father that he was afraid? Would a father ever express to his son that he was afraid! I doubt it! How many wives have ever seen their husbands shed a tear? A Country and Western song asked: "do grown men cry?" And the answer to that question is that grown men indeed <u>do</u> cry but generally only in private. Yes, grown men do cry! Does God see their tears?

It was in my journals that I could write about how I often felt like just sitting on the floor and crying my heart out—something I could not and would not admit to anyone. I could write how there were times when I just felt like I would not be able to take the emotional pain of a broken heart and broken life for even another minute—again it was something I could not and would not admit to anyone. It was only in my journals that I would reflect on how I often felt like I should never have been born. I even wrote of the thought that I wished I had died aboard the Oriskany in its fire. That is how intense the pain was for me at times. It was unbearable! There were certain songs that when I heard them—well—they caused my eyes to fill with tears. There was such a deep sadness within me. I could write about it in my journals but not speak about it to anyone. While grown men may cry they do hide their tears. Men are very reluctant to express their thoughts and feelings to anyone—even to their wife. I sure failed to communicate with my wife while I was married. I often remarked, when asked how was I: "that I was okay and that it was important for a man to be okay even when things were not okay." Wasn't it a mask that I wore in order to hide how I really felt? Don't husbands hide most of their fears and even hurts from their wife? Men/husbands don't talk much! It certainly had been one of <u>my</u> major faults and failures within my own marriage. When the sales representatives that I managed asked me about my age I often answered that I: "was 1000 years old." What did I mean by such an answer? Despite the mask that I wore there were days in which I was overwhelmed by a deep sense of sadness. I hid it well most of the time.

Isn't one of the main causes of divorce a failure to communicate between husband and wife? More often than not isn't it the husband, the man, who fails to communicate? What is it about men that they remain so close mouthed? Is it fear itself that causes men to remain such private beings? I was of a generation, which admired the strong silent man who was self-reliant, independent, not afraid of anything, and who kept his thoughts, feelings, and fears to himself. Wasn't that the way a man was suppose to be? And wasn't that the way most men were in their marriage? A man was supposed to be the fearless leader and provider for his family. He was supposed to be able to handle any and all adversity. He was supposed to handle it all without showing any weakness or having to turn to anyone for help—wasn't he? Who was it that decided such a role for a man and a husband?

How many men in past generations thought of their wives as being their best friend? Didn't men consider some other man to be their best friend? And what of women—in past generations did any woman consider her husband to be her best friend? Why was it that in past generations a husband did not trust his wife to be his best friend and a wife did not trust her husband to be her best friend? Was it a lack of trust or was it a matter of that was just the way such relationships were supposed to be back then?

My Son remarked to me that he had: "married his best friend"—that he and his wife had been friends before they had even started dating. Wow! That is great! That is the way it should be for a husband and a wife today. Shouldn't they be lovers <u>and</u> friends? Perhaps relationships were changing for the better? I am very proud of my Son and very proud of my Daughter-in-Law. They indeed appear to be best friends, true helpmates, and mutually supportive of each other.

While going through my divorce, a friend of mine cautioned me to remain friends with my soon to be ex-wife. My Son who was only nine years of age at the time overheard the comment and remarked: "If mom and dad were friends they wouldn't be getting divorced." Wasn't that the truth! Friends try their best not to hurt each other. Friends remain friends through thick and thin. True friends don't get divorced. Of course friends do not cheat on each other and they do not lie to each other.

In my aloneness I often reflected on those times when I had actually been very successful but that I had no one with whom to share such success. I thought of a particular award trip in 1984 for outstanding sales performance that I had won while at Xerox. At the banquet dinner the main speaker remarked how the wives and husbands of the winners should also be congratulated and thanked for having helped and supported their spouses who had won the award trip. One of the single woman, an award winner like me, stood up and asked: "what about us single women and single men who had to do it all on our own?" In talking with her later, she expressed the sadness that she felt because she did not have anyone with whom to share her success. I had felt that same sadness. There were times when it really hurt to be alone.

> **"Success is most satisfying when you have someone you love to share it with"**

A few stories came to my mind as I rubbed my left bicep. I still wondered how I could have experienced such a wound. Could I have visualized the cut? Was my dream more of a mental visualization than a dream? All of these stories and incidents experienced by others came into my own mind as a potential explanation for what I was possibly doing to myself? Was I creating a reality through visualization? Could I actually cause a wound to myself?

There is the story of the experiment conducted with three groups of basketball players in an attempt to improve their foul shooting percentages of shots made versus those attempted. One group actually practiced shooting foul shots for 30 minutes per day for 30 days—their percentage of shots made improved. A second group did not practice at all—and as expected their percentage of shots made did not improve. A third group sat for 30 minutes per day for 30 days with their eyes closed while imagining and visualizing themselves shooting and making foul shots—their percentage of shots made improved as much as the first group that had actually practiced taking foul shots.

The technique was referred to as visualization. It is a technique that had actually been pioneered by the East German Olympic teams. Their athletes had competed very successfully in the Olympics, and they often won near as many gold medals as did the strong US and Russian Olympic teams. It involved practicing their events in the mind and imagining success in the event while programming the mind and body to repeat that visualized success on the field of competition. It worked!! Professional golfers, after making a bad shot, will generally go back and take another imaginary swing while visualizing that imagined shot to have been corrected and good. The idea is to have the mind remember the good shot in order to repeat it during the next round.

Many of the American POW's, during the Viet Nam war imagined and visualized their selves to be playing golf, or playing musical instruments while spending years in captivity. Once released, they were able to play golf with scores in the low 70's and 80's, or to actually play the musical instruments on which they had practiced playing in their minds. What they had imagined and visualized their doing successfully in their minds they were able to actually do once released from the infamous Hanoi Hilton. It is an excellent example of the power of visualization.

During his service in WWI, General Douglas MacArthur, often scouted the terrain up close near enemy positions—much like Confederate General Stonewall Jackson did during the Civil War—while constantly being exposed to enemy fire. He was never wounded despite bullets and rockets whirling all around him. Had his mind somehow visualized his safety and brought it about no matter what the danger was around him? He was the most decorated American soldier of WWI, very often exposing himself to danger, and yet he was never wounded by enemy fire. He repeated such boldness in WWII. For whatever reasons he was never afraid. Had it just been his fate and destiny not to ever be wounded in battle? Could his visualization and expectation that he would never be wounded or killed in battle have become his reality?

General George S. Patton believed that he had previously fought battles all throughout Europe during some previous life prior to his service in World War I and especially prior to WWII. He believed that he had been reincarnated—that he had been a warrior who had actually lived a past life or several past lives. He had also read of virtually every battle that had ever been fought in Europe. Had his mind played a trick on him? Could it have been that the memory of all that he had read then somehow became etched onto his subconscious mind to have been returned to his conscious mind as a memory and a belief that he had actually fought in all of those battles? Patton had a strong belief in reincarnation. Is it possible that he actually fought in those battles in some past life as he believed, or, had his memory of all that he read become an actual experience within his mind? Had Patton merely imagined that he had fought in various battles throughout Europe? It had all been real to him but had it actually taken place in another time in which he once lived?

Ironically nearly seventy five percent of the world does believe in reincarnation. Edgar Cayce—the sleeping prophet—and a devout Christian believed in reincarnation. Cayce read the Bible from cover to cover for 56 years in a row—from the age of eleven until his death at the age of sixty-seven. Although he was a devout Christian, Cayce believed that there were passages in the Bible that supported the concept of reincarnation. Could it be that my other dimensions of time and space into which I often escaped was merely the memory of my past lives? Had I once upon a time actually been a gladiator, a knight, a gunfighter, a fighter pilot as I imagined?

Obviously visualization with expectation can have a positive affect on a person but it can also have a negative affect on a person too. Sadly as one's mind creates the expectation of harm that expectation can become self-fulfilling. I remember one of the young pilots aboard the USS Oriskany who slept in the junior officers' bunkroom. This particular pilot had nightmares all during the night before his next mission over North Viet Nam. As I was leaving the bunkroom to go stand a watch I asked the pilot, who was just sitting in his bunk in sort of a daze, if he was okay? The pilot responded that he: "would probably get shot down that night." Sadly his plane did go down on his next mission and the young pilot was killed. Had the pilot visualized in his mind his own death? He expected to be killed and he was! Had his subconscious mind fulfilled his expectation of getting killed? Or was it just his destiny?

There was another incident during that 1966 deployment of the Oriskany that was similar. A pilot was in his plane at the catapult ready to take off for a mission over North Viet Nam. The pilot then asked not to be made to take off because he feared that: "his next catapult shot off the ship would not be good." He was an experienced Navy pilot with many combat missions. It was <u>not</u> combat that he feared. He was relieved of his duties and was to be sent back to the states. As the plane, which delivered mail and personnel to and from the ship, was catapulted off the carrier with this pilot aboard, the harness restraining him broke. He was thrown backward and he was very severely injured with major head trauma. It had been his next catapult shot off the aircraft carrier! It had nearly killed him. Had this pilot visualized such an accident and thus made the expectation of it self-fulfilling? Or was it just some coincidence that he was injured during his next catapult shot off of the aircraft carrier? Was it his fate?

Where is the line drawn between what is real and what is imagined?? What was real and what was imagined, and, how did the mind distinguish between the two? Can the mind tell the difference between a real and an imagined event? We've all heard the phrase that: "your perception is your reality." Do we truly create our reality out of the thoughts we have in our minds? Does that perception have the power to positively and negatively affect our lives? In the experiment with the basketball players trying to improve upon their foul shooting percentages, it appears that the minds of those who did the visualization did not distinguish between what was visualized and what they had practiced only in their minds. Despite only visualizing within their minds that they were practicing shooting foul shots, the scores improved for the one group who spent their time in visualization. Their positive expectation became their reality.

What about Generals MacArthur and Patton—had their subconscious minds controlled their realities and kept them safe in combat? What about the two Navy pilots on the Oriskany—had the subconscious mind of one caused him to be killed while the subconscious mind of the other caused him to be severely injured? Did thinking create a positive experience for some while creating a negative experience for others? Do our thoughts and especially the thoughts that we feed our subconscious minds create our reality? Do our lives play out as per our thoughts and expectations? Or do we merely fulfill each of our destinies that are predetermined for each of us?

People going through sales training generally practice role-playing as a function of their training. The idea is to create within the minds of sales representatives a successful experience that will be remembered out in the field. The concept of practice makes perfect is that practicing a skill leads to the later perfect execution of that skill. The Marine Corps basic training concept is one of repetition, repetition, repetition, and more repetition until the desired skill is so ingrained in one's mind that one does not have to think about doing it—that one just does it! One would not want to have to think before acting in combat! Thinking in combat could get a man killed! ALL military training is meant to program a soldier to act and not to think!

An example is what happened to me and to all of my classmates in my company at Naval Officer Candidate School upon our graduation and receiving commissions as officers. For sixteen plus weeks as officer candidates we were accustomed to saluting our company commander who was a lieutenant and to also saluting our company chief. As per Navy regulations it is the junior officer who extends the salute first and who holds his salute until the more senior officer extends his salute and then is the one who first breaks the salute. Here we all were newly commissioned officers and we saluted our company chief—much like in the movie 'Officer and a Gentleman'—and we all held our salute until the chief reminded us that he was now junior to us and that it was now our responsibility to first break the salute as being senior to him. Sixteen weeks of programming just did not get broken in one brief commissioning ceremony.

Although Navy OCS was not Annapolis, it was quite tough on the officer candidates. We got up at 0530 hours each morning; stood at daily inspection; marched everywhere, to classes, to the chow hall; etc. Although, unlike the Annapolis students, virtually all of us were already college graduates and post college age, the military indoctrination and academics were quite challenging. Then there was the constant fear that if we failed and busted out of OCS we would end up as an enlisted man, as a white hat instead of a commissioned officer. How would we explain that failure to our families? Many did fail and did not receive a commission. Unlike college there was no late night studying past lights out in the barracks.

The candidates stood watches; marched on Saturdays in a 'Pass in Review' ceremony—the sound of 'Anchors Aweigh' still puts a smile on my face! It was during a midnight watch that I learned a valuable lesson. I stood the watch with an upper classman. Upon returning from making my rounds I made a log entry: "all secure." The upper classman then asked me if I had checked behind all of the locked offices, which shared a part of 'Nimitz Hall' barracks. Of course I had not. I was then advised to make my next log entry to be more correct, that: "all <u>appeared</u> to be secure"—not only to cover myself but because it really was the correct log entry. The lesson was learned and has lasted a lifetime.

At Navy OCS all of the candidates learned a new language. A floor now became a deck; a wall became a bulkhead; a door became a hatch; the stairs were referred to as ladders; and of course one went to the head and not to the rest room. And then there was the chit—the correct form with the required signature. It was all an interesting and most memorable experience—and a great challenge.

I have constantly asked of myself: "why am I the way that I am?" Have my thoughts created me to be the way that I am? Have I visualized myself to be the way that I am? Has my mind created me to be as I am? Have all of the hours that I imagined myself to be a warrior, create me to be a warrior? Have I role-played myself into being a warrior in my dream world only to have such a role carryover into my waking world? In searching for answers to these questions I have often considered the following for how my thoughts; for how my conscious mind; and for how my subconscious mind have all shaped me.

Didn't role-playing prepare one for actual events by programming the mind for those events by imagining them first in the mind? I had had a career in sales—hadn't I role-played before many an important sales call? As a sales manager, hadn't I visualized in my mind and practiced in my mind how I would conduct an important sales meeting—preparing for every possible contingency and how I would respond by first imagining them in my mind? One of the reasons I was so controlled in various confrontations was that I had visualized and practiced such control in my mind. Wasn't the goal—in practicing, in repetition, in visualization, in imagining events—to imprint on the mind the successful execution of a particular skill? Where and what was the line drawn between what was imagined and what was real—could the mind tell the difference? Was there a difference?

Does the subconscious mind merely accept as real whatever the conscious mind feeds it? Can the subconscious mind tell the difference between what is real and what is imagined? IF the subconscious mind believes and accepts an event as being real, does it then become real in one's mind? We are told that the conscious mind is the gateway to the subconscious mind and we are warned to guard against allowing negative thoughts from entering our minds less they take hold in the subconscious and then affect us adversely. We are further warned that we move in the direction of our most dominant thoughts regardless of whether they are positive or negative.

How does the saying go: "your perception is your reality" fit into this? Don't people act as if? I relate the following stories because I am looking for an explanation of why I woke up from a dream with a cut on my left bicep? Did my mind create such a wound due to my thoughts? Could I have believed myself wounded by another gladiator in a dream and such a belief actually caused the wound? Did I do to myself what those in the following stories apparently did to themselves?

For example, there is the story of a man who had entered a railroad refrigerator boxcar; the door slammed shut behind him and locked; and he found himself to be trapped in that boxcar. The man thought and believed that the refrigeration was turned on in the boxcar. It was not. Acting as if the refrigeration was actually turned on, the man expected that he would freeze to death and indeed the man froze to death. Unknown to him the refrigeration was broken and the actual temperature in the boxcar never dropped below sixty degrees, which would not have caused him to freeze to death. The man acted as if the temperature in the boxcar got below freezing temperatures and his body responded by freezing to death. Wow! His belief became his reality. When workers opened the boxcar the next day and found his dead body they were mystified as to why he had died. He died because he expected to die.

What about people who are suffering from a life threatening illness? Some are given a placebo and told that the pill that they are given will cure them of their illness. With their belief that they are being cured, many are actually cured despite the fact that the placebo having been given to them had absolutely no curative powers. Again it is proof that attitudes are more important than facts and especially in the minds of those who are suffering from life threatening illnesses.

A prominent TV preacher told how his own Mother had been sent home to die from cancer in 1986, as her doctor gave her only weeks to live. The woman prayed daily; displayed pictures of her healthy and happy throughout her house; and every day repeated the mantra that she was being healed and that she was being restored to perfect health. She is still alive today in 2007 despite being told by her doctor in 1986 that she had only weeks to live. How does one account for such a 'miracle'?

What happens when a so-called curse is put on a person, especially a so-called 'voodoo' curse that threatens the person with death? IF the person believes in their mind that the curse will kill them, they generally will die. IF the person shakes it off as nothing, they will not be affected by the so-called curse. Whatever they believe and expect will happen to them is what will happen. As Dr. Wayne Dyer has said: "IF you believe it you will see it."

Paul Harvey in his 'now you know the rest of the story' radio broadcast several years ago told the following: Elvis Pressley was extremely close to his mother who had died around her age of 40. The story is told of when Elvis was in the Army serving in West Germany. In the middle of the night he and another soldier got lost in a terrible snowstorm while driving their jeep and inadvertently crossed the border into East Germany. Not wanting to be captured by the Communists they parked their jeep and left the engine running so as not to freeze. Both Elvis and the other soldier fell asleep in the closed-up jeep. Elvis' mother came to him in a dream and awakened him—preventing he and the other soldier from dying due to carbon monoxide poisoning. That was the end of Paul Harvey's story. Years later the follow-up story of Elvis Pressley ends in a tragic manner. Unfortunately Elvis Pressley always had the expectation that he would die at about the same age that his mother had died—and he did! He died in his early forties. Was it a tragic drug overdose that killed Elvis or was his premature death the result of a self-fulfilling expectation of his that he would die young at near age forty? Was it just his destiny?

What about people who are put under hypnosis? While under hypnosis a strong man who can ordinarily lift hundreds of pounds of weight is told that he cannot lift a feather. Because his subconscious mind accepts what he has been told as fact, when asked to lift the feather, he actually is so weak that he cannot lift it while under hypnosis. Another person while under hypnosis is told that they have placed their hand on a hot burner and their hand actually blisters with third degree burns. They and their bodies acted as if what their subconscious mind was told while under hypnosis was fact. Subconscious minds actually do believe and accept as fact whatever they are told under hypnosis. Isn't this what occurs while visualizing? The subconscious mind accepts as fact the visualization. Doesn't brainwashing occur under a variety of circumstances?

How many children grow up in a household in which they are repeatedly told that whatever they can put their mind to they can achieve—and—they go on to very successful lives as adults. How many other children are told repeatedly that they are dumb, stupid, and that they will never amount to anything in their life—and—they fulfill that negative expectation. I am so very proud that my Son was teaching his three boys to pray daily: "the favor of God is upon me; I can achieve whatever I set my mind to accomplish." Isn't that a powerful daily prayer and expectation? Shouldn't everyone pray that prayer every day as a positive affirmation!

There is the saying: "the outcome of any contest is decided in the minds of the combatants long before the first blow is struck." Do we create the world in which we live through what we feed our subconscious minds which, through the acceptance of our thoughts and visualizations, brings them to reality? Do we have the power to change our lives by changing our thoughts? Or, are our lives determined by destiny?

While Vince Lombardi was head coach of the Green Bay Packers he had that championship team believe that they had never really lost a game; that time, had run out on them in some games; and that given more time they would have won those games. The players expected to win every game that they played. They had a winning attitude! Doesn't winning or losing first occur in the mind? How does one create in their minds a winning attitude instead of a losing attitude? Is it done by choices we make? I wonder about myself in reflecting on this—did I expect to win or did I expect to lose?

Why is it that some men turn out to be model citizens, law abiding, with good moral character while other men turn to a life of crime, stealing and murder? What is it that separates the two men? Is it environment? Or is it a result of the internal battle between good and evil, which is fought by all men?

There is that story from an email that someone sent to me of how one evening an old Cherokee Indian Chief told his young grandson about a battle that goes on inside of people. He said: "My son, the battle is between two wolves inside of us all. One wolf is Evil. It is anger, envy, jealousy, sorrow, regret, greed, arrogance, self-pity, resentment, inferiority, lies, false pride, superiority, and ego. The other wolf is Good. It is joy, peace, love, hope, serenity, humility, kindness, benevolence, generosity, truth, compassion, and faith. The grandson thought about it for a minute and then asked his grandfather: "Which wolf wins the battle?" The wise old Cherokee Chief simply replied: "The wolf that you feed."

"If a man can conquer his own darkness, he can defeat any enemy"

Are we the masters of our fate by what we think and feel? Do we create our dreams or do our dreams create us? Is there a separation between our dream world and our real world? Are they the same world merely existing at different levels of consciousness? How does one affect the other? Do they eventually merge into one world? These are the many thoughts that dwell in my mind as I question life itself and what meaning does it have for me?

It had been a productive day for me as I mailed out another four resumes while answering newspaper want ads; I'd sent a get-well card to an Aunt who was ill. I'd spent time talking with a fellow-out-of-work neighbor. I was active today and it made me feel good about myself. I recognized that activity alleviates stress.

There were no phone messages from anyone today and there was no real progress made in finding a job. If I had a job and an income, I could afford to date and I really desired to be in a relationship with a woman who would be my lady, my friend, and my lover—even my helpmate. Being out of work without an income seemed to preclude any social life for me. I had been alone for far too long. I laughed at myself—heck, even when I had a job and an income I still had no social life and was not dating!

Then there was the matter of my not sleeping well at night. There was no one to watch my back as there had been aboard the Oriskany in Viet Nam. Who would wake me if my townhouse caught fire? I did not fear fire. What I did fear was being caught in a fire and dying in it because there was no one to tell me to get up. Was it the <u>demon</u> of the Viet Nam War that kept me awake at night? Most likely I do suffer from Post Traumatic Stress Disease. Prior to 2007 I had never been previously diagnosed or treated for PTSD. I had never sought any help or medication for my restless/sleepless nights—I seemed to suffer from a mild case of it as so much revolved around my Viet Nam War experiences and the fire. The war experience is one, which continually haunts my mind. Ironically in late 2007 I actually went to the VA and did receive a few counseling sessions for PTSD. It was determined that I had mastered the ability as a young boy, after the death of my father, to suppress and bury my pain deep within myself, and further to shut down all of my emotions as a sort of defense and survival mechanism. No feelings = no pain! It does not really work, but it allows me to function from day to day. I was doing the same thing to my war experiences. I was trying my best to shut down all emotions involved in my memory of the war.

I'd had a mid-watch the night before the tragic fire that occurred aboard the Oriskany on 26 October 1966 off the coast of North Viet Nam. I had gone to the wardroom to have a hamburger afterwards; and then had gone to sleep about 0500 hours in the morning. At exactly 0728 hours I'd heard the general alarm that had echoed throughout the ship: "this is a drill, fire, fire, this is a drill." Immediately the alarm was again sounded: "this is no drill, fire, fire" and the ship's frame number was given for the location of the fire. I'd heard both alarms but just turned over in my bunk. Fires aboard ship were somewhat ordinary occurrences and I wasn't going to get up. Ron, the A-4 pilot who slept in the bunk below mine, then pulled the curtain on my bunk and told me: "it's really bad you have to get up." I turned over in my bunk to see the young pilot zipping up his flight suit and then he was gone. Ron had rushed out of the junior officers' bunkroom and went aft unknowingly right towards the fire, which cost him his life. He was only 23 years of age. Going aft was almost a reflex for all of the officers whose quarters was the 01 level bunkroom. The wardroom, the pilots' ready rooms, assigned duty stations for ship company officers; everything was aft. It was the only direction in which the officers went after leaving the bunkroom or their staterooms.

For the ship company junior officers who slept in the 01 Level Junior Officers' Bunkroom it was often the case that they would leave the bunkroom to go their duty station and not see the light of day. Often I went from the bunkroom to the Communications Department and didn't know if it was 0400 hours or 1600 hours? There were often days when I did not go topside and just did not see the light of day.

I very slowly got out of my bunk; I put on my trousers; then sat down in a chair to put on my socks and shoes. I was in no hurry despite the darkened bunkroom beginning to fill up with smoke. Finally I put on a shirt and then took the few steps to the door exiting the bunkroom. An officer—or was it a guardian angel—then directed me forward. I would have gone aft right into the fire and been killed as I did not know the location of the fire. Upon closing the hatch behind me there was fire on the other side in the passageway! The bodies of four junior officers were found in the 01 bunkroom after the fire was extinguished. It was not determined whether they had stayed in the bunkroom, or whether they had sought safety in it from the fire?

Knowing the frame number most likely didn't register in anyone's mind except perhaps in the minds of those officers and sailors assigned to damage control parties. IF there was a failure or glitch in Navy procedures it was in giving the frame number of the fire instead of warning everyone that the fire was in the hangar bay and for all to stay out of that area except for damage control parties. There had been no drills for the crew about how the frame number would be given in such a fire and no drills that explained to the crew as to how to identify a frame number with a particular part of the ship. Pilots and members of the air wing certainly were not accustomed to associating frame numbers with any part of the ship. It was an adherence to Navy procedures, which in all probability proved fatal to all too many?

Unlike the Destroyer Escort, the Thomas J. Gary (DER-326), on which I had initially served, when the aircraft carrier left port it did not undergo a general quarters or a man over board drill after securing the sea detail—an exercise that was standard aboard Destroyers *every* time they left port. No wonder the master chiefs at Naval Officer Candidate School referred to the Destroyer Navy as: "the real Navy." Of course the DER had only 150 sailors and 12 officers—the Oriskany had a total crew of 3300 with the Air Wing!

Had I gotten up more quickly I too would have gone aft and I probably would have been the 45th casualty of the fire aboard the Oriskany. Had Ron not shaken me to tell me that the fire was bad and that I needed to get up I would have probably died in the fire right in the bunkroom while still in my bunk. Ron had watched my back and had saved my life. Now I was alone and there was no one to watch my back. I felt like a fighter pilot without my wingman to watch my six—my back and my rear! It made for many restless and sleepless nights for me.

As I was about to climb through a hatch to reach the catwalk and then the flight deck, the flare locker exploded and sent a concussion throughout the forward part of the ship. I was very nearly blown off the ship into the sea. Once I reached the flight deck I looked back at the ship engulfed in flames and smoke. My first thought was that I would die. My second thought was that perhaps I should have accepted the medical discharge from the Navy that had been offered to me in 1965! I knew that the fire was very serious and that all of our lives were in grave danger. And here we were off the coast of North Viet Nam!

It had taken all morning and the extremely brave efforts of the crew for the fire to be brought under control and to be extinguished. It bears repeating—it took the very brave efforts of the officers and the crew and *all* aboard to save the Oriskany! There is probably no greater threat to a ship at sea than fire. The ship was damn near lost due to the fire. IF any ordinance had gone off the Oriskany would surely have been lost. Tons of bombs were thrown overboard off the ship from the hangar bay, which is where they were stored and they were in proximity of the fire. After the fire had been successfully put out it was while eating K-rations that officers and sailors began to find out how many had been killed in the fire. A total of 44 officers and sailors died in the fire. It had swept through the forward part of the ship through officers' country and that is why so very many of the men who died were officers. Pilots who had survived surface-to-air missiles and anti-aircraft artillery being fired at them by the North Vietnamese lost their lives in a tragic fire. Some who died had just returned to the ship the day before the fire. Others who were waiting for a plane to be scheduled to take them off the ship died in the fire. Sadly the fire had been caused by the carelessness of a sailor mishandling flares. A flare was dropped and began to burn. The sailor then kicked it into a flare locker with hundreds more flares. It was a very tragic and careless accident, which killed 44 brave men. It just should not have happened! After an investigation it was determined that the configuration of the flares was at fault and they were redesigned.

The worst aspect of the fire is that the Oriskany was supposed to have been, in Japan on a scheduled ten days of rest and relaxation the day the fire happened. Due to the mechanical problems experienced by another aircraft carrier, which was supposed to have relieved the Oriskany on the line, the tour of The Mighty O that month was extended. Instead of rest and relaxation for the crew and pilots of the Oriskany, there was death and destruction. Was it destiny? The Oriskany returned home a month early, yet had put more days on the line off the coast of North Viet Nam than it had been scheduled for in 1966.

I had come very close to getting killed. The days that followed the fire are mostly a blur to me. I cannot remember sleeping or eating or anything about the next few days after the fire. It was all a blank in my memory. I can vividly remember the burial at sea of one of the officers who had died in the fire. It was a very somber ceremony. It was a scene and ceremony that I just never thought I would ever witness in my life. I had grown up watching the Victory at Sea television series. I could remember watching scenes of burials at sea; I remember the scenes of aircraft carrier operations against the Japanese; and I remember watching films of the aircraft carrier Lexington getting hit and then the massive fires aboard that aircraft carrier before it was sunk. The master chief who taught seamanship at Naval Officer Candidate School told stories of having served aboard the aircraft carrier Lexington during WWII and being aboard it when it was hit and it caught fire. They had fought fires for three days without being able to put them out. They finally had to scuttle and sink the ship.

When I thought of that master chief it brought a smile to my face and I laughed out loud. There was the day during Seamanship class when the chief in all seriousness asked the officer candidates what would they do if their ship were at ground zero of a nuclear bomb attack on the fleet? All of the candidates gave serious answers about how they would batten down the hatches of their ship and how they would secure the watertight and airtight integrity of the ship. The chief sort of smiled and told the class that our answers were all wrong. He then told the class, that under a nuclear bomb attack on the fleet the only thing that they could do was: "to drop your drawers, and to bend over backwards and to kiss your dirty-asses goodbye." It broke up the entire class into laughter. Some things and people one does remember with a smile!

It was years later that I read a story about John Gavin's experiences aboard the Oriskany. The actor had visited the ship just days before the fire occurred. As the story went: the night before leaving the Oriskany on a scheduled departure after having been aboard for a few days, Gavin had two separate dreams of friends of his who had been Navy pilots and who had served aboard the Oriskany during the Korean War. The ship had won two battle stars for service in that war. Each of the pilots had been killed during the Korean War while flying off the ship. In each of the two dreams the pilots warned Gavin to leave the ship because he was in mortal danger while aboard it. Not thinking of those two dreams at the time he departed from the ship on the morning of 25 October 1966 as he was scheduled to do. Had he spent one more night aboard the Oriskany—Gavin may have also been a casualty in the fire—he was quartered in an officer's stateroom which was in the forward part of the ship in officers' country. That is the area through which the fire swept and where most lost their lives. Did Gavin receive a message from the grave? Do the dead exist in some other dimension of time and space and have the ability to enter our dimension and world? How did his two dead friends know of the danger? How were they able to use a dream in which to communicate with Gavin? Weren't figures in the Old Testament of the Bible contacted via dreams?

What exactly are dreams? What are thoughts? Is there a connection between the two? Is there a 'spirit world' in which the dead exist with the ability to come back and interface with us in the real world? Where do our souls or spirits go after we die? Do our thoughts live on? Do we live on in the thoughts of others who knew us? The Buddhists believe that a person suffers two deaths: "one death when they die and a second death when all those people who ever personally knew them die."

My maternal Grandfather had always expressed the question about the dead and the concept of Heaven: "If it is so wonderful on the other side how come nobody ever comes back to tell us so?" It does make one wonder about Heaven and the other side doesn't it? Just where do the spirits of the dead go? Just exactly what are thoughts?

"Thought—a dimension of being beyond our form in a spirit world"

That I had very nearly been killed in the fire aboard the Oriskany did not quite register on me at the time. As with the death of my Father I just suppressed memories of the experience deep into the recesses of my mind where they lay dormant for several years only to surface and to haunt me years later. I was then only twenty five years of age with my whole life in front of me. I still had hopes and dreams about what I would accomplish in my life. At the time I was looking forward and not backward at my life. The backward glance would come later after I retired from an active job/work career and had gotten old.

My close brush with death aboard the Oriskany in its fire had not been my only close brush with death. After all I nearly died in childbirth, as I had weighed barely four pounds at birth. There had been many other close calls for me both before the fire and afterwards but in each of those so-called close brushes with death no one else had been killed or had died. It was only during my close brush with death in the Oriskany fire that others had died. For very many years after the fire I did not even think about it or how I had been spared from death while so many others had died. Any feelings of guilt over having survived did not come until much later in my life.

Eventually I would begin to be haunted by memories of the Oriskany's 1966 deployment to the Viet Nam war. There were memories of the pilots I personally knew who were lost in that war—memories of those empty bunks in the junior officers' bunk room when it was one of the younger pilots whose plane had gone down over North Viet Nam. The memories of the fire and of my nearly getting killed in it would especially haunt me. The memory that 44 others had lost their lives while I had been spared from death in the fire was a haunting demon in my mind. Eventually it would have a very significant affect on how I would come to later look back at my life and on how I would come to terms with how my life had turned out. Having nearly been killed in the fire aboard the Oriskany in 1966 at my then age of 25 got to be one of the demons that tortured my mind in the dark of many a night. It has been best said of the Viet Nam War and it is appropriately said of all wars: "some gave all and all gave some."

Ironically as the years have passed since I had served in the Viet Nam War and survived the fire aboard the Oriskany, the memories are becoming much more vivid with each passing year and more prominent in my conscious thoughts. I remember encountering more than one pilot who was in the midst of writing a just in case letter to his wife back in the States—a just in case that pilot came home in a body bag or didn't come home at all. I had not written such a letter to anyone. I didn't have a girlfriend or wife back home to write such a letter. So many other memories of the 1966 deployment and of the fire fill my mind daily.

While working as a sales manager with a uniform services company in 2001 I was in the field making sales calls with one of my sales representatives. At a tire shop I noticed a customer about my age with a small Navy emblem on his tee shirt and I remarked about the emblem to the fellow. The man responded that as many times as he had worn that tee shirt that I was the first to ever remark about the Navy emblem. I explained that I recognized it because I had served in the Navy during the Viet Nam War. Both of us openly shared our experiences as we both had served in the Navy in that war.

Then the fellow made an interesting comment. He said that his wife had recently told him that she was surprised that he still remembered his Viet Nam War service experiences; further telling him that with such passage of time that she thought he would have forgotten all about it by now. Both the fellow and I shared the same current experience—that memories of the war were becoming much more vivid with the passage of time and were surely not forgotten. Just the opposite was happening, as the memories were more vivid than ever before despite the passing years. Didn't the Navy advertise that: "the experience lasts a lifetime?" For those who gave some—it seemed that the giving indeed continued for a lifetime!

I thought more about my service aboard the Oriskany in the Viet Nam War. After the ship left port the red nightlights would come on in the junior officers' bunkroom and they would remain on for 24/7 while the ship was at sea. At all times there would be junior officers asleep, as the bunkroom remained dark and quiet. Pilots would try to get some rest and sleep before their next mission; ship company officers would also try to get some rest and sleep before their next watch, as they were on a 12 hours on watch and 12 hours off watch duty schedule. While not on watch officers and crew performed their assigned duties.

I thought of the pay that we all received—very meager in those days! As a lieutenant junior grade I was paid a salary of $297 per month plus $48 per month food allowance that was paid into the officers' wardroom mess and another $65 per month combat pay when the ship was in the war zone. A pilot of the same rank and pay grade received the same pay plus another $110 per month flight pay—a whopping $3.67 more per day for flying over North Viet Nam and getting his plane shot at by the enemy. WOW!

Civilians who have never served in the military just do not know what that experience is like because there is absolutely nothing in civilian life that compares to military duty. And to serve in a war—one has to really have been there and done that to comprehend such duty and the sacrifices involved. The courage demonstrated by the Navy pilots to get in a plane loaded with bombs and to fly over North Viet Nam knowing that they would face extremely intense anti-aircraft fire; surface to air missiles; and MIG interceptors—how can a civilian possibly comprehend such courage without witnessing it in person as did I? And for these same pilots to see firsthand a fellow pilot go down on a target knowing that their comrade has lost his life or been captured—and then to fulfill their duty the next day just the same—how does one measure such courage? And for a pilot to be shot down himself and then to go right back up in the air on a mission the next day—wow—how could any civilian ever comprehend such courage and sense of duty? All wore their uniform with pride and performed their duties!

I remembered one of the F8 Crusader fighter pilots—a commander who had been shot down early in the deployment but who had been rescued. Later on during the deployment this same pilot shot down a North Vietnamese MIG 23 fighter interceptor. While Secretary of Defense Robert McNamara was aboard the Oriskany during a visit he awarded a well-deserved medal to this commander and asked him if he was proud to receive the awarded medal? In true professional fighter pilot fashion the commander answered McNamara that: "seeing that SOB get blown to bits was all the reward that I needed." While attending the Oriskany reception in May 2006 in Pensacola I asked about this commander and was very sorry to hear that he had died a couple of years previously. The professionalism of the Navy pilots was fantastic. The entire ship's crew and air wing personnel were all great! The hard work performed by all to support the pilots was just amazing! It was indeed a 24/7 job for ALL! Only one who has served in the military and in war could possibly relate to that which those who served in war experienced! War is indeed—as correctly described by Union General William T. Sherman—"all Hell."

A civilian could not possibly imagine how extremely dangerous aircraft carrier operations are to the crew. One night aboard the Oriskany a terrible accident occurred. The A-3 Tanker landed aboard the flight deck and the arresting cable it caught with its tail hook snapped. It sliced through the thighs of a third class petty officer—he lost both legs; and it sliced through the leg of one of the lieutenants—he lost the leg just below the knee. With armed missiles and bombs being constantly loaded onto aircraft; with flight operations often twice a day; with the ship being on the line for thirty—forty days at a stretch—it is amazing that more frequent serious accidents did not occur. One could not possibly measure the bravery and dedication, in the face of everyday danger, of all of the officers and crew aboard the USS Oriskany in its service in the Viet Nam War.

The 'Mighty O' had been the smallest aircraft carrier that served in the Viet Nam War. It had been the last of the Essex class of aircraft carriers built—all had been named for Revolutionary War battles—the Oriskany for a battle that had taken place in upstate New York in the small town of Oriskany. It had been awarded two battle stars for service in the Korean War and five battle stars for service in the Viet Nam War. It was sunk off the coast of Pensacola, Florida on 16 May 2006 to become an artificial reef—the 'Mighty O' continues to serve.

Could the demon that kept me awake so many nights be that of my <u>divorce</u>? Had I not ever recovered from my own divorce? Other men had gone through a divorce and they had gone on with their lives. One friend had married and divorced three times. I know many men, and women, who had divorced only to marry again within just a couple of years. The second marriages that lasted seemed to be when the individuals had taken the time to recover from their first divorce. Why had I not fully recovered, or have I? I was and am damn particular when it came to women. It would take a very special woman for me to ever marry again. She'd have to be pretty, shapely, with high moral values and principles; and she'd have to be a woman who did not lie or cheat! She would have to have what I refer to as that little girl enthusiasm that made her so very special in my eyes and heart. I could love her only if I valued her. I still believe that love and marriage were forever. Yes, I am a true Taurus even in love!

I subscribe to the Ayn Rand concept that to say that you valued someone was at a higher level and more meaningful than to say that you loved that person. To value someone meant that you truly knew who and what, they were. To value someone meant that that person's personality, their character, their morals, their own sense of value and values were compatible with oneself. IF that person had value and values, then it meant that they would be valued and that they would be truly loved in the highest sense of the word love. Unless I could and would value <u>and</u> love a woman, I would remain alone. Was there a woman out there for me? Or would I remain alone for the rest of my life? Either way I was not going to lower my standards.

Would any woman value me? Would she value my honesty and integrity, my faithfulness, my high ideals and principles, and my self-discipline? What of my warrior personality—would any woman value that within me? What of my serious nature—would any woman accept that in me? What of my inability to make a woman laugh and my inability to really have fun, would any woman really value that in me? I realized that the fact that I had always been faithful to my wife had meant nothing to her! And my values sure didn't matter to her either. Sadly after her first known affair before we had children she never even said that she was sorry for cheating on me. She had left me during her affair. I sure had been a fool to take her back! Hell, she had not even asked to be taken back by me. She was never sorry that she had cheated on me! Damn! That hurt still remained in my heart. Again, she never even said that she was sorry for hurting me! Interestingly enough when I called the wife of the man with whom my wife was having an affair, which actually exposed the affair, my wife got angry with me! The man's wife later told me that my own wife had had a problem at her previous job. Was the affair in which I had caught my wife her second of our marriage? Heck we had been married only 1 ½ years at the time. What was I thinking by taking her back? Damn what a stupid decision that had been! Obviously she had never intended to remain faithful to the marriage vows. She apparently cheated on me from the first that we were married. Damn that hurt me deeply! Some wounds are not healed by time.

I often reflect on why I have remained alone. And, I have repeatedly stated that it was the characteristics within me that enabled me to survive alone that also kept me alone—my toughness, my hardness, my aloofness, my independence, my warrior mentality, my seriousness, and my seemingly keeping people at arms length from myself. And I am not a fun guy. I am and have always been far too serious! In defense of my ex-wife, I am sure that it was not much fun being married to me. I would often repeat this observation to myself and to others. Perhaps I had too much hurt and anger within me to ever love again or to accept being loved? Of course my being so very selective about women was and continues to also be a big factor in my being alone. I refuse to be with just any woman—she would have to be special! IF it was and is my fate to remain alone, so be it!

As our I had stated to a few: "my ex-wife is no worse off for how she has led her life and I am no better off for the way I have led my life." It appeared that she was out enjoying her lifestyle while I was alone brooding about all of those dreams which never had come true for me and which might have meant something IF they had come true. Wasn't I just like Ethan Edwards from 'The Searchers?' There was the warning: "Do not brood over your past mistakes and failures as this will only fill your mind with grief, regret, and depression." Hadn't I done just that? All of the hurts of my past continued to pain me! Like 'Sergeant Stryker'—the John Wayne role in the movie 'The Sands Of Iwo Jima'—I was and am a deeply sad and lonely man.

At my current age of 66 in 2007 most people thought me to be in my early to mid 50's. I tend to remark that I looked much younger than my age due to my: "clean and boring living"—there was much truth to that! Ha! Ha!

As my ex-wife had hardened in her own way I have also hardened in my own way. Today, if I had remarried, no matter how much I may have loved a wife, I would not take back a cheating wife. When my ex-wife had cheated on me and I had taken her back it was as though I had gone against my strict set of rules and it had burned me badly. It was as though I had broken some code of honor that had protected me. I would never do that again. There would never again be a second chance for a liar and a cheat. I recognized that cheaters cheat and liars lie—it is what they do. They can't help it! How does the saying go: "the leopard can not change its spots."

It was only after our final separation in 1980 after twelve years of marriage that I discovered the extent of my ex-wife's lies and it shattered me while ending our marriage. A neighbor had even remarked to me that my ex-wife was a pathological liar; that the neighbor's own father had been one; and that she knew from the fluttering of the eyes, from the shifting from one foot to the other, from the body language, and from the failure to look one directly in the eyes—all were signs of a pathological liar. I was stunned! I could <u>never</u> believe or trust my ex-wife again.

I am reminded of the story of the scorpion and the frog. There was this scorpion, which was on the banks of a large pond and it wanted to get to the other side of the pond. Now the scorpion could not swim so it asked a frog if it could ride on back of the frog as the frog swam to the other side of the pond. The frog objected telling the scorpion that it was afraid that the scorpion would sting the frog causing the frog to die. The scorpion told the frog that it would not sting it because after all if it did the frog would die and the scorpion would also drown. So the foolish frog believed the scorpion and allowed it to ride on its back as it began to swim across to the other side of the pond. While they were halfway across the pond the scorpion stung the frog. The frog asked the scorpion why it did that for now the frog would die but the scorpion would also die. The response from the scorpion was that it could not help itself after all it was a scorpion and that is what scorpions do they sting. The frog died and the scorpion drowned. The scorpion could not help doing what scorpions do. It could not help being what it was. It had to fulfill its role.

My ex-wife was who and what she was—she could not help it doing what she did. I am who and what I am—I couldn't help that either. Each in our own way seemed to be fulfilling our destiny.

For whatever reasons (seemingly unknown to me), I have always visualized that I was to be a warrior, who was tough, courageous, unyielding, a straight arrow who lived by a strict code of honor. I have always identified with movie roles and characters in books who were warrior types and hero types, i.e., the gladiator; the knight in shining armor; the gunfighter; the fighter pilot; and those who fought for what was right and honorable; and who were always the hero who walked a straight line.

The John Wayne role in the movie 'Sands of Iwo Jima' was one with which I identified very strongly as was Wayne's role as Ethan Edwards in the movie The Searchers. Neither man won the woman. One died in battle while the other just rode off alone. Why did I identify so strongly with those roles in which the <u>hero</u> did not win the girl, but instead road off alone into the sunset? For whatever reasons it was more important for me to be the hero even if that meant not winning the girl. Why was that? What within me caused such thoughts and feelings? I really did not know. Certainly in that other dimension of time and space into which I often escaped—the dream world—I was always the warrior and the hero!

In the movie 'The Man Who Shot Liberty Valance' John Wayne plays the role of the strong hero who saves Jimmy Stewart's life but Wayne loses the woman he loves to the character played by Stewart. It so devastates Wayne in the movie that it destroys him and his life. Why does the hero <u>not</u> win the woman he loves in so many movies? Why did I so closely identify with the role of the hero who loses the woman he loves? That I didn't win the woman surely became a self-fulfilling expectation that kept me alone. Why did I feel that way? As with the movie characters with which I so strongly identified, I was a sad and lonely man. Wasn't it possible that my negative thoughts were creating my world?

"Thoughts are things—we become what we think about and imagine ourselves to be"

It was frustrating for me to be able to successfully mental image in my toughness, as I was indeed tough, yet not to be able to mental image in the successful satisfaction of the needs and desires of my heart. I recognized that mental imaging worked to shape me into a tough warrior type, why wasn't I able to be successful in other areas of my life? Were other men affected in the same manner?

How did other men view themselves? How did other men relate to the John Wayne characters he played in his movies? How did other men view 'Ethan Edwards' from the movie 'The Searchers?' Did other men prefer to be the strong hero who unfortunately loses the woman he loves? Did other men prefer to be the weaker man who walks away with the woman? What are the thoughts and feelings of other men in such matters? What common thread is woven through all men? Is there one?

What about the men who declared that: "God had blessed them with the fulfillment of the desires of their hearts." Such men enjoyed love, happiness, success, and financial wealth. Had God blessed them? Had fate blessed them? Was it a fulfillment of their destiny? Or had they imagined and visualized and expected such for themselves and all that they enjoyed was merely a self-fulfilling expectation? Did such men who appeared to have it all have any demons deep in the recesses of their minds?

During 1993 I had a conversation with my parish pastor. I expressed to the priest the desire to be blessed with love and happiness, with success and financial wealth, and with what so many other men seemed to enjoy. My pastor stated that he had the: "perspective of the confessional." I asked what did he mean? The pastor explained that he knew of men who had achieved and enjoyed what most men wish for in their lives. But in hearing their confessions the pastor was made aware of the demons that tortured them in their minds. That other men also suffered from demons in their minds did not provide any answer or satisfaction to me as to why I was alone and why love and happiness, success and financial wealth had eluded me. It still appeared to me that other men had been greatly blessed by whatever God there was while I had not been so blessed. That disappointed me and made me angry! It certainly weakened my faith in God.

And what of the men who did not enjoy the fulfillment of their heart's desires? What had gone wrong in their minds and thoughts and expectations? Could it be that such men had sabotaged themselves by their stinking thinking? Is that what I had done to myself by the manner in which I escaped? Had I been so negative in my thoughts that they created a negative life for me? Why did I think such negative thoughts? Why did I have such negative expectations? Was it my fate or destiny to live the life that I did? And what of God? Could it be that God chose to bless some men and not others? Why? Didn't I think that NO man ever got what he deserved in life—not the good and certainly not the bad! Surely I had not deserved to survive the fire aboard the Oriskany and Ron had surely not deserved to die in that fire. The Bible does clearly state: "all that a man has comes from God." Is each man predestined to live out the life that has been assigned to him by God or some force? Didn't the Book of Sirach in the Catholic Bible state: "all human success comes from God?" In 'The Godfather' it is Vito Corleone, the 'Don' who states that: "a man has but one destiny."

No man asks to be born. No man decides when to be born. No man decides to which parents to be born. No man decides in what country he is to be born. No one decides that they will be born a man or a woman. No one decides the color of their skin, or the color of their eyes, or the color of their hair, or their height. Some are born to kings and queens while others are born to paupers. Didn't God tell Job in the Bible that: "I knew you before you were in the womb?" Is the Don correct in believing that a man has but one destiny and that it is not determined by him but by powers beyond his control? Is a man's success or failure, happiness or sadness, and all that happens to him in his life all a matter of destiny? Is a man's life all predestined by God or by some other Force that has control over a man and the events in his life? These are the questions I ask myself almost every day. That there are no answers seems to haunt me.

The author of the book—When Bad Things Happen to Good People—Rabbi Harold Kushner—seemed to have based the book and his other books on The Book of Ecclesiastes in the Bible, which was supposedly written by King Solomon. In his own books, Kushner appears to place a limit on God similar to that placed on God by the German philosopher Nietzsche. It was Nietzsche who stated: "Either God can prevent evil but He will not or God wishes to prevent it and He can not." Kushner relies on Ecclesiastes in which Solomon observed: "I have seen the good get what the evil deserve and the evil get what the good deserve." Is a man's life a matter of fate, destiny, the stars, or does shit just happen to some men while other men seem to always step into a pot of gold? Neither the books by Kushner, or Ecclesiastes in the Bible, or the cynical observations of Nietzsche were any consolation to me. I still hurt! And I still had a growing disappointment with God.

The disappointment with God stemmed from all of my prayers that went unanswered; from all of my wants, needs, and desires that went unfulfilled. I remembered the story told by one of my favorite singers from the Rock and Roll era. This singer had much early career success and developed some unhealthy addictions. One day he dropped to his knees and cried out to God to heal him of those addictions. Immediately he was healed! Seemingly God answered his prayer right then and there!

It disturbs me greatly that there was a God Who could and would answer the prayers of some but not my own prayers. Why did God not answer my prayers? Was I not deserving of having my prayers answered? Did I lack sufficient faith in God? What was the reason that God did not seem to answer my prayers nor my needs, wants, and desires? Why was God not a loving Father in Heaven to me? Did God just not love me?

Did other men feel such disappointment with God because of their own unanswered prayers; and because of their own unfulfilled needs, wants, and desires? Did other men lack faith in God? Were there any real connection between a man's prayers; his faith in God; and what Life and God seemed to dole out to him in his life?

Damn! I wished that I didn't even ask such questions. Did other men, especially war veterans, ask such questions? Did other men find a semblance of truth in the cynicism of the philosopher Nietzsche?

And so we have my memoir filled with redundant questions for which there just does <u>not</u> seem to be any credible answers! Is there no answer to the why question?

That other dimension of time and space into which I try to escape the hurt and in which I existed as a warrior, was it real? I laughed at the thought, but the concept disturbs me. As per the author of the book—Men are from Mars and Women are from Venus—men escape stress and confrontation by withdrawing into a cave. I escape hurt, pain, sadness, and sorrow by withdrawing into what I referred to as another dimension of time and space in which I am a warrior—it was a sort of cave for me. Yet, ironically in that dimension it is almost as though I sought out confrontation rather than escape it. I sought out situations in which I would be the hero rescuing a damsel in distress. Was it just a fantasy? Was I just playing John Wayne is some imagined movie role? Was I simply dreaming about who I desired to have been? Was I just trying to escape the pain? A man alone receives no comfort from anyone.

One of my favorite songs was: 'Have you never been mellow' by Olivia Newton John. In it she asks the question: "Have you never let someone else be strong?" It seemed that I was not mellow and that I had never let someone else be strong—I had to always be the strong one!

What was real; what dimension was real; and where do I actually exist? How could there be any connection between what I often imagined in my mind and in my dreams? And the cut on my arm, did it actually happen in a dream only to exist in my waking world? Were the two worlds of dreams and waking beginning to merge into one world? Now that really frightened me as I thought, what would happen if my dream world took over my waking world? What would happen IF I disappeared into that other dimension of time and space—my dream world—never to return to whatever was the real world? Could that even happen? Had it already happened? What world was even real? Could my mind still distinguish the difference between the two worlds?

I thought of Stephen King the author—how did he come up with the concepts for the books that he wrote? Did he imagine those weird story lines? Did he dream or imagine those story lines that he wrote about in his books? Now that was a question, which I found to be interesting! From what part of an author of fiction's mind do the stories which he/she write come? I was really intrigued by that question. The reason it intrigued me is that I was looking for some connection to others and to what others thought and felt, and to what others dreamed and imagined. Once again I asked the question so redundant in my own mind and herein—did other veterans of the Viet Nam War think and feel as I did? Just how did other men, especially war veterans, think and feel? And what do others do about their thoughts and feelings? How did other men deal with their hurt, pain, sadness, and sorrow? What did they do to escape the pain? What about those men who had survived the Oriskany fire—what did they think and feel all of these past 40+ years of borrowed time?

There had been 3300 officers and sailors aboard the Oriskany at the time of the fire. That included the ship's officers and sailors also the pilots and crew of the air wing. How many of those 3300 had come as close to getting killed in the fire as I had? What have been the thoughts and feelings of those men, who barely escaped death, all of these years since the fire? Did any of those men have demons in their minds due to the fire? What about all of the 3300 men who had survived the fire? What had been their thoughts and feelings all of these years since the fire? What kind of demons did other survivors have in their minds due to that tragic fire? Damn war!

Union General William T. Sherman was to have said: "war is all hell." Confederate General Robert E. Lee was to have said: "it is best that war is so terrible less we grow too fond of it." Damn all wars!

"War doesn't make boys men, it makes men dead"
—Ken Gillespie

I changed the bandages on my left arm. The wound was healing quickly. I still could not figure out how I'd injured myself. I dismissed the dream of being a gladiator, putting it out of my mind, but somehow I still felt the intensity of the battle I had experienced in that dream. It had seemed and felt like a real experience.

I was all dressed up with nowhere to go, except to the State Unemployment Office. It appeared that I would not be eligible for any benefits, even after my severance had run out. To have been downsized out of my job at age 51, after having worked over 20 years for my employer, now that was depressing! What would I now do? I had no idea as to what to do with the rest of my life. The year was then 1992. Years later at age 66 and retired I still did not have an answer as to what to do with the rest of my life? I suspected that I was not the only man in the world without an answer to that question. The year was now 2007. The question remains without any answers!

Didn't many other men change careers in midlife, at ages forty and fifty, seeking to do something different with the rest of their lives? Didn't many men and women reach a mid-life crisis only to give up a well paying corporate job, in order to do charity work or to teach in order to make a contribution to society? What were men chasing? Didn't men want to have a significant purpose to their lives? Didn't men want their lives to have had some important meaning? When a man came to the end of his days, didn't he want to look back and be able to say with pride "**I did it**?" Just what was 'it?' Was it fame or fortune, or to have started a company, or to have made a significant contribution to society, or to have written a book, or was it some other venture that was 'it?' Nike shoe company advertises: "**just do it**" but what is **it**?

In professional football was 'it' the winning of a Super Bowl championship? In professional basketball was 'it' the winning of an NBA championship? In professional baseball was 'it' the winning of the World Series? In all of sports at all levels was 'it' defined only by winning a championship in what is a team sport? How many truly great players in all levels of team sports, whether it was high school, college, or professional were never on a team that won a championship? And those athletes who were on a team that won a championship, was that 'it' for their lives? The majority of professional sports careers end by the age of forty. And today we hear the term that: "life begins at the age of forty." There has got to be more to 'it' than winning a team championship! What did these champions do with the rest of their lives? I have often thought that if I had been a professional athlete by the age of forty my career would have long ended and then what?

At a very young age has the golfer Tiger Woods already done 'it?' Had Arnie Palmer and Jack Nicklaus done it in their own golfing careers? Had the late Rocky Marciano done it in the world of boxing? The list of champion athletes could go on and on. Of course the list of non-champions is a lot longer.

Then there is the fame and fortune achieved by so many Hollywood stars who, then went on to commit suicide. Obviously they had not achieved it! For them, there had to be something a lot more to 'it' than achieving fame and fortune. Why had they become so dissatisfied with their lives in which they had achieved the fame and fortune supposedly desired by many others that they prematurely ended their own lives?

What was 'it' for other men? How does each individual man decide what 'it' is for him? What gives a man satisfaction when he looks back at his life? When a man says: "I did it" what is he proudly saying that he did? And if a man did not do it—was he just not able to do it? How does that make him feel? How inadequate does that make a man feel? Certainly it appears to be true that: "men are extremely sensitive about feeling inadequate as one of man's deepest needs is to feel adequate." I look back at my own career with a sense of failure. I wonder about other men in order to establish some connection between them and me—wondering if we share any of the same thoughts and feelings?

Ted Williams had a Hall of Fame baseball career and is the last baseball player to bat over .400 for a season—he batted .406 in 1941. But he was never on a team that won a World Series. Failing to win a World Series ring sure does not define his baseball career. Karl Malone and John Stockton had Hall of Fame NBA basketball careers but they were never on a team that won an NBA championship. Surely their failure to win a NBA championship ring does not define their careers. They did do it—it as having had long careers as great professional basketball players.

What about Wilt Chamberlain, was 'it' for him winning an NBA Championship or the bedding down of 20,000 women? Is 'it' for some men that they were able to screw over co-workers in their rise to the top of the Corporate Ladder of so-called success? Is 'it' for some men that they got away with repeatedly cheating on their wives over many years of marriage? What was 'it' for other men?

I remember the college football coach Joe Paterno being asked, after one of his Penn State football teams had gone undefeated and had won a national championship, if that had been his best team ever? Paterno answered that he could only answer that question in twenty years after he had seen what kind of men his players had become and what kind of lives they had lived. For Paterno 'it' seemed to be successfully teaching boys to become good men who went on to lead good lives—a worthwhile it! Is 'doing it' something different for each individual man? How is it determined? Does each man determine what 'it' is for himself or does society determine it for him?

I admire and respect heroes who had put all on the line for a greater purpose than they. Of all that I have ever done with my own life, I am most proud that I had turned down an offered medical discharge and that I had served in the Viet Nam War. And I was quite proud that I had served out my three years commitment upon being commissioned at Naval Officer Candidate School; and that despite two Medical Boards during those three years in each instance I had returned to full duty. At the end of only three years service I was on the early selection list for Full Lieutenant despite the two medical boards. Yes, I had served with honor and of that I am very proud. It was the feeling that I had been true to myself that made me feel some pride. It was the sense that I had lived my life as a man according to the high ideals and principles I had set for myself as a boy. I could respect myself for that! It wasn't 'it' for me but it was how I had lived my life. I would go to my grave one day with a sense of pride that I had served in the Navy and in the Viet Nam War. John Kennedy said it best:

"And any man who may be asked what he did to make his life worthwhile, I think can respond with a good deal of pride and satisfaction: 'I served in the United States Navy'"

Had it not been for my suffering motion sickness I just may have made a career out of the Navy. But I would have wanted to have earned the captaincy of a ship, which I could never have achieved suffering from motion sickness. So I left the Navy after my three years commitment had been fulfilled. My life was to take a different path. I have often wondered—what if I had joined the Marines instead of the Navy? What if the Navy had allowed me to transfer to the Marines out of OCS as I had verbally requested after receiving my orders to a DER? I had expected to suffer from motion sickness on such a small ship and I had! I remembered with a smile that one of the most treasured compliments I had ever received was from a UPS delivery truck driver. While I was out jogging on the street one day the driver stopped and asked me: "are you a retired Marine?"—that I "looked like one." I know as much about the history of the Marine Corps as did any Marine! Had it all been part of my destiny that I had suffered from motion sickness? Could I have been a Marine or a Navy Seal? Did I have it within myself to be either? I wondered about that. I would never know the answer to that question.

John Wayne had actually wanted to attend the Naval Academy at Annapolis and to make the Navy a career. His family's move to California and his subsequent football scholarship to USC all changed that. Ironically, for all of the war movies that Wayne made, he never served in the military or in World War II. For the rest of his life he regretted his failure to serve in the military. Yet, his appearance as Sergeant Stryker, the tough Marine, in the movie—The Sands of Iwo Jima—probably saved the Marine Corps from being disbanded and eliminated as a branch of the Armed Forces. The US Congress had planned to eliminate the Corps after WWII.

What made other men proud of themselves? Was it a successful work career? Was it having served in the military? I had not really met any man who didn't have some pride in having once served in the military and in war despite war's horrors. Maybe it was a man's thing to have been able to do it—to have served in the military while knowing that there is NO experience in civilian life that even comes close to military service and especially that of serving in a war. Nothing but nothing compares to serving in a war! And for those who were draft dodgers and who avoided service to their country in time of war—Shakespeare's Henry V said it best in referring to those not there for the great battle as men who: "shall think themselves accursed they were not here, and hold their man-hoods cheap."

It was interesting how in recent years so many men running for political office and even other men claimed to have served in the Viet Nam War—even claiming to have been awarded medals for bravery. When the truth was known—so many of these same men had not served in the military; had not served in the Viet Nam War; and certainly had not been awarded any medals. It is as if Shakespeare was correct—these men felt less as being real men for not having served in the military and especially for not having served in the Viet Nam War. Then there are the chicken hawks—men who were draft dodgers during the Viet Nam War and then became warmongers all too willing to send other men off to wars of their making!

There was even a TV and movie star who had claimed that he had served five tours of combat in the Viet Nam War and that he was wounded with shrapnel. When the truth was finally told, for which he did apologize, he had actually served in the Marines but was stationed in Japan the entire time. He had not ever served in the Viet Nam war. What possessed him to tell such a blatant lie? Did he feel like less of a man because he had not served in the Viet Nam War? How many other men told such lies?

Sadly, in recent years, an Admiral who was the Chief of Naval Operations had committed suicide after it had been revealed that a medal he wore had not been awarded to him. The shame of that revelation was too much for him to bear. Why had he claimed the award? He rose to the top of the Navy only to fall in complete shame.

There are others who actually served in the military and in war but who did not brag about such service. The late movie star Lee Marvin had served in the Marines in World War II. He was involved in the initial assault on Iwo Jima and was awarded the Navy Cross. How few people ever knew about Marvin's war service, as he never mentioned it and certainly did not brag about it. He was proud of having served! Yogi Berra—yes, the Baseball Hall of Fame New York Yankees catcher—had been a seventeen year old seaman aboard a Navy ship at Normandy. One of my favorite Yankee baseball players was Hank Bauer who had served in combat during WWII in the Marines. Of course there are so many others like Ted Williams and Jerry Coleman who had served as Marine pilots in both WWII and Korea. During the Korean War it was Coleman who brought down his plane with a 500-pound live bomb hung up that would not release itself—and—Williams who had brought down his plane in flames.

I remember that most of the Marines in the contingent aboard the Oriskany were pretty pissed off that they were serving aboard an aircraft carrier off the coast of North Viet Nam instead of serving in combat in country in South Viet Nam. That was more of a feeling that they wanted to be with their fellow Marines.

While out jogging and walking I often wear a tee shirt with NAVY screen—printed across the chest. I wear that proudly. I often wear it on days that I am emotionally down as a reminder that I am alive and have been blessed with 40+ years of borrowed time since the Oriskany fire. Despite my admiration for the Marine Corps I would _never_ wear a Marine tee shirt and I would _never_ wear a Navy Seal tee shirt—I had not earned the right to wear those tee shirts!

It is probably best to preface the following by saying that my ten years old Granddaughter recently asked me if I "listened to any modern music?" She told me that I really needed to upgrade my life by wearing more casual clothes; not to be so serious; to listen to music other than what I did; that I needed a new television; and she had many other suggestions. Bless her heart and accurate observations about me being far too serious and having my seriousness expressed in my lifestyle. She is correct! Sadly I just do not seem to have it within me to change. I am stuck being me and I can't get out of the mold. I mention her observations, as I did not seem to go through any mid-life crisis when I turned age forty and I seem to be unchanged from my youth. I laughed when I read that General U. S. Grant did not dance—darn if I don't either! Was I an old man at the age of twelve?

Why do so many men go through what is referred to as a mid-life crisis? Is it the onset of growing old that prompts such men to try to act young again as though they could really recapture their youth? NO offense to any man, but the sudden wearing of earrings, gold chains, the growing of a beard or mustache, the drinking and carousing that some men do as they reach the age of forty—what does it accomplish? Does it really make such men feel any better about who or what they are? Can any such man truly say that such activities give any real purpose or meaning to their lives? Does it really make them feel better about who they are? Or are such actions indicative of their not being able to feel good about who and what they are no matter what?

Do men suffer through a different crisis as they reach old age? What about when a man reaches retirement age or so-called old age and as he looks back at his life he concludes that he did NOT do it? How does he then think and feel about his life? At what age is it too late to do it? Colonel Sanders at age 70 started a business based on his special recipe for fried chicken. Wow! Is it ever too late to do something?

Is it ever too late to have what a man has never had before in his life? Is it ever too late for a man or a woman to find and share love in their life? Is there some age that when passed men and women no longer consider love or marriage? There was an interesting saying from the TV program—Doc—that went like this: "When we get past what we want, we're often provided what we need." Don't we all want and need love? Didn't I still desire and need love? Had I become so hardened that it destroyed my ability to be loved and to accept being loved?

Could an old age crisis be more serious than a mid life crisis for a man? What to do about it especially with time running out? Even in the midst of a mid-life crisis a man can console himself with the thought that there was still time to do something with his life; maybe to do something that he had always wanted to do; and maybe to do something different from what he'd ever done before? At midlife it appeared still possible to have what one had never had before. But what of an old man—has time run out on him preventing him from ever doing it or from ever having it?

Gatorade asks: "is it in you?" Nike recommends that you: "just do it." And what IF 'it' is not in you and you just cannot do it? How does a man handle the reality that it is not ever going to happen for him—whatever *it* is? What if a man realizes that he is like Al Bundy from the television program—Married with Children—that he's not going to ever make love to a beautiful woman; or reach the ladder of career success; or own that big spacious house; or drive that expensive sports car—then what? How does he resolve all of those never going to happen things in his life? How does a man handle the reality that, for whatever reasons, he has missed out on love and happiness, success and financial wealth? Who or what is to blame for a man's failures? How does a man handle his failures? How do they affect a man? Every one of these questions is what I ask of myself! Isn't it true that:

> "There is no greater loneliness greater than
> the loneliness of a failure"
> —Eric Hoffer

I never did go through any such mid-life crisis—none that I can remember. Even after the failure of my marriage my behavior remained the same as it had been before. There were no changes. I was too disciplined to allow myself self-destructive behavior. I did not need any such distracting activities. I accepted who and what I was. I realized that none of those activities would give me any meaning or purpose to my life. It just was not me! Reluctantly I accepted that, at the age of 40 when my divorce became final, I was no longer a man of age 25 while accepting that I was, right now, a man of age 66. I do seem to be going through an old-life crisis as I realize that there are, too many never going to happens in my life. I am not a happy man and others have observed my sadness. Had I been so demanding of myself that I just would never be happy? Had I thought that I could achieve perfection and my failures caused me to be very unhappy and sad? Didn't I once think that I was going to achieve great things in my life? What went wrong? Why had I failed? Had I measured myself against impossible goals?

How am I going to be able to resolve that perhaps I just did not have it within me to be a winner at the game of life? How can I resolve that I did not achieve in my work career what I once thought I was capable of achieving? Damn! It really sucks to feel like a loser at the game of life. How can I accept my failures in so many aspects of my life?? Again it is remarked that my nearly getting killed in the Viet Nam War and remembering those who did die eventually provides the answer for me, as the reader of this will find out much later on herein.

> "Demand perfection of yourself and never be happy; expect perfection in
> others and never be satisfied"

The above phrase comes from a TV movie that I had watched with my Daughter. Upon hearing those words my Daughter immediately turned to me and said: "dad, that is exactly how you are." I cut neither myself, nor others much slack. While I was beginning to get a little less demanding of others (<u>not</u> much less) I was still too damn demanding of myself. It was a cause of unhappiness and deep sadness within me. And I really was still too demanding of others. I continued to expect too much of others. It has caused me problems in my relationships with others. My perceived failures as a father and a daddy damn near destroyed me! I was a broken man. I felt like a total failure as a father and that was a terribly deep hurt within me. I am very proud of both my Son and my Daughter. The bigger and more important question for me was—had I made my children proud of me? I wondered and worried about that! And I felt like a failure! I certainly had not achieved perfection.

What about other men as they reach age 66 and retirement, what do they think and feel as they evaluate where they are now and where they had hoped to be and when they look back at their lives? IF they did not achieve the success that they once thought that they were capable of achieving in a work career what do they think and feel about that failure? Do they look upon themselves as having been failures or as just having failed? Do they just chalk it all up to having been cursed by bad breaks? Do they just all accept it that it was their destiny? What even defines success and failure for other men?

Even in the Bible it states that a man should: "not get all puffed up because of his success" in life because "all comes from God." So, it appears that success is a blessing that comes from God? Why then do some men receive it and other men do not? Does it mean that no matter how hard a man works—success is then granted by God irrespective of how hard a man works or despite his lack of hard work? How does God decide whom He will bless? Can God even bless any man? They are questions that are very disturbing! It appears to explain why the philosopher Nietzsche was so cynical about God and why the author Kushner seems to limit what God can and does do in this world.

Does a successful and happy marriage override a less than successful work career? Heck, at retirement age the work career is over but at least the wife is still there for some men. Married men do live longer than do single and alone men. What if there has been failure in both areas of a man's life? How does a man think, and feel when his work career is over, and it has been viewed by him as having been a failure and he is alone? Again the question is asked: "How do men think and feel when it appears that love and happiness, success and wealth have all eluded them?" Do they hope that there is really such a thing as reincarnation and that perhaps in some future life they will be blessed, as they desire? It certainly appears that in this life there are no second chances? I can tell the reader—I do not feel so good when I look at my failures and aloneness.

My Granddaughter at the then age of 4 or 5 had remarked to me: "Pop-Pop, you won't have a woman to love in this life but when you get to Heaven you'll have a woman to love." As she admitted when asked a couple of years later—her remark stemmed from her desire not to share her time with her grandfather. Then again, maybe she knew something that I didn't know?

For my recent 66th birthday I was quite surprised to receive a happy birthday email from a woman who remembered me after all of these years—we had met while I was at OCS in1965 and then dated while I was at Communications School in early 1966. She had gone on to marry a Navy Officer—the marriage had ended years ago. Wow—she remembered me! Unknown to her—she had been in my daily prayers for many years. I'd had not forgotten her!

I laughed as I remembered my company chief at OCS who had warned the Officer Candidates to: "look out for those Bristol Barracudas and Fall River Debs"—young women who flocked into the Viking Hotel in Newport on a Saturday night to meet Officer Candidates. Some found husbands! I remember meeting the wife of one of my fellow Communication Department Officers—I had not ever previously met her but I did remember her face from the Viking Hotel in Newport! I often reminded those who had seen the movie—Officer and a Gentleman—that it had been a realistic portrayal of life at Navy Officer Candidates School!

My company had been the best in its class at OCS after the twelfth week and had earned the right to a Friday night liberty in addition to the usual Saturday night liberty. As Murphy's Law would have it that night Newport was hit with a terrible snowstorm and minus 10 degrees temperatures. The only people at the Viking Hotel were the officer candidates—none of the girls came into town that night. I guess nights like that is why God made beer.

What does a man think of himself when it appears that he has been a failure and other men have been successful? Do men compare themselves to other men? It was something that I had always done and such comparisons have adversely affected me. In the television program 'Everybody Loves Raymond' there is constant competition between the two brothers Raymond and Robert to outdo each other. In one segment Raymond wins an award, which is indicative of his career success and Robert declares: "Raymond, your success is not my failure." But do not men allow the success of other men to reflect on their own failures? I sure do! Don't all men measure themselves against other men? Do other men agonize over their perceived failures while reflecting on the perceived successes of other men? How do men console themselves over their failures?

The question was asked: "what would a man prefer—an income of $50,000 per year with everyone else making only $25,000 per year—or—an income of

$250,000 per year with everyone else making $500,000 per year?" How would any of us answer that question for ourselves? How do we measure success and failure? Is success for us to do better than others? Is that how most of us measure success?

Most men do buy into the concept that: "a man is what he does." Don't most women buy into the concept that: "a woman is how she looks?" Is that why retirement from a work career is so difficult for most men? After his work career has ended then what does a man do to give him self-worth? What is a man to do? Of course absolutely **no** work career success could or would ever make up for a man's failure as a father and daddy! Vito Corleone was to have said: "no man is a real man who is not a father to his children."

Wasn't there a NFL coach whose team won Super Bowl championships? That was the epitome of his career success! But at the time he admitted that he didn't even know the birthdays of his children? Wow! While <u>not</u> knowing the details of this coach's relationship with his children—and also not wanting to throw stones at him—it sure appeared that he placed no value on being a good father or daddy? He bragged about having "put his wife on waivers" when he left coaching a college team to take the position as a NFL coach—he had divorced his wife. Vito Corleone would not have viewed this man as having been successful—would he?

Somewhere I once read that every man should do three things in his life: have a son; plant a tree; and write a book. I've had a son and a daughter. I think that I once planted a tree? As for writing a book—it seems that 81 percent of Americans feel that they should write a book but only 2 percent actually do! I am making a best effort to write this book—a memoir. And even in this endeavor there is the question of whether I have the talent for such an enterprise? I sure have a knack for questioning myself—don't I?

It was Friday and another laundry day for me. It had been another unproductive week, as I still had not found a job, and not even a job prospect. Things change, I reminded myself, there is always next week for dreams to come true. I often wished that my dreams would come true, now more than ever before. Of course, I wondered about some of the dreams that I had been having, did I really want some of those dreams to come true? Could it be that there was a danger that lurked within my dreams? I suffered a terribly restless and sleepless night. At 1:00 am I went downstairs to watch TV, finally returning to bed at 3:00 am. As usual I did not sleep well at all.

I had a dream in which I was still married to my ex-wife. "Do you want to see a counselor?" I asked her in the dream, feeling more pity than love for her. "Yes, I want to go to counseling." She replied to me, looking sad and disturbed. While in this dream, I was thinking that it would be best for me to just divorce her, to get out of what had turned into a bad marriage, and to get on with my life, even thinking that I night marry again. Although still married (in my dream) we had been living apart. I thought of the promiscuous lifestyle that she had been living. At the risk of 'STD's' I realized that I could <u>never</u> again have sex with her. IF ever again I felt any desire for her, well, it could not ever be realized, not ever! It was best that I divorce her, but her sad eyes made me reluctant to tell her. I started to reach out to take her in my arms, but backed away instead. I realized that it would have been an empty gesture. Although I don't like it she too often enters my thoughts and my dreams—far too often! She would laugh at that!

Still within the dream, I thought of my Son who was still in high school. I'd have to ask him to make a decision about with whom he would live after the divorce. Would he stay with his mother and younger sister? As it actually turned out, my Son remained with his mother—neither of my children ever chose to live with me. That was a disappointment to me.

It was a strange dream. It was just a dream, <u>not</u> quite like the reality of my actual divorce. In life my children had been young, ages 9 and 6, when I got divorced. After a bitter custody battle, which I lost, and in which I believed that my own attorney had betrayed me, my ex-wife actually did go on to live a very promiscuous lifestyle, bedding down countless men as if she had something to prove. I had learned later on that the judge "did not like you" (meaning me) and that is why I apparently lost the custody case. At the time my ex-wife was dating a rich and prominent boyfriend who may also have had some affect on the case? She won—I lost! The children also lost!

Another major difference in the dream, between it and the reality of life, was that it had been several years since his ex-wife looked as good as she did in my dream. I <u>no</u> longer found her to be attractive as I once did. The love and especially the desire for her were gone! I no longer saw her in the same way that I once did. The image of her that I once held in my mind had been badly tarnished and was gone. I now saw who and what she really was. I was reminded by the saying by Goethe that: "love is an ideal thing; marriage is a real thing. A confusion of the real with the ideal never goes unpunished."

I had truly loved my ex-wife and had always been faithful to her—something that she could NOT claim. I thought that I had seen beauty and goodness within her—and—I had fallen in love with the image of her that I held in my mind.

Unfortunately, the image of her conflicted with the reality of her. She was a pathological liar, a cheat, and I had come to realize that she had never really loved him. And unlike what Kenny Rogers sung in his song—she did NOT believe in me.

While we were still married I had coached my young son in both church league basketball and Little League baseball. At the end of each basketball season I bought trophies for all of the players and took the team out for pizza, all at my own expense. It was years later that it occurred to me—I could not ever remember hearing my wife tell me that she was proud of me for anything I ever did. When a wife does not love her husband it does not matter what he does—she just does not give a damn!

I remember when I had coached my Son in basketball at the YMCA on Saturdays. After the morning practice the two of us would then stop at a Dunkin Donuts. Comically there always seemed to be police officers at the donut shop—really! They always asked my Son if he was able to eat both of the big donuts before him. He always did! One Saturday when we got home my wife got angry with me for not buying any donuts to bring home to her. Perhaps I had been thoughtless and wrong? Perhaps she was envious of the time I had shared with our Son? The attention did have to be all on her or she pouted!

I have never claimed to my children that I had been the best of husbands—I surely had my faults. I did have a negative attitude and a melancholy disposition. But I had never lied to my wife during the marriage; I had never cheated on her during the marriage; and I had truly loved her. And, as the Willie Nelson song went, she "had always been on my mind." I was too serious natured and I did not make anyone laugh. I remember watching an interview of Joanne Woodward and Paul Newman. They've been married for a very long time. She was asked what kept them together? She told the interviewer: "Paul still makes me laugh." That is something that I failed to do—I was just too damn serious natured. I did not make anyone laugh. Would it have made any difference in my marriage? I doubted that it would have made any difference to a woman who didn't love me or believe in me. Hell—we were barely into their marriage when she first cheated on me!

Unknown to me during our marriage—she had criticized me to everyone, even to my best friend. The telltale sign and indication that she was having an affair was when she raised her level of criticism of me. She had once met with my best friend for lunch. This was early in 1970. The purpose of the meeting was for her to express the concern that she didn't think that I would ever be successful in my career—she was having an affair at the time with her boss at work. This was very early in our marriage before we had any children.

Near the end of our marriage she had stated to the wife of this same best friend that I was suicidal. When my friend was told that by his wife his response was that my wife was having an affair again. How did he know? He knew that I would never do such a thing because I loved my children too much to do to them what my Father had done. He knew that it was her usual smoke screen to hide that she was running around again. There was no doubt that my wife was indeed again having an affair at work with her boss at the time.

Also towards the end of our marriage she became openly flirtatious with other men. I remember her asking one of my co-workers after a softball game—"you need to come by the house to teach me how to dance." What blatant flirting in front of me! Obviously she did not equate marriage with faithfulness. Did so many of her subsequent relationships and marriages fail because of her continued infidelities?

No matter what I did she always criticized me. I drove a subcompact car as an in-the-field sales representative and generally drove 3000 miles every month in a sales territory. My Son called it "the toy car." It was a Datsun model 1200. It enabled me to afford a large family car for my wife and children to insure their safety. Even in that the wife was critical of me—as she asked why didn't I buy a sports car for myself? That I might be sacrificing my own safety for the benefit of my family didn't matter to her. While we were married I had never criticized her to anyone!

In looking back, I realized that I should have divorced her when I found out about the first affair and before we'd had any children. Love sure is blind!! Love is also very stupid!! During 12 years of marriage, it is unknown to me just how many affairs that she did have while working? Did she frequently change jobs because she had been having affairs at each of her jobs and when they ended she left that job? What a dreadful thought to have, that my wife had numerous affairs while we were married. There is no question that she again was having an affair at work when the marriage ended—it was like déjà vu all over again from her first known affair!

Could I have been a better husband and helpmate?—YES! Could I have been a better father and daddy?—YES! Could I been less serious and smiled more?—YES! It is very doubtful that the marriage would have lasted no matter what I had done differently or how differently I had been. I certainly felt a sense of guilt that I had failed at my marriage; that perhaps if I had been a better husband the marriage would have been successful. The reality is that it probably would not have mattered however different or better I had been as a husband. There is the saying: "loving the wrong person in the right way just won't turn out right." The marriage was doomed to failure from the start. Judging from the activities of my ex-wife since our divorce—apparently she was not exactly right for any man? I've always stated that it took two to make a marriage and two to break a marriage. I have also always stated that it was important to look at the activities of the two after their divorce—it told a lot about them in their marriage!

In defense of my ex-wife, my seriousness, my negative attitudes, my not being a fun guy—all made me a most difficult guy with whom to live. In many ways, except for a few very serious 'flaws, she once was a good wife and mother. I just don't know what drastically changed her?

I have two children whom I love and four grandchildren and a daughter-in-law <u>all</u> whom I love very dearly. Despite a broken heart that just will not heal, and despite a deep sadness within me, I am very thankful for my children and my grandchildren and my daughter-in-law. They are the good that came out of the marriage. Despite any sadness they all give me great joy.

It was unfortunate that I had never found another to love—worse that I often feel like I will go to my grave NEVER having been truly loved by a woman. I accept that my wife of 12 years had never really loved me. My heart remains broken. I feel like 'Humpty Dumpty' from my childhood rhymes as all of the king's men and all of the king's horses could not put my broken heart together again nor could all of the angels and saints in Heaven put my broken life together again. The old songs from the early 'Rock and Roll' era often stated that: "only love can heal a broken heart." There was no love to heal my broken heart. Having had children while married sure made a divorce most difficult and it made it heart wrenching for a man! Isn't it true that: "if you have children, a divorce will affect you emotionally for the rest of your life." It sure has affected me!

Morning came and I awoke very tired as though I had physically experienced the events of my dreams. I often awakened with such a feeling of tiredness after many dreams, like my body had been transported into the activities about which I had dreamt, and as though my dreams had been real and had actually happened.

Was I the only man who lived alone and who often went days without any conversation with another person? I had recently talked on the telephone with a friend from college who did remark that he too went days in his house without any contact or conversation with other people. What about other men who live alone? Do most or all such men experience days of isolation? Do they go days alone without any conversation with anyone? Do they, like me, think: how different would they be and how different would their lives be if they shared love with a good woman? How does it adversely affect a man to go day after day without anyone telling him that they love him? Didn't married men live a lot longer than single men? At least when old married men got ill they had a wife to drive them to the doctor—I had no one.

The next day, while out jogging, my mind drifted to thinking about how my ex-wife had looked in last night's dream. She looked as she once did when we were still married; she was slim, pretty, and attractive. She no longer looked like that anymore as the years and her lifestyle had hardened her. The years of marrying—divorcing—marrying—divorcing—with a promiscuous lifestyle in between her numerous marriages—had spoiled her looks as she had become quite hardened. It showed on her face. Of course with graying and thinning hair, I no longer looked the way I once did.

I reflected on the woman I once imagined her to be. It was this image of her within my mind that I had grown to love and value. Maybe it wasn't her fault that she did not fulfill such an image, perhaps no woman could? I had never really known her as I had only a glimpse of her lies which were much more extensive than I ever knew. And she had cheated on me from the very first that we had been married. The truth of what she was like, well, it was a horror! It was really a lie that the only way to get to know someone is to live with that person. You could live with someone for years and still <u>never</u> get to really know that person. Doesn't everyone wear a mask?

After our divorce my ex-wife dropped her mask and the real woman emerged. It turned out that she was a pathological liar; a cheat; and a real selfish self-centered woman who, showed little concern for her own children. She had even cashed in our Daughter's US Savings Bonds in order to pay for the girl's braces for her teeth. She no longer had any regard for either child. Bringing her many lovers home to sleep with her in front of her children did not matter to her. No one mattered to her!

All of her energies went into living a wildly promiscuous lifestyle that included more marriages and divorces; marriages that lasted six weeks, six months, and two years, five years—she was currently with yet another husband as she had tied Elizabeth Taylor's record for marriages. I wonder how long that marriage would last? She seemed to hide her previous marriages, divorces, and multitude of affairs from her subsequent husbands—did any of them know how many times she had been married or with how many men with whom she'd been? Had she been married and divorced once before she and I were married?

I cannot imagine my finding any woman on this Earth, who had been married seven times previously, to be attractive no matter how she looked. I cannot imagine myself ever being the third or fourth or fifth, etc., husband of any woman on this Earth. But then that is just the way that I am!

Was she now happy and blessed, as she seemed to claim? After all of her affairs and previous marriages had my ex-wife finally found what she might have been searching for all of the years since our divorce? Why had she not found happiness in any of her previous relationships? Certainly if she had wouldn't they have lasted? I wonder if she cheated on all of her other husbands and lovers as she had cheated on me in our marriage—is that why none of her subsequent marriages lasted very long? Could the following saying be true and possibly applicable to her?

"It is the mind that first makes the marriage; and the mind that breaks or <u>adulterates</u> its marriage cannot possibly find happiness in any human relationship"

Our twelve years of marriage together only seemed to indicate that I was the most blind and dumb man of all of her lovers. All of the years that her other seven marriages had lasted barely added up to the twelve years she and I had been married. I had truly loved her and it seemed that no other man had been so dumb to have really loved her as I did. How could I have been so wrong about her? The woman I had imagined her to be; had thought her to be, had never really existed. In my mind and in my dreams, she had been a better woman, mother, and wife. I would <u>never</u> have expected my ex-wife to go on to live such a sexually promiscuous life after our divorce. Wow! Had I been really wrong about her! How could I have been so blind? I sure had deluded myself badly! Love sure defies all reason and rational thoughts of the mind!

What if, after our divorce, she had married and that the marriage had lasted all of these years—how would I then feel? Wouldn't I have really felt bad about myself; wouldn't I have felt guilty; and wouldn't I have felt that our divorce had been all, of my fault? Wouldn't I have felt that I had really been a bad husband? But, my ex-wife was on marriage #8 and she experienced six other failed marriages besides our divorce. Could it be that she was not such a good wife to these other husbands? Had she lied and cheated on all of her other husbands as she had done to me? Didn't I feel some justification in believing that perhaps our divorce was more her fault than it was my fault? Actually it did not really console me nor make it any easier for me to get over my love for her, nor to get over the pain of our divorce.

A former neighbor had speculated that my ex-wife had suffered an emotional breakdown. Could that have been possible? After our separation she changed completely from the woman I thought that I knew. There were little things like her wearing earrings, which was something that she had never done before. She had no earlobes. Then she turned to drinking wine at night, which again was something that she had never done while we were married. Another little thing was that she began to wear sleeveless dresses, which was something that she had never done while we were married. And she often stayed up late at night with her subsequent lovers watching television—she had very often gone to bed early each night while we were married.

It was all speculation—I will just never know what went wrong in our marriage or what made my ex-wife change into a totally different person than I thought I knew her to be? Perhaps she reverted to what had been her behavior—unknown to me—before our marriage? Her post divorce behavior did make me feel less guilty about my contributions to our divorce.

There was something that she had said at our engagement party—after she had too much to drink—which nearly caused me to cancel our marriage. I cannot remember exactly what she had said that night but I do remember my misgivings about marrying her. I sure made a terrible mistake to have married her.

Then again I do have some fond memories of our years together—our marriage was not all bad from my perspective. Perhaps it had been bad from her perspective? I don't know?

I removed the bandage on my left arm. The wound had healed completely. I still could not remember or determine how I had been injured. Forgotten was the dream of being cut by an opponent's sword in the arena as a Roman gladiator.

After having received a call from a friend, in response to her request for help, I wired her $1500 no questions asked. Now, after two weeks had passed, there wasn't even a thank you note or call from her. I never heard from her again. That hurt! It made me trust people even less. As a Taurus I was not particularly trusting of people to begin with nor were Sicilians very trusting of people.

To avoid the hurt and the pain I drifted more and more into what I called my "warrior dimension", which was that different dimension of time and space in which I suffered no adversity, no failures, no heartbreak, and no loneliness. I was most comfortable in that other dimension. Sure, I was alone when I was a warrior, but there was no pain associated with my aloneness. It was an existence devoid of all emotion. Actually, here it was best to be alone in order to avoid all distractions; it was best in that it allowed me to fully concentrate all of my senses in facing battle. Combat took all of one's concentration to survive. Wasn't: The strongest man the man who could stand alone?"

Survival, victory, defeating his opponent—these could be the <u>only</u> thoughts of a warrior in the midst of battle. He could not afford to think of love, of a woman, of children, of anything that would make him vulnerable to defeat. To survive and to win, he must utilize all of his strength, courage, power, and senses on the battle at hand—all of the resources of mind and full concentration.

I sensed a creeping danger, the hardness and toughness, that I imagined in my so-called warrior dimension that was necessary for my survival; that it was becoming a dominating aspect of my character and personality in my real world and in my waking hours. I feared that I was losing my sensitivity and caring for other people. More and more I asked myself the question—what does it matter? All that I was, thought, felt did not seem to carry over into my imagined dream world of the warrior, but there were characteristics of the warrior in the dream world that did carry over to affect me in my waking hours. The two worlds in which I escaped and in which I actually lived were merging! Was it true that: "a man is what he thinks and what he thinks he becomes."

Since being out of work I had become very withdrawn, often going days without any conversation or social interaction with anyone. That concerned me. I was alone too much, alone with the imagination of my mind. Essentially I was <u>not</u> a loner but I spent too much time alone. Didn't the nuns in parochial school warn all of the students: "an idle mind is the Devil's workshop." Damn if that was ever so true! It seemed that the nuns were correct on all of their warnings.

I wanted and needed a good woman; I wanted and needed love; and I sure needed some TLC. I wanted a woman to love; to care about me; and to value me. I accepted the saying: "there's nothing worse than being alone". I had needs, desires, and it hurt me deeply that none were being fulfilled. I hurt emotionally and spiritually. Of course, I did accept that "bad company was a lot worse than no company"; that having a woman who did not love me and who cheated on me was so much worse than having no woman at all. The warrior in my mind did not hurt.

I remember a segment of the TV program—Stingray—in which the hero, 'Ray', drove an older model Corvette Stingray. In the segment remembered, Ray, is told by a pretty young woman that he shouldn't be alone in life and that no one should ever be alone. Ray answers her that he didn't plan on being alone but that is the way it has worked out for him in his life. I sure identified with 'Ray' as I had not planned to be alone but I was now alone. And that is the way the cookie sometimes crumbles! What of other men and how their life turned out—did the life of other men turn out just the way they had planned? Or, was the life of other men best reflected in the saying: "The plans of mice and men often go astray?" Was life just all chaos? A younger cousin of mine repeated what our maternal Grandfather was fond of saying: "Man makes his plans and God laughs."

Except for a few minutes of conversation with a store clerk, I talked with no one yesterday. Yet, I felt comfortable with and in my solitude, not feeling the pain of my unfulfilled wants, needs, or desires. What I did feel was hardness, toughness, all of the attributes I constantly imagined myself as possessing, the qualities of a warrior. I felt a real comfort in this! I could be alone and I could survive alone!

Did other men have such thoughts and feelings? Did other men imagine themselves to be warriors? Did other men imagine themselves to be heroes? Once again I asked the redundant question that appears time and time herein—what did other men think and feel? Were the thoughts and feelings of other men anything like my thoughts and feelings? How did other men act towards what they thought and felt? How did other men deal with the reality of their lives? How did other men deal with their aloneness? How did other men, especially war veterans, deal with the demons in their minds? Did other war veterans even have many demons in their minds? Did they do better than me?

One of the negative legacies of the Viet Nam war was that so many veterans dropped out of society completely as they went off to live in the woods alone. All too many other veterans had become homeless, wandering the streets. Many suffered from mental problems seemingly brought on by what they had experienced in that war. Obviously many other men did not deal very well with the demons in their minds. Of all of the homeless people in America 23 percent were veterans. That is sad!

I remember watching the black and white TV program Superman as a boy. I often dreamed of my being a Superman; and of living my own life being "for truth, justice, and the American way." As a boy I had even prayed to God for the fulfillment of such a dream! I always wanted to be a hero!! Didn't every man want to be a hero? Could I have been the only boy who had had such prayers and dreams? Surely other boys wanted to grow up to be heroes? Surely other men dreamed of being heroes? Didn't they? Heck, I laughed to myself, why do men join the Marine Corps? It had to be more than the spiffy uniform! Could it be that they joined the Corps to be heroes? Do all boys want to grow up to be heroes?

One of the questions I often asked job applicants when I was a sales manager was: "Who are your heroes and why?" The answers that job candidates gave me generally provided great insight to the values and character of the applicants.

The movie—The Great Santini—was on TV and I watched most of it as I liked the story of a tough Marine fighter pilot who was a true warrior in every sense of the word. At the story's end—'Santini' becomes a real hero by sacrificing his own life to save the lives of many others. The engine of his plane flames out and he steers it over water to avoid the plane crashing into any housing and possibly killing people on the ground. He stays with the plane and goes down with it getting killed. As I watched the movie—I, the imagined warrior came to tears. I do have another side to me.

I remember taking my Son and my Daughter to see the movie when they were just little children. I sat in the middle of them as I held their hands and cried with them through the sad parts of the movie. My taking them to see that movie had been my way of trying to tell my children that I recognized that I was too much like 'Santini' in the movie—tough on them and so very demanding. It was sort of an explanation of the way that I was and also an attempt to apologize to them. In the 'Taurus Character Analysis'—it states how: "the Taurus father is strict with his children and may even appear to be tyrannical to them." I feared and greatly regretted that I had been too much like the 'Taurus father' and that I feared that I had been tyrannical to my own children. I had been harsh. Damn I was so sorry for that! And now my Granddaughter complains that I am "too tough" on her. Will I never chill out and mellow?

Yet at the same time I often felt that I had been doing all that I knew to do to prepare my Son and my Daughter for life—much in the way that Sergeant Stryker had prepared young Marines for battle. If they would end up living successful lives then I would feel that my efforts were rewarded and that I had done the right thing. I often warned both children that as their father I was more forgiving than Life would be. I further warned them that they would make mistakes in life—everyone does—but for them to try to avoid the mistakes for which they would pay and regret all of their lives.

I greatly love both my Son and Daughter more than anything, more than my whole life; and I feared losing them, after the divorce, by my toughness and I feared pushing them away. IF only they could know, as my friends knew, that I was much tougher on myself than I was on anybody else. I was very demanding of myself, and often too demanding of others. I had at my age of 66 begun to mellow just a little bit—only a little bit! At long last I was beginning to learn how to laugh at myself. Wow! I was making progress—not a lot but some!

In the movie The Great Santini the mother's admonition to the children to be strong in public, to not cry at the funeral, reminded me of my own Father's funeral. I was just a boy of age 12 at the time when my Father died. I could not remember having cried at the funeral. I still could hear an aunt telling me "to be strong like a soldier" and I had been strong. I did not cry during or at my Father's funeral.

Did I ever really get over the death and loss of my father? I recognized that my Father's suicide in the house with me present on another floor defined me as an adult. I could still hear my Uncle shout—"no, Joe, don't"—and then the sound of the German Luger handgun going off. I had never really gotten over the loss of my Father and I accepted that I probably never would. Something within me died with my Father that night. It was yet another 'demon' with which I had to deal in my life. Damn the demons! They cause ruin in one's life.

I found it curious that here I was, the imagined tough warrior, crying while just watching a movie. My tears were over my own Father and for all of the moments stolen away from both of us, which were never to be shared and enjoyed. And my tears were over my own Son and my Daughter because of the moments stolen away from us due to the divorce, their childhood moments lost forever. I dwelled on all of the nights I did not get to tuck them in bed and all of the days I did not take them to school or pick them up from school—so many moments that we never got to share together. The opportunity to have shared those precious moments was lost for all time. NOT even Almighty God could give anyone back yesterday and any of the moments that were lost for all time. It all created such a deep sadness within my heart and within me that a few were able to observe despite my attempts to mask the hurt with a persona of toughness and hardness. My Daughter-in-Law has observed that: "you have a deep sadness within." A friend had also observed and stated the same. Had I given up on love? Did I exist only in the past and in my dream world? Had I given up on life?

It was the year 2006 when I was age 65 while I watched the movie—Field of Dreams—with my Granddaughter—she observed that my eyes watered during the movie. I told her that I always came to tears while watching that movie no matter how many times I watched it because it always reminded me of my Father. My Granddaughter remarked—"Pop-Pop, your father would be very proud of you."—a beautiful and highly treasured compliment from such a precious and beautiful and most special Princess! She is really an extremely bright and sensitive young lady—she was very intelligent and bright from the day she was born! Like ALL of my grandchildren, she is very special to me.

The legacy of my Father was his expression of love through the words: "I love you as high as the sky and deep as the ocean." Despite how very tough my Father had been on me, and he had been, he always expressed his love for me, and his pride in the excellent grades I made at school. My Father had always told me: "you're going to go to Princeton University and become a doctor." The year that my Father died I had just started 7th grade. That year I achieved the highest average grades that I had ever made in eight years of grade school. My Father was not there to witness my winning the academic excellence award plus three other awards as I graduated from grade school.

An uncle, who was one of my Father's brother's, always offered to take me to father-son communion breakfasts at the parish church, but I always refused to attend, as I had no father. I felt that I didn't belong and would not attend such events. This same uncle often took me fishing which I greatly appreciated.

I remember that I had always felt different from other children. The feeling seemed to have started even before my Father had died and intensified with his death. I remember that other children had a scar on their arms from their smallpox vaccination, but that I did not. I had often wondered why did I not have a scar on my arm while it seemed that all of the other children had a scar? And after my Father had died, it seemed that I was the only boy in the entire neighborhood who had either parent who was dead. That disturbed me greatly. Isn't it a wonder what young boys think about and what affects them all of their adult lives?

Playing sports, graduation from high school, later from college, and especially when I received my Commission as a Naval Officer—so many times I had wished that my Father had been alive to share those moments with me and I did envy those others whose fathers had been there for them.

My Father would have been a good mentor to me. Throughout my life and in my work career, I had NOT ever had a mentor. I'd made career decisions on my own without the benefit of any advice, and there had been many mistakes. Every job that I had ever worked at I had found on my own. No one had ever really given me a break. I had been on my own throughout my career. One job interviewer once asked me who had been most influential in my life and career? I thought long and hard then remarked that there hadn't really been anyone.

Would I have been allowed to continue playing football in high school IF my Father had been alive? I was an excellent running back as a junior varsity player. I just never got to know how good I might have been as I gave up all sports in order to work and save money for college. A classmate who had played football with me supposedly remarked to a cousin about me—that he thought I could have been one of the best running backs that the school had ever had. While that sounded nice—I didn't quite believe that myself. Having quit football to work was another deep hurt and a demon! I never found out how good I was or might have been?

Do other men wonder what they would have and could have been? Do other men wonder what their lives might have been like if such and such had happened or had not have happened? Isn't all of a man's life a question of could have, should have, and would have? Could any man's life really have been different, or does each man live out the life that was determined for him by fate and destiny?

How else could I survive such hurts that I carried deep within my heart and within my soul except to imagine myself to be a warrior and to try to exist in some other dimension of time and space? How did other men survive such hurts? Into what cave did other men withdraw in order to lick their wounds and try to heal their hurts? Were other men warriors? Were all men warriors or just a few men?

How were other men affected by the death of their father? Ty Cobb had been one of the greatest of all professional baseball players and his lifetime career batting average is still tops for all players who have ever played professional baseball. He was one of the charter members to be first inducted into the Baseball Hall of Fame. Cobb was probably the meanest man ever to play the game and was certainly hated and disliked universally by all players of his era. While he was a boy Cobb's father was accidentally shot to death by Cobb's mother upon his father returning home unexpectedly. His father was thought to have been a burglar. Did the death of his father, while Cobb was still a boy affect Cobb in such a way that it made him a very mean and hated man?

Larry Bird's father committed suicide when Bird was nineteen years of age. Yet Bird went on to be one of the great college basketball players and a Hall of Fame NBA professional basketball player. Had he been able to deal with the death of his father in such a way that it did not affect him so adversely? Of course no one knows what is in Bird's heart and mind in regards his thoughts about the death of his father.

Does how a boy's father die have a different affect on the boy as he grows into a man? What if a boy's father died in combat in a war—how does that affect the boy? What if a boy's father dies in an accident or of a heart attack—how does that affect the boy? What if the boy's father has committed suicide—how does that affect the boy?

How does a boy handle the suicide of his father? Does it create the fear within the boy that he carries many of his father's genes and that the possibility of his own death by suicide exists? As I reached the age of 37 at which my own Father had committed suicide it did make me fearful. I was greatly relieved with the passing of that year. I was much like my Father and yet very much different from him. I did have some of his weaknesses, but I had strengths never possessed by him. If he had died by other than a suicide how would that have affected me?

In order to deal with the death of his father does it force the boy to become a warrior in order to survive such a loss? Do any such circumstances create warriors? Are all men warriors no matter what has happened to them as boys? Do men choose to become warriors or is it just their lot in life to be warriors? I had thought about having cried while watching the movie—The Great Santini—and the tears did not disturb me. After all there did exist another side to me, a gentler softer side that had needs, wants, desires, hopes, and dreams; a side of me that needed a woman and love. It was only in my imagination in which I was a warrior, wasn't it? Besides I was a 2nd generation born in America Sicilian. I had witnessed the older men in my family cry tears of hurt and tears of joy. They were no less men because of such expressions and shedding of tears, nor was I.

Restless is the warrior who is between battles. I was very restless indeed! Besides missing a paycheck from Xerox, the only other thing that I actually missed were the battles that I had fought with so many managers who had been hateful to me and who had been incompetent. I always challenged my incompetent managers. That apparently was part of my Taurus personality.

My friends within the Xerox Division for which they all worked called me "the G. Gordon Liddy of Xerox." I was a legend due to the many battles I'd fought with the Company and which I had won or at least had survived. What the Company had never understood about me was that I imagined myself to be a warrior; that I liked being a warrior; and that I had to an extent enjoyed the battles. I was not one to ever turn down a challenge, especially from some incompetent manager. Of course I probably brought a lot of 'battles' upon myself.

It is in the midst of battle that a warrior feels most alive. It is while the battle rages on that a warrior is at his best. It is what he has prepared himself for physically, emotionally, and mentally, and he finds an inner strength with which to survive and even win. It took all of his concentration to do battle.

No one ever seemed to have detected the telltale comments in my conversation, my references to having "battle plans" when involved in a confrontation with the Company. I did seem different. I did give the appearance of almost enjoying the confrontations. My friends within the Division never suspected my true warrior mentality. They wondered why I would even battle the Company? It is doubtful that there was another employee of the company quite like I had been?

While many other sales representatives backed down in confrontations with incompetent managers who had taken advantage of them I never backed down and always stood up for myself no matter what the costs. It didn't matter to me what level of manager that I had to confront—I had no fear and would not be intimidated by titles. As I often remarked—the company wasn't the Mafia and they didn't break kneecaps otherwise I'd been prudent enough to keep my mouth shut. The worst that they could do was fire me from my job and that just never intimidated me.

With a couple of close friends I did reveal my enjoyment of the battle; of matching wits, with managers who were mostly incompetent, with managers none of whom were as tough as I was, and that I felt comfortable with sword and shield in hand doing battle. These close friends had a suspicion as to what I was.

The last manager I'd had at Xerox in 1990 and 1991 was also one of the best I had ever had, an excellent Region Manager and Leader, and who was most competent! Upon reviewing my personnel file, this manager had stated that I "took shots" at people. I refuted this observation by giving a sort of analogy to this manager.

I stated that I was like a tiger in the jungle minding my own business when a hunter came into the jungle and took a shot at me, hit me, and wounded me. At that point it was the tiger (me) that became the hunter and the hunter had become the hunted. I had had all too many managers who had treated me unfairly, who had taken shots at me. I always returned their fire!! I would NEVER have won or even survived the many battles IF I had ever been wrong. And I always seemed to have the proper documentation to prove that I had been mistreated. I'd had a different manager for darn nearly every year I had worked for Xerox.

It was in 1989 that I had had a major confrontation with a Region Manager. Although I had pre-qualified for President's Club by the end of June this RM had tried to intimidate me and had tried to run me out of the company. This same RM had presented me with my Annual Performance Appraisal for 1989 several months after it was due in 1990 and had given me a poor evaluation despite the fact that I had achieved President's Club award for my performance.

Most disturbing to me were the lies that the RM had put in the Performance Appraisal about me that questioned my integrity. I took the situation up to the vice president level. The VP sort of dismissed me and displayed a certain amount of arrogance—sort of like with an attitude of why am I having to deal with this lowly employee. But, true to my nature, I persistently pressed my case. I would not have my honesty or integrity sullied by lies.

Upon resolution of my case by the Division Personnel Manager, the VP admitted that: "they had put someone in a position of management who did not belong there"—in reference to the Region Manager with whom I had had the confrontation. My excellent documentation had served me well. The RM had lied and even put such lies into my Performance Appraisal. The lies and incompetence of the RM were exposed. He was subsequently demoted and was not put in a position of management again. I even received a retroactive raise in salary.

Confrontations just seemed to follow me, or perhaps I had a way of creating them and bringing them upon myself? It must have been me because I certainly seemed to be confrontational. I guess it was the warrior, within me, that was always looking for and creating battles for myself? It must have been me because other sales representatives did not have the problems that I continually encountered with my managers. It wasn't just at Xerox—I also had a confrontation in the Navy with a commanding officer.

When initially assigned to the Oriskany in the Communications Department my Commanding Officer also assigned me to be the Registered Publications Custodian. This assignment involved responsibility for all of the Top Secret, Secret, and Confidential Communication codes including those distributed to the pilots monthly. I was told that it was just an automatic re-assignment from the previous officer who held that responsibility. With some excellent guidance from the Intelligence Officer aboard the Oriskany I demanded that an inventory needed to be taken with a formal written acceptance letter of the responsibility. My Commanding Officer protested such a procedure but I stuck to my guns.

I submitted a letter to the Captain of the Oriskany via the Communication's Officer, via the Operations Officer, via the Executive Officer further requesting a formal relieving procedure with documentation. I was just an ensign at the time and I was bucking a lieutenant commander. With the advice of the Intelligence Officer I stood my ground. After all I had come off a Destroyer Escort and I did have some experience in proper Navy procedures. I was quite proud to have been rated "exceptional" for "moral courage" on my Navy Fitness Report by the Captain of the Oriskany. I could be a pit bull at times when I believed myself to be right! The Navy had proper procedures for such a challenge by me to do the right thing in the right way.

To the credit of Joseph Wilson the founder of Xerox—the Company had an open door policy, which was similar to communication procedures in the Navy. Such procedures worked to protect its employees. In many ways it was a special company. Another region manager, at a region dinner in the early 1980's, stated that: "Xerox was one of the three most difficult companies for which to work." This was measured by mental and emotional breakdowns by employees, stress, divorces, physical ailments, and pressure put on employees to perform, etc. The three companies he listed were Xerox, Johnson & Johnson, and ITT. I laughed as I remarked that I had worked for two of the three companies—Johnson & Johnson and Xerox—and could attest to their being most difficult for which to work! I also prided myself for having worked for both companies. They may have been very difficult companies for which to work, but they both were also very excellent companies.

When I had started my career with Xerox there was the dreaded charge back pay system for its sales representatives. When rental equipment, which was on a thirty day rental agreement, was cancelled by a customer Xerox would charge back to the current territory sales representative the current commission rate despite that sales rep not having placed the equipment nor having been paid any commission for its placement. It was possible to not make money during a month and to go in the hole, and lose money during a month. Many a sales representative had to leave the company because their reconciling commission balance—what they owed back to Xerox—was so large due to cancelled equipment charged back to them that they had no recourse but to leave Xerox. They would never have been able to work their way out of such a hole. Yes, it was one heck of a tough company for which to work! Only the very strong and the performers survived a lengthy career with Xerox! I somehow managed to put in 21+ years with Xerox! I wonder how?

After I had been downsized out of the company, I remarked to friends that I had never had any illusions that I would win the war. Although I won and survived many battles I always recognized that I would lose the war. As I often reminded people—"you actually can fight City Hall, you just can not win."

I left the company with my head held high and on good terms. I was part of a 2500 employee reduction in force in 1992. I left feeling that the company was never going to allow me to do more than I had already done in my career. I regretted that the company had never given me the opportunity to become a sales manager, which I had always aspired to be. Although I had been designated a ready now candidate for promotion to sales manager—the opportunity just never was presented to me. Ironically, after I left Xerox, I never again worked as a sales representative. Other companies _did_ give me the opportunity to be a sales manager, and I was quite good as a leader.

How did I become to imagine myself to be a warrior? When did it all begin? Had I been a warrior in some previous life? As one of her criticisms of me—my ex-wife often told me: "You can't help it the way that you are." And what way was I?

Why did I think the way that I did? Why was I the way that I was? Was I crazy? My ex-wife, throughout our bitter separation and divorce, claimed that I "had mental problems." My response was always to laugh off her claims. I never denied her claims; I just stated that she did not have the medical degrees or training for her to make such a determination. Maybe I did have mental problems?

My ex-wife's attorney sent a letter to my own attorney claiming that I had "mental problems." In a very calm and controlled voice, I asked my own attorney if that meant I could kill both my ex-wife and her attorney and get away with murder by claiming insanity since the proof of my insanity was in their own letter. Surely I could get away with their murder, couldn't I? I was joking but my attorney saw no humor in it. How ironic that it was that others did not see humor in situations as I did.

My own attorney became greatly frightened and concerned that I indeed would commit such murders. Perhaps it was the icy cool control that had alarmed my attorney most, as it could be frightening because it was so unsettling. People were use to emotional outbursts of anger under such circumstances and not a cool icy controlled demeanor. I showed no emotion at all. My stone face showed no expression of any kind. The question and concern of others was always—what danger lurked beneath that calm exterior of his? What could he be thinking? What was he capable of doing? I could be a scary guy.

I was a Sicilian in every aspect of the term. In my own mind I was Michael Corleone from the book and movie—The Godfather—icy cool and calm and most dangerous! It was a practiced persona. Actually that was yet another trait of the Taurus character—"it is dangerous to deliberately make a Taurus angry." Was it all a result of the stars as to the way that I was? For me it was a practiced persona that started long ago as a boy watching my heroes in movies who were always calm and controlled no matter the circumstances and danger around them. It just wasn't natural as most people responded in emotional outbursts under the same conditions in which I often found myself. That is why I often frightened others. I seemed to have a control over my emotions not exhibited by any other men. The Stoics were some of my favorite philosophers.

One of my favorite books was by the Roman Emperor and Stoic philosopher The Meditations of Marcus Aurelius. I also liked reading the Sayings of Epectitus, which expressed the philosophy of the former Greek slave and Stoic philosopher. I remembered that the late Admiral James Bond Stockdale—who had survived seven and one half years as a POW during the Viet Nam War—had often quoted from the philosophy of Epectitus. Stockdale had been awarded the Congressional Medal of Honor for his acts of bravery while a POW. He had been a true hero! Ironically he had been shot down while flying off of the USS Oriskany in 1965. He was a true American hero.

There was still another incident that occurred after my divorce. My ex-wife apparently tried to sell our jointly owned house without my knowledge. Upon learning that my house had been put up for sale by my ex-wife I called the realtor with whom the house had been listed. The realtor was quite arrogant and almost verbally abusive in telling me that it wasn't my house but that it belonged to my ex-wife with whom he had a contract for sale. Another man just might have gotten very angry upon learning that his ex-wife was trying to sell their jointly owned house from under him and would have expressed his anger at the realtor. In a calm icy cool voice I stated to the realtor that, he had been lied to by the ex-wife; that the deed on the house still had my name on it; and that the house could not be sold without my approval and signature. I further told and warned the realtor that if he attempted to sell the house with all proceeds, of the sale going to my ex-wife that I'd bring criminal charges against the realtor. Without ever raising my voice or expressing any anger on the telephone I advised the realtor to call my attorney and to also check out the deed on the house. When the realtor called back later he was very apologetic—he had found out that my ex-wife had indeed lied to him about the house. The realtor sounded almost frightened as he apologized repeatedly and said that everything would be handled in the proper manner with my approval. When the matter came up in a subsequent court hearing—my ex-wife's attorney was shaken by the potential harm to his career by any accusation that he might have been part of her attempt to defraud me. Oh what an awful web we weave when first we try to deceive! It was another example of my ex-wife's shenanigans! It was also yet another example of my ice-man persona and self-control.

During the year of my divorce I worked for a young female Sales Manager whose initial inclination was to fire me for my negative attitudes. I did indeed have very negative attitudes! Upon informing me of her intent, I very calmly asked when would she fire me? There were no outbursts of anger and no emotion of any kind expressed, not even a defense of myself or a pleading to keep my job, just an icy cool asking of when would I be fired. I just seemed to be resigned to such a fate. She thought for sure that I was on the verge of a nervous breakdown, what with my going through a divorce and now about to be fired from my job; and through it all I was not expressing any emotion at all. Surely I must be going through a nervous breakdown as no one could have such an icy calm control of his emotions, as I did, while in the midst of such adversity, or so she thought. She advised that I seek therapy.

To her credit, she did not fire me despite my having a poor unproductive year. Her support of my efforts was later vindicated when she became Region Manager and I was one of the top sales reps in her region and in the division.

I never forgot the support that she had given me, and the patience that she had with me. Years later, after I had been downsized out of Xerox and was a sales manager for other companies, I always supported my sales reps and had great patience with them. I often told my region managers that I'd been to Canton, Ohio to the Pro Football Hall of Fame and that there were players honored there for their careers who had been cut by other teams who had not been patient enough with their early development. I cautioned other sales managers not to fire a sales rep who could end up being another company's star performer. I advised that if a sales rep showed an excellent work ethic and had a positive attitude, be patient with them and support them—it was what I always did. My last manager at Xerox ran an entire region via the motto: "Attitude + Activity = Achievement."

I had often put my own job at risk by defending and supporting my initially under performing sales reps, yet I had always been rewarded and vindicated by their later excellent performance. As long as they worked hard and exhibited a positive attitude, I had always backed them completely!

I remember Carol who worked for me when I was a Branch Sales Manager for a company. While out making numerous cold sales calls one day together, she asked me if she was in trouble due to her initial poor performance as at the time as she had gotten off to a slow start in writing business. I told her not to worry; that I recognized her hard work and positive attitude—and that her efforts would soon yield rewards in her achieving business. I further calmed her fears of possibly losing her job by telling her that she had my complete confidence and support—the business would come! And it did!

She had an excellent work ethic and a great positive attitude—she worked harder than any other sales rep I ever had managed before or afterward. Despite pressure from my Region Vice President, I continued to defend and support her. That summer she went on to be the top producing sales rep in the region.

After I had moved on to become a Sales Manager for another company I recruited Carol who came to work for me. Once again she got off to a slow start and once again I was pressured to terminate her. And once again my faith and confidence in her were rewarded as due to her work effort and attitude for the next six months she was the top producing sales rep on my sales team. She again rewarded my faith in her!

When her husband was offered a job in a state near his young son from a previous marriage, Carol sought a transfer within the company to that state. I'm not sure if Carol ever found out how much I had supported and assisted her transfer by giving high praises of her to the sales manager who covered that area. I was really proud of her when her new sales manager reported to me that she worked harder than anyone else he had on his team. That was Carol! I was very proud of her.

I worked in the field with my sales reps often enough that I got to know each of them very well. I got to know whose positive attitude and strong work effort would result in their achievement. I knew whom to cut loose because they did not exhibit such qualities. I had often warned my sales reps that just because I didn't always remark about something didn't mean that I had failed to observe it. There was very little that I failed to observe. I got to know what made my reps tic and how to best motivate each of them.

At one company as a Sales Manager—one of my sales representatives turned in her resignation from the company. She complained that she just wasn't making enough money. I offered to keep the rep on and for her to work out her two weeks notice. I then offered that she could stay on as long as it took her to find another job. In less then two weeks she came to me; asked if she could rescind her resignation; and would I give her extra training and help. Of course I did all that. I was very proud of her, as when I left that company she was one of the top performing reps on the team. I knew her well enough to know what motivated her and I knew that she really did not want to leave the company. She just wanted to do well and to make good money. My support of her was rewarded by her performance.

I discussed what had happened with this sales rep to my fellow sales managers in the company—not mentioning her by name—and what I had done. Every sales manager and even the personnel manager all stated that they would have let that sales rep leave the company when she had first turned in her resignation. None of them would have done what I had done. It didn't matter to me what all of the others thought. I knew that I had done the right thing—proof of it was in the rep's turnaround performance. In many ways I was very different from my sales manager peers.

When I interviewed job candidates I was especially interested in their value system—determining that if they had good values and that if they were good people they would make good employees. I was generally correct. I was a pretty good judge of character—a trait that my Father had demonstrated. Every candidate whom I had hired because they seemed to be good persons rewarded me with excellent job performance. Their good personal qualities led them to be good employees.

I often expressed the attitude that the best military officers were true leaders who knew how to take care of their troops first—and that is what I always tried to do as a manager. My experiences in the military as a Navy Officer were always with me. I expressed to my sales reps—and practiced such—that I was willing to do with them side-by-side what I expected them to do on their own when I wasn't with them. Many of my sales reps were particularly loyal to me, even more so to me than even to the company for which we worked. Good troops always took care of a good leader! When the Navy's fleet goes off to war the Admirals and Captains down to the lowest rated seaman all go off to war. I felt strongly that it made the Navy a special branch of the military. ALL were put in harm's way in the Navy—not just the lower ranks. I felt that was the way it should be—all should be exposed to the same dangers.

As a sales manager I always worked in the field with my sales representatives making cold calls with them. Many sales managers had the attitude that they had paid the price by making such cold calls as a sales representative in the field to get to be a manager and that they declined going back into the field. I had no such attitudes. I was willing to continue to do what I had once done as a sales representative in order to support my sales reps. I believed that I best supported them by being with them in the field! That I had earned my stripes didn't make me reluctant to do all that I once did to earn my management position. If supporting my reps meant being in the field making cold calls with them—I cheerfully did it! Plus, it was a great training opportunity for both. It also provided excellent observation of their abilities and work ethic.

I worked with my top performers in the field more so to learn from them than to lend them support that they seldom required. I would buy their lunches and when it involved an overnight for me, I would take the rep out to dinner. It was my way of thanking that sales rep for their performance and making them feel part of the team. The poorer performers I worked with more often and seldom failed to turn their performance around into good performance. It was not unusual for a sale rep to have had a bad sales week and to apologize to me for having let me down. That was the kind of loyalty that I inspired among my team members.

I am a great fan of Alexander the Great having read several biographies of the greatest military leader in all of History! Alexander always led his men into battle. He even wore special plumes on his helmet so that the enemy would recognize him. He trained with his men; he ate with his men; and he went through all of the rigors that he expected of them. He built up such a loyalty amongst his men that, they followed him halfway around the world. I admired Alexander's leadership greatly.

My personal feelings were that what was very wrong with Corporate America was a lack of leadership skills displayed by CEO's who had never been in the military. All too many CEO's had the attitude of screw their employees instead of wanting to take care of them. It was no mystery why employee loyalty to the companies for which they worked was at an all time low in America. Loyalty worked both ways. One earns what one is willing to give. I always told my region managers that when my sales team performed credit belonged to the sales reps and when the sales team failed to perform the blame was upon me.

Essentially I really never felt that any sales representative had worked for me when I was a sales manager, but that we had all worked together and that they had worked with me and me with them. I really had no ego about having the title of sales manager. I told all of my reps that I still had to pay 99 cents for a cup of coffee at a convenience store just like everyone else—my title wasn't worth two cents at a convenience store. That didn't diminish my responsibility and authority as a sales manager—I always felt that I was a sales representative with a title as I liked selling and did all I could to support my sales team members in the field. I was a hands-on, in-the-field leader and motivator. I also had a certain intimidating presence. While I never ever enjoyed having to fire an employee for poor performance, I did it when it was necessary. It generally was done because of an ethics violation for which there was never a second chance, or because of their negative attitude or absence of a work ethic. I never shirked my responsibility to the company for which I worked.

I remember what happened to me when I had first reported to the DER—the Thomas J. Gary (DER 326)—I was assigned to right out of Naval Officer Candidate School. The First Class Petty Officers aboard that ship tactfully, but in no uncertain terms, explained to me that I was a green wet-behind-the-ears newly commissioned Navy officer and that <u>they</u> ran the Navy. They further explained that they would support me; that they would not disrespect or disobey me but that I needed to understand who ran the Navy. I responded that I knew and I accepted that <u>they</u> did indeed run the Navy. I further responded that it was in both of our interests not to play any games; that I did outrank them green as an officer that I was; and that I just wanted for all of us to just work together for the benefit of their ship and the Navy. I always got along very well with the men!

When I worked as a Production Supervisor in a manufacturing environment at Johnson and Johnson I had that same attitude towards the union blue-collar wage employees I supervised. I again demonstrated by my actions the attitude of "let's all work together" as a team to get the job done. I <u>never</u> looked down on anyone no matter what his position, and I <u>never</u> felt superior to anyone. When necessary I would exert my authority but only to get the job done and never in an egotistical manner. I was very loyal to my men and to their credit they were loyal to me!

While working at Johnson & Johnson I supervised a father and son team that operated one of the production machines. Initially when I took over the shift the father was a rather quiet man and not very friendly towards anyone. What I began to do was after I filled out the break and lunch schedules for the men on the shift I would then go ask the father to look at the schedule and to approve it. As the Supervisor it was not something that I was required to do. But it was a show of respect to the father who was also the union shop steward. It wasn't long before men from other departments came up to me and asked me: "what are you feeding him?"—meaning the father. The father changed into a man who had a nice smile and was friendly to everyone and he responded with the respect to me that had been shown to him. The men I supervised were <u>all</u> good men worthy of my respect.

When one of the production machines at the plant caught fire—I very calmly grabbed a fire extinguisher and put out the flames. I did not panic. I had no fear. I very calmly did what needed to be done. The Navy had sent me to fire fighting school upon my return from Viet Nam and I used the training that day.

I made every effort to be a leader first and a manager second while recognizing that I had to accomplish both responsibilities. I was extremely well organized and I certainly knew how to manage things.

The District Manager who had initially interviewed me at Xerox responded to my question about what it took to be successful as a Sales Representative for Xerox—"you have to juggle all of the balls in the air and not drop any." A Captain who was a member of the 82nd Airborne Division gave me another version that had been given to him by his Colonel—"you have to juggle all of the balls and keep them in the air and if you dropped one of the balls you have to make sure that it was not one of the glass balls."

It is very true that "leaders lead and managers manage."

My control was something I had worked on since I had been just a little boy. For some undetermined and unfathomed reason, I always feared that if I lost control of my emotions that within me was the capacity to kill someone in a fit of anger. As I got older I realized that I was nearly incapable of such an act, but the thought and fear remained within me. It was as if I recognized a dark side within me, which I must control always at all costs. This was a feeling and a fear that I had felt long before the movie, Star Wars, came out with its theme of the battle between the 'dark side' and the 'good side' that takes place within a man. Didn't every man face such a battle within himself? The Captain of the Oriskany had once remarked to me that I "had a quick temper and a sharp tongue", and indeed I had such at the time. Over the subsequent years I worked hard to control my temper recognizing that it was my 'dark side.' I had made progress with my temper—control of my tongue was more difficult! It was a battle with an even darker side of me! I was not winning that battle.

I often joked and reflected, had even written in my private journals, how I had become 'Michael Corleone' from 'The Godfather'—icy cool, calm, and under control at all times. Some people found me to be 'intimidating.' I frightened them. I was one whom they could not intimidate and that frightened them. It also made some men very pissed off at me! I laughed—hell, wasn't it a whole lot better to piss off some men than to have them piss on you or even worse shit on you! Yet another character trait of the 'Taurus' was that one "may make enemies due to your uncompromising nature." I was not afraid to make enemies and I often did!

A Xerox Region Manager, at a sales team meeting, took each sales rep in on a one-on-one meeting in which he loudly shouted at and was verbally abusive to each sale rep with each sales rep shouting back at the RM. When it came to my turn, I stood very silent and did not respond back to the verbal abuse of the Region Manager. That I remained quiet and controlled so angered the RM that the RM shouted—"I can't get through to you." I smiled inwardly. Unlike all of the other sales reps, I had remained icy cool, quiet, controlled—I essentially had 'won' the confrontation by remaining under control of myself. I showed no fear and would not be intimidated.

There was the time when I was eighteen years of age and working as a delivery boy for an electronics distribution company down the street from where I lived, I had an encounter with a drunken man who accused me of cutting off his car while he was making a turn. At age 18 I weighed barely 140 pounds at the time. The drunken man was a much larger man weighing about 200 pounds. The man took a swing at me, which barely caught my lip. My back was to a plate glass window in the front of a store. I remember thinking that if the man swung at me again, I would side step the man and then I would trip the man into the plate glass window. The proprietors of the store came out before there was any further fighting. Again, I remained calm, cool, and very controlled while not feeling any fear. Maybe it was my youth at the time, as young men tend not to feel any fear? I had not yet met G. Gordon Liddy nor had yet read any of Nietzsche and certainly had not yet subscribed to the saying:

"That which does not kill me, makes me stronger"
—Nietzsche

My ex-wife hated this aspect of me. She detested my self-control. Yet, once when I responded to her urgings that I should see a psychiatrist for help, by pounding my hand down hard on the arm of a chair—she actually jumped back and was visibly shaken by my angry outburst. For an instant I had lost control of my emotions and it had really frightened her. It had also frightened me!

Ironically, she relied on my self-control throughout our divorce battle and thereafter. For all of her promiscuous behavior, in my own house in front of my own children, I never lost control. Another man just might have killed her and would have been justified by such an act possibly even getting away with it! Yes, there were times when even I resented my own self-control. I <u>never</u> wanted to find out what I was capable of doing if I lost control of myself.

Didn't the nightly news on almost a daily basis have the report of a husband murdering his estranged wife at her boyfriend's house? 'Jealousy' did appear to be an emotion from which all men did suffer. The image of their estranged or former wife in bed having sex with another man did drive most men to go 'crazy' and to even do something really crazy. That emotion was something <u>all</u> men seemed to have in common with each other. There indeed was a common thread of emotion, which was woven in all men. There was the reluctance to have to give up the former wife and to be greatly disturbed by the images of her having sex with another man—a dark emotion suffered by all men. Heck, I certainly felt that way initially. Did women not feel or suffer from that dark emotion? Didn't I hear a woman on one of those talk shows say: "when your husband leaves you for another woman, the best way you can get revenge on the other woman and on him is to let her have him." I laughed at that! It seemed that it was rarely reported in the news that a scorned wife went to kill her ex-husband. Yes, I did feel that jealousy emotion initially—it passed as I came to realize that I didn't want to have sex with her anymore. All of those other men were welcome to have her!

Hell I did <u>not</u> want her anymore! The shock of discovering the reality of her destroyed the image I once had of her and all desire for her. I didn't look at her or see her in the same way as I once did. She had changed! Perhaps I had also changed?

> **"When you change the way you look at things—you change the things you look at"**
> —Wayne Dyer

I smiled as I remembered an incident that had occurred after my divorce. Because of the actions of my ex-wife at the time and how it all disturbed me, I called my best friend to complain: "what am I to do when my wife keeps bringing men home to sleep with her in front of the Children?" There was a long moment of silence on the telephone and then my friend simply said: "Your wife?" I never again referred to her as "my wife"—never! She was forever afterwards "my ex-wife." Such is life!

The anger 'genie' was kept locked tight in the bottle. I recognized and greatly feared that, once let loose, it would never return to the bottle. Thus, more and more, I tried to become the icy cool and controlled 'Michael Corleone' from 'The Godfather.' It was a daily battle with the darkness within me. I remembered a saying from a movie that I had watched while alone: "If a man can conquer his own darkness, he can defeat any enemy." Wasn't it a battle that every man fought? Did other men recognize such a battle within themselves? How did they fight their own battle?

The thought of my losing control of my emotions and of myself greatly frightened me. Of what could I possibly be capable? I did not want to find out by losing control, by unleashing the dark forces, which, I, and every man, has deep within himself. I often referred to myself as "the Iceman"—a man who under great stress and danger remained icy calm. I had no idea what mental, emotional, or physiological strain it might be putting on my mind and body by maintaining such control? I just believed that I must keep myself under control at all costs.

Obviously too many other men were quick to lose control and to do harm to others and to themselves. Again the question is asked—what do other men think and feel and how do they handle their emotions. Why do some men lose control while other men do not? Why do men act as they do? Did men fulfill in reality what they had imagined themselves to be? Was it education, or training, or values, or morals, why was it that some men lost control and others did not lose control?

I remember hearing the observations of a news reporter who had interviewed G. Gordon Liddy several years ago. Intrigued by Liddy's apparent toughness, the reporter asked Liddy what he would have done if he, the reporter, had walked into the room with a gun pointed at Liddy. Gordon calmly replied to the reporter that he "would just take the gun away from you." The reporter said that looking into Liddy's calm eyes was like looking into the eyes of a cobra ready to strike at him. That G. Gordon had been so calm and that he had not been intimidated at all had really frightened the reporter! Men who refuse to be intimidated appear as being very dangerous to others.

In his autobiography Will' Liddy details all that he did as a child to make himself to be strong and fearless. In his case the boy surely did become the father of the man that he became. He made every effort to face and to conquer all of his fears. The title of his autobiography 'Will' is sort of a takeoff from Nietzsche's philosophy as coined by the phrase: "Will to power." Liddy became the tough guy that, as a boy, he once imagined and visualized himself becoming as a man! He even dealt with his fear of God. Liddy was to coin the phrase: "Defeat the fear of death and welcome the death of all fear." He is an excellent example of the following quotation:

"There is nothing more empowering for a man than to meet his fears and to overcome them"

In 1981 I actually got to meet G. Godon Liddy at a book signing and to hear him speak later on that night. From the afternoon to the evening there appeared to be a transformation of Liddy from a mild mannered man signing books to a man who exuded a great physical and mental power.

While my outward appearance was that of a man who was relaxed and calm I was like a coiled rattlesnake—always ready to strike. Once while at college, I had borrowed a friend's car in order to take a date to a movie. The movie theater was downtown. After the movie, while my date was getting into the car, with my holding the door open for her—I heard the sound of footsteps behind me. I heard voices saying, "let's get him." My date screamed! I turned to see three young men running towards us. They were at first just a blur and I did not initially recognize any of them. I calmly cocked my right fist prepared to hit the first of the men to reach us. All three men pulled up. It was three friends of mine. They were pulling a joke on me. I was ready to strike at them!

Was it the 'darkness' within me that was ready to strike? Was it the warrior within me that was prepared to strike? Or was it that 'knight in shining armor' who was going to protect his date at all costs to himself? In making the choice between fight-or-flight, at that time, I chose to fight. Heck, I would not and could not have run and left my date behind! Actually it was not really a 'choice' that I had made. It was my reaction to danger. Luckily it was only friends playing a joke and not real muggers. I do not remember feeling any fear at the time.

I had often stated that, if I'd become a priest that I would have been a very good priest, probably making it to 'Cardinal.' I also stated that if I'd been a Mafia hit man, I probably would have made it to 'Don.' Somehow I sensed that the capacity for both was within me—the 'light' and the 'darkness' and both were strong within me.

Wasn't it Darth Vader from the Star Wars movies who, had succumbed to the dark side after initially having been a 'jedi warrior?' Didn't Yoda train Luke Skywalker to continually combat the dark side within him? Although it was just a movie—doesn't the battle between good and evil; between the darkness and goodness; occur within every man? Were the Star War movies so popular because they presented a theme to which every man can relate? Were there not 'two wolves' doing battle within every man?

It was within my imagined world of the warrior, a world so very often reflected in nighttime and daytime 'dreams' that I existed, survived, and actually lived. I was, for all intents and purposes, a 'warrior!' It was a role in which I was most comfortable, for in my world of the warrior there was no adversity, no failures, no aloneness, no women or children, no love, no unfulfilled needs, no unfulfilled wants or desires, no unfulfilled hopes or aspirations. All of my being was fulfilled in my role as a warrior in this dream like dimension in which I existed and survived. It was my 'escape', the 'lair' into which the lone wolf retreated to heal his wounds.

And there were wounds, many scars, and a heart that was broken. Above all I needed love, a need born out of my first conscious moments as a baby. It was a need that exposed all of my vulnerabilities and a need I kept well hidden from virtually all people behind a hard crusty self-reliant and independent exterior.

A couple of incidents come to my mind, one when I was at college and the other when I was in Viet Nam with each affecting me in a similar manner. I remember once while at college going to my campus mailbox and actually seeing a letter in my mailbox. It had been so long since I had last received mail from anyone that I had forgotten the combination to my mailbox. I had to ask the campus postmaster to retrieve the letter for me. I also remember my Commanding Officer aboard the Oriskany while in Viet Nam chewing me out for not checking my mail, as I'd let a letter set for nearly two weeks before I had retrieved it. I had explained to my Commanding Officer that I never received mail from anyone, thus I never bothered to check it. While others, may have gotten 'homesick' at college or while in the military, I had never experienced any homesickness anywhere or anytime.

Returning from a day of consulting work in Raleigh for my old employer, I stopped at a convenience store off the interstate for something to drink to soothe my sore throat. The young woman behind the counter was pretty with a very sweet smile. She had that special look which I always found attractive. Walking out the door I turned to look at her one more time. I started to go back to tell her that she was pretty, but I didn't. I hadn't even noticed if she wore a wedding band? Anyway, she was too young for me, but she was so pretty and with such a nice smile.

Once again on the highway I thought of the pretty young woman and how I wished for and how I needed a woman with whom to share love, life, and passion. I thought of my unfulfilled desires and needs, and I hurt. Quickly I escaped the hurt by daydreaming and by entering my private world of the warrior, a world in which, I reminded myself, there were no needs and no hurt.

I remember, after my divorce, having lunch one day with a co-worker at a Shoney's restaurant. The next table over from us was a young, pretty, very pregnant, woman, having lunch alone. After finishing her lunch she had ordered a big piece of chocolate iced layer cake for dessert, giggling to the waitress that she "was eating for two." I looked at her and how she 'glowed' from being pregnant, which is what some women do. My ex-wife had 'glowed' with each pregnancy. My heart stirred. As I, and my co-worker were leaving the restaurant, I went over to the table at which the young woman was seated and picked up her bill. I told her that, if it was okay with her, I was going to pay her bill; that she glowed; and that she would have a healthy beautiful baby. She bashfully smiled at me and thanked me. She was a reminder of how my ex-wife had glowed while pregnant. It is funny how I did such things—how for all of my apparent hardness I, once in a while, allowed my soft and tender side to be revealed.

Of course, my Daughter had often remarked and observed in reference to me that "all it took for a grown man to act silly was his grandchildren." Around my Grandchildren I did act silly. I had enjoyed having imaginary 'tea parties' with my precious Granddaughter. I had enjoyed 'buddy's days' out with my oldest Grandson during which I took him out bowling and then to lunch together. I had enjoyed getting down on the floor and wrestling with my three Grandsons.

They liked to 'attack' and to 'tackle' me, as they were all rough and tumble boys! We had taken walks together. I had pulled a wagon with them in it giving them a ride. I had cooked lasagna together with my Granddaughter. We had made brownies together. In the company of my Grandchildren I was a different man. I was not a warrior in their presence. I did *not* keep them at arms length. They were allowed in and welcomed within my 'walls' as I needed no 'protection' from them. I knew that they loved me and they knew that I loved them. I had remarked to my oldest Grandson who had told me: "Pop-Pop, you're silly"—yes, I was silly when I was with my Grandchildren but that once I got back home and was alone that I was again 'serious.' I enjoyed it when I was silly.

My three Grandsons called to wish me a happy 66th birthday. My five-year old Grandson—a Taurus like me—proudly told me that he had just learned how to ride his bicycle without training wheels. I reminded my own Son that the boy would surely surpass both of them in his achievements and that whatever he put his mind to accomplish he would succeed! He was handsome and extremely intelligent—also very personable and loving—a really good boy!

I love my four Grandchildren so very, very much. As I often told them—I "loved them as high as the sky and deep as the ocean." They were the great joys in my life. Ironically I often wrote in 'journals' to each of them—what I referred to as a 'leave behind'—notes of love to each of my Grandchildren so that they would know that I loved them dearly! I was already on my second notebook to my Granddaughter. After I was long 'gone' they could read my notes of love to them!

As I often mentioned to my Son: "my life has not turned out the way I would have liked, but I guess it all worked out the way it was supposed to." Deep down I was very thankful for my marriage that resulted in my two Children and my four Grandchildren. I just wished that the marriage had been successful, happy, and had lasted. I had seen glimpses of beauty and goodness in my ex-wife during our marriage. I had loved her greatly—and—I still loved the woman I once had thought her to be.

While out jogging (it was 1992 at the time) and walking my mind turned to my Son who was 21 years of age at the time and who was an exceptionally fine young man. I thought of years past when I was just a young man himself. I thought of when I was just 23 years of age and of getting my commission as an Officer in the US Navy at Naval Officer Candidate School in Newport, Rhode Island in March 1965. I was just a young man, at that time only two years older than my Son was now.

Upon receiving my orders to a small Destroyer Escort (USS Thomas J. Gary DER 326) stationed in Newport, and because of my anticipated problem with motion sickness aboard such a small ship, I actually had gone back to my Company Officer and requested that I be allowed to transfer to the Marine Corps. I said that I would ever volunteer for ground combat duty in Viet Nam if allowed to transfer to the Marines. The Navy could not allow such a transfer. I had to follow my orders and report to the Destroyer Escort, a 306 feet long ship, which was top heavy with radar equipment and which was capable of taking 45 degree 'rolls.' The ship was assigned to Operation Deep Freeze, which required it to operate out of Christ Church, New Zealand in the Antarctic Sea area off of the South Pole.

I attended Combat Information Center School at NAS Glynco, Georgia that summer and then reported back to the Gary as it prepared to leave Newport for Operation Deep Freeze. It was then September 1965 and I was 24 years of age. I was the CIC Officer and the Registered Publications Custodian.

I remember the First Division Officer ordering a gross of baseball bats. When I asked what the baseball bats were for—I was told that they were for breaking the ice off the hull of the ship. It would indeed be that rough a cruise!

When the ship left Newport, Rhode Island, it encountered very rough seas, which caused most of the crew to get seasick. I remained very sick the entire way to Panama—the Navy referred to it as 'motion sickness.' Within a week I had lost 15 pounds and was on intravenous by the end of the week due to dehydration. The Captain of the ship recognized that I would not be able to serve aboard that Destroyer Escort—certainly not in the rough seas of the Antarctic. In Panama I was transferred off the ship and ordered to report to the Navy Hospital in Charleston, South Carolina, which I did after a three week stay in Panama.

I reported to the Navy Hospital on a Sunday night after a long eight hours flight from Panama aboard a 'Military Air Transport Service' flight. On Monday morning a Navy doctor came to my room and informed me that "motion sickness" disqualified my Commission and that I would be offered a medical discharge from the Navy. In a decision that would later very nearly cost me my life—I refused the medical discharge and requested that I be allowed to remain in the Navy and that I be assigned to a West Coast aircraft carrier as I had originally requested on my 'dream sheet' at OCS. For two months I basically fought with the Navy to remain on active duty. Finally, after the completion of a 'Navy Medical Board', I was assigned to the USS Oriskany CVA-34 a West Coast attack aircraft carrier. My 'Medical Board' read that I would be assigned for "a six months trial period" aboard the Oriskany—something I was aware of but did not mention to anyone aboard the Oriskany. It was an oversight that nearly proved fatal to me!

How many young men in 1965, with the Viet Nam War heating up, would have turned down a medical discharge from the military, only to request service aboard a ship that meant certainty in serving in that war? I was very fortunate that such a decision had not cost me my life. I knew that there were men, who had volunteered to go back to Viet Nam for a second and even a third tour of duty, but I have not ever encountered any men who had turned down a medical discharge in order to serve.

Pat Tillman, the former professional NFL football player, who volunteered for Special Services and who served in the Afghanistan war, did lose his life. And I had met a Marine, Clebe McClary, who, although he had been past the age of being drafted into the military had joined the Marines and who had served in combat having lost an eye and who had suffered other serious injuries, which had nearly gotten him killed. Obviously there were other men who were 'warriors.'

Perhaps many men were the same? Again, I have often wondered IF there was another man like myself anywhere in the world? It seemed that I had never really encountered anyone quite like myself. It was a redundant question often repeated herein. Do men ever cease asking questions of themselves and about their lives? I don't know?

Are not these the questions that men ask of themselves: "am I so unique that I am not like other men?" Am I like other men? How am I different from other men? How am I like other men? Do other men think and feel like I do? Do I think and feel like other men do? Are all men alike? Do all men think and feel alike? Why am I the way that I am? Why are other men the way that they are? How did I get to be the way that I am? Am I 'connected' to other men in any way? Are all men connected to each other in any way? How did I get to be as I am? Could I not help it the way that I am?

Then there are these questions: What do other men actually think and feel? How do other men deal with their failures and disappointments? How do other men deal with getting older? What do other men think and feel as they look back on their lives and realize that they did not do it and that it was not in them?

Of course there are a multitude of questions that men ask of themselves—are any of them ever answered? Then there is the one great question for which there is no answer—why? King Solomon, for all of the wisdom granted to him, did not have an answer to the 'why' question! Don't we all ask the "why" and the "why me" question?

"In the book of life, the answers aren't in the back"
—Charlie Brown

Why did I not die in the Oriskany fire? Why did Ron die in the fire? Why did any of the 44 die in the fire? Why am I here? Are there no answers?

While remembering this event in my own life, which occurred when I was age 24, I thought—did the 'warrior mentality' exist within me at an early age, while I was just a young man of 24? I had been young then when I had turned down an offered medical discharge from the Navy. My Son was young and now age 24. Did my Son have such thoughts? At what age did I transform my being and persona into that of a warrior? Was it in grade school while studying ancient history? In reading and learning about the Greeks, the Spartans, and the Romans—wow—it had excited me.

Why did I develop a 'warrior' persona? What about all of my classmates—did any of them develop such a persona as I had done? What was it that 'clicked' in my own mind that resulted in my becoming the man that I had become? I didn't know. What further caused me to think as a warrior and to often 'escape' into a world of dreams and daydreams, into what I referred to as that "other dimension of time and space?" Why was I, in my own mind and even outwardly, a tough hard warrior personality? How many other men had seen the movie 'Sands of Iwo Jima' with John Wayne? Of all those young men who had seen the movie, how many young men consciously chose to be like John Wayne's portrayal of the tough Marine?

Of course, for the sake of bravado, many Navy pilots and Marine ground troops thought themselves, to be like John Wayne's movie roles, while serving in the Viet Nam War. How many of them had internally transformed themselves into warriors in both their dreams and conscious thought as I had done? At the time I was reflecting back with such thoughts, I was age 51. I continued to reflect on such thoughts and would for the rest of my life.

Was I 'crazy' as I joked that I was to my friends? More likely, I suffered from PTSD and deep depression, as how often had I prayed for the Angel of Death to take me while I slept. Too frequently I sunk into the depths of deep depression and hopelessness. I appeared to exhibit the classic signs of manic depression—withdrawal, no social life, in private I actually cried during sad movies, and had no real enthusiasm for life and living. Yet, the paradox was that I took pains to take care of myself as I ate right, I exercised a few times every week, I jogged and walked almost daily, and I did have sustained intellectual interests. I was simple yet very complicated—a paradox! I actually was an intelligent and an interesting man!! I was well read and very knowledgeable of current events—that was something observed and even reported in one of my Navy Fitness Reports.

Lately, the more depressed I became about my 'real' life, the more that I escaped into my imagined and dream world of the warrior. I was not depressed in that 'other existence' and that was something of which I took note. I often wondered—could I remain permanently in that dream world and other dimension of time and space into which I escaped? Did, my own mind know the difference between the two worlds? Was I losing myself in a dream world? In which world did I prefer to exist? I'd had several dreams during a restless and mostly sleepless night, but I could not remember any of them. All that I could remember is that I'd had dreams.

I woke up to reality, the reality of my aloneness, my unemployment, to how discouraged I was about all aspects of my life. Slowly I was sinking back into the depths of depression. I was alone and sad, I hurt, and I wanted to cry.

This 'reality', this depression is what I tried to avoid by entering my dream world and my existence as a warrior where there was no pain. I recognized my vulnerabilities and never denied them. I merely masked them with a tough exterior.

I was actually very sensitive, something my Father never seemed to have recognized in me when he was a boy, or did he? Perhaps my very demanding Father did recognize that his son was very sensitive and that he was merely doing all that he could to prepare me for a tough life?

There was an incident, when I was about 8 or 9 years of age, when I was beat up by the neighborhood bully and I came home crying. My Father was furious with me, not for losing the fight, but for coming home crying. My Father, after calling me a "baby", sent me out of the house to fight the bully again, which I did, and I was beat up again. But, I did not return home crying. I can't remember if my Father had ever called me a "baby" again? It had been a very cruel thing for my Father to call me a "baby"—it was the absolute cruelest and most hurtful thing that could have been said to me by my Father. Being called a "baby" hurt more deeply than if my Father had told me that he didn't love me anymore. It really, really crushed me.

Many years later when upon her questioning about how my Father had died, I told my (at the time) 9 years old Granddaughter how my own Father had actually died; that he shot himself to death. She asked me—"didn't your Father love you?"

At best that I can remember the incident, I do not recall getting angry with my Father. I do remember that being called a "baby" by my Father had greatly shamed and embarrassed me. It had made me feel that I had failed my Father. That I came home after being beat up again and wasn't crying—that made me feel a little pride in myself. I can't recall what my Father's reaction had been at the time? The summer before my Father's death I had gotten into a fight with the same bully. This time I sent the bully home with a bloody nose and split lip. When I got home and told my Father of the fight—the man got angry with me. There just was no pleasing the man at times, or so it seemed. That boy never bullied anyone again!

Years later I read a book co-authored by Navy Admiral Elmo Zumwalt and his son. The Admiral was the Chief of Naval Operations during the Viet Nam War who made the decision to drop 'agent orange' on areas of the South in which the River Patrol 'Swift' Boats operated. At the time their book was written—the son was dying from cancer caused by 'agent orange.' The grandson was also ill with the same cancer.

The son, Elmo Zumwalt Jr., recalled a story of when he was just 8 or 9 years of age and the family was living on a Navy base. Upon being chased home by a neighborhood bully who was much larger than he was, he got to the front door of his house only to have his father lock the door on him. He thought in terms that his father was merely teaching him a lesson—the lesson being that he would have to stand up for himself and that his father would not be there always to protect him.

I read that story of the Zumwalts with great interest. It made me feel connected to the younger Zumwalt, who had been a young Lieutenant in the Navy aboard a River Patrol 'Swift' Boat in the Viet Nam War. Each of us tried to honor our fathers and to make our fathers proud of us even as little boys. Each had had a similar incident occur to us as young boys and each had responded in the same manner. What was it within each of us that caused us to react to such an incident as we had?

After that incident, ironically, I never again backed down from a fight no matter how big my potential opponent. Whether it was a physical confrontation or a mental confrontation, I never again backed down from anyone or from any situation. The boy became a man—my Father was not alive to witness my growth.

In sharing the story with a local college football coach, the coach relayed a similar story to me. The coach had been in a fight and had come home crying. The coach's father sent him out to fight again, telling him "get back out there and kick that other kid's butt", or something to that effect. How many other men can relate and can tell their own story of having been in a fight as a boy, of having come home, and only to have their fathers send them back out to fight again? I suspect that it is an event and story to which many, many men could relate and tell. Was I really so different from other men? To a great degree, weren't all men the same? It seemed that it was only when such stories were shared that men realized how very alike they are. Perhaps this was the purpose of this book—to try to get me to understand that no matter what our varied experiences all men are really alike; that essentially we all think, and feel, and hurt in the same manner; and that essentially we are all connected to each other—that I really am like other men.

Didn't all boys want to please their father? Wasn't that a driving force within every boy—the strong desire to please his father and to do all that he could in seeking the approval of his father? Then later on as the boy became a man—didn't all men want to surpass their father; to 'beat' him in life by becoming more successful; bigger and stronger? Didn't a boy then later on as a man—didn't, all boys and men want to please their father? How does a boy/a man feel when he fails to gain the approval of his father? How does that affect him in his life?

I recalled sharing a few stories about what I had gone through in my divorce with other men who had also gone through a divorce. Did all ex-wives act the same? Did all men have the same experiences in going through a divorce? Even the verbiage of the ex-wives appeared to have been scripted out of some 'wives book.' Each divorced man with whom I had talked told of his personal story, which was different yet really was the same as had been my own.

It just seemed that there were incidents that occurred and in which I acted that exhibited my attempts to still prove to my Father that I was not a "baby."

While in the Navy in Panama, in 1965, I was walking down a street when I happened to look across to see a man, on a 2nd story balcony, who had a rifle with a scope that was pointed right at me. As I walked down the street the man continued to point the rifle at me, following each step I made. I was age 24 at the time. I remember the incident like it had happened yesterday.

I was the only person on the street. There was no car traffic. As I continued walking I stared up at my apparent assailant. I refused to flinch even when I heard the hammer of the rifle hit an empty chamber as the man squeezed the trigger. The rifleman gently nodded his head, sort of in recognition of his apparent target's firm resolve, or as if to say that he had respect for me and for my toughness. I nodded back at the rifleman, more in relief than anything. Perhaps my Father had prepared me well? I had not flinched! For the next three weeks that I was in

Panama, I did not leave the Navy base. I may be tough, but I was not stupid as there was no need to tempt fate again! How would another man have acted under the same circumstances?

Today sadness and depression gripped me. After several days of not hurting, the pain was uncomfortable and unsettling. I sought relief from the pain by trying to enter a dream like state of mind in which I was a warrior in the midst of battle. For a few moments there was no pain, no sadness, and my aloneness did not hurt. I had 'escaped' into that other dimension of time and space which was 'real' to me but which was merely imagined. And so my <u>daydream</u> went as follows imagined and told in the second person as though I was observing myself in the dream in the role of "our warrior":

There were police lines surrounding the bank with a swat team on site, police snipers, and several patrol cars with a crowd watching. He recognized the bank as the one in which Shirley worked. He stopped and got out of his car to join the onlookers. Then he saw Tom, Shirley's husband, who seemed to be visibly shaken and distraught. He went to Tom and asked him: "what is going on?"

Tom, in a shaky voice with tears running down his cheeks, replied that three armed bank robbers had entered the bank, were holding hostages, and that Shirley was one of the hostages. Before anyone could stop him, our warrior bolted through the police lines and entered the bank through the unlocked front door to the shock and surprise of the bank robbers.

"Who the hell are you?" One of the bank robbers asked him as he put a gun to the warrior's head. While he answered the robber that he "was no one", his eyes scanned the situation, locating Shirley and the other hostages, and targeting the other two robbers. Then with the lightning speed and quickness of a rattler striking its prey, but with no advance warning, his left hand rose to grip the robber's handgun, snapped it back hard breaking the robber's wrist, pulling the handgun from him, and gripping it in his own hand. A swift kick to the robber's left kneecap with his thick wing tip shoe caused it to crack and the scream of pain from the robber resounded throughout the bank as he fell to the floor writhing in pain from a broken wrist and shattered knee cap.

The other two robbers turned towards him in shock and surprise, completely stunned by the sudden turn of events. It had all happened too quickly for them. Everything seemed to be moving at slow speed for them except for our warrior who was moving at lightning speed.

As the two robbers, each in stunned shock, began to raise their handguns to aim at him, he all too quickly for them fired at one and than at the other. An expert marksman could not have had a better 'hit' as each robber was felled by a 9mm slug that slammed into their heads hitting them right between their eyes, shattering their heads and spraying blood and bone fragments on the hostages.

It had all happened so suddenly that none of the hostages even screamed, as they were still so stunned and in a state of shock. A couple of the hostages fainted. Some then did cry in relief as they quickly ran to the front door. Who was this man, their hero who had rescued them each wondered, as they scrambled out of the bank past him as he held the gun on the third robber who was writhing in pain on the floor from a broken wrist and smashed kneecap.

Shirley saw him and cried out to him, ran to him, and warmly embraced him. "What ... how ... what are you doing here?" she asked, sobbing and shaking as he held her. The other hostages asked her "do you know him?" "Who is he?"

Everyone outside of the bank had feared the worst when they heard the sound of the gunshots. When they saw hostages running out of the bank, the police rushed inside only to find our warrior still holding a gun on the injured third robber while he still held Shirley in his arms. As they took the remaining robber away in cuffs and saw the bodies of the other two robbers, they asked what happened? He explained that he had taken a gun from the one robber and that he had 'terminated' the other two robbers.

As he walked out of the bank with Shirley, the police and Press mobbed them. Who was he? What had happened inside of the bank? How had he rescued the hostages? How had he overpowered the one robber while shooting the other two? Who was this guy who had calmly walked into the bank; who had disarmed the one robber while 'terminating' the other two? Why had he even gone into the bank?

When he saw Shirley, Tom came rushing to her. They hugged and kissed; he held her tightly; relieved that she was okay. They both looked at our warrior and asked him. Why was he in town? How had he come by the bank? Why had he entered the bank? Why? Why? He just smiled with that sort of half grin of his as he answered them. He was in town on business and was just coincidently passing by the bank when he saw the commotion and stopped as he remembered that Shirley worked there. Tom wanted to know why he would risk his own life for Shirley? He smiled and simply said that, with knowing that she was in the bank, he just went in to rescue her for Tom.

After his divorce he moved into an apartment and it was at that apartment complex that he had met Shirley. He still remembered the day that he had met her at the swimming pool—he was there with his Children. He had gotten a lounge chair for her. From the first moment that he saw her, he took to her, as did his Son and Daughter. She was pretty, sweet, a very special young woman whom he grew to value very much. They became friends—<u>no</u> more to his disappointment. She had married a really good guy in Tom. She never knew how much he 'valued' her. He thought of the song by the group 'The Four Seasons'—as it seemed appropriate—"My Eyes Adored You"—from afar as "I never touched you." He had just valued her from afar!

His Granddaughter had asked him during her week stay with him in 2007—"didn't you tell her how you felt about her?" He had not.

The police came to him. They wanted to know who he was; and how could he have disarmed the one robber while felling the other two robbers with a single shot each to the head? He explained that he'd practiced those shots a thousand times and he tapped his head as he said: "Up here." The police looked at him strangely, like he wasn't real. No one could have done that in that situation, they reasoned. No one was even that crazy to risk his life as he had done and why?

Although he knew the answer to all of their questions, he really could not and would not even attempt to explain his actions to them. What he knew down deep within his soul was that a 'warrior' such as he would do such a thing as he had done. It was his 'destiny' to be as he was and to do what he did.

Shirley came to him again, hugged him, and kissed him on the cheek, and thanked him for rescuing her. She then walked away in the arms of her husband. They were lucky to have each other. Shirley was a very, very special young woman and Tom was a really good guy. They were blessed to have each other and to share a special love. He was very happy for them. They were both special people. That they had been married for 22 years confirmed in his mind just how special Shirley was and just how good a guy Tom was. He was right about her from the moment he had met her—she was special!

He walked away <u>alone</u>. He was alone. There was no special woman for him and no love shared. He may be a 'hero' but he was a warrior and he was alone. He felt very much like 'Ethan Edwards', the John Wayne role in the movie The Searchers.

While it was just a 'daydream' it was very real to both my subconscious and conscious minds. I 'felt' as though it had all happened just as I had dreamed it. The memory of it was just as vivid as anything else that I had ever actually experienced. Yet, in a sense it was as though I was watching a movie in which I had appeared in the starring role as 'our warrior'. How strange! It had felt real!

"The dream is real while we are dreaming it"
—Edgar Cayce

I awakened and returned from my daydream, one, which I had a thousand times, or so it seemed. Why did I even imagine such dreams? And why did I have this particular dream? I had been in my daydream, a hero to a woman whom I had only adored from afar. I had been the hero, the warrior, and the lone wolf who had walked away alone as I always seemed to do in such dreams.

In what I called "the dimension of the warrior", I was the lone gunfighter, the lone fighter pilot, the lone gladiator, and the lone warrior. It just seemed appropriate as a warrior for me to be alone. There was no pain in my aloneness in this dimension. Outside of this dimension in the reality of my life, there was hurt and pain.

As I have previously stated herein, a warrior needed only to think of battle plans, of survival, of the battle and the opponent he faced. All of his senses and skills must concentrate on the battle. The best warriors, the very best, were always alone—weren't they?

In my daydreams I was okay being alone and I accepted my aloneness. In my awakened reality, to be alone hurt me deeply. For ordinary men there was nothing worse than being alone. Once again I was sad and hurting. I felt so deeply sad as I was aware of so many unfulfilled needs and desires. I was very alone and it really hurt.

It had been just a daydream. For a few moments I had entered into another time and space in which I was okay. It was a means of survival for me and, for a few moments, an escape. What about other men, did they have such 'daydreams? Did other men imagine themselves rescuing a woman whom they only loved from afar? What did other men daydream about? Again the question is asked—how did other men deal with their aloneness?

Sadness began to envelop me, returning me to a world of sadness, hurt, and aloneness. I was very alone and this night I felt the hurt. Perhaps it was my Father's suicide that caused such deep hurt within me, a hurt that caused me to withdraw deeply within myself and to shut down all emotions and feelings. I built thick 'walls' around myself. Had I ever allowed anyone ever within those 'walls?'

I remembered Linda from college. She was a classmate and a very pretty young woman. We had never dated. She appeared interested in me, or so it seemed? She attempted to get within those thick walls, which surrounded me, but I did not allow her to enter. Too bad I now thought, as she was a very nice young woman.

There were others who had tried but I seem to have kept everyone at arms length distance from myself. I did not allow anyone within my inner self and did not permit anyone to get too close to me nor I to get too close to anyone. Was I afraid that I would lose them as I had lost my Father? Was I afraid that they would abandon me, as did my Father by having committed suicide? What did I really fear?

Had I ever allowed my wife within my 'walls?' Hadn't I greatly contributed to <u>her</u> unhappiness within our marriage by my 'warrior' and my 'ice man' persona? How close to me had I allowed her to get? I am honest enough to reflect my own part in what had turned out to be an unhappy marriage for both of us. Reluctantly I do wish her love and happiness in her current marriage. Just because I was filled with sadness was no reason for her not to enjoy happiness—or so I thought. I had not seen her in four plus years and assumed that she was indeed happy? Heck, her happiness is not my sadness and her sadness would not be my happiness.

I remember a friend of mine at college, Stuart, who had chewed me out one day. While Stuart complimented me for being a strong and loyal friend, he also complained that that I had never asked anyone for a favor. Stuart further explained that my friends needed to know that they could be depended upon for favors and that they wanted me to need them as they needed me. The asking of favors would express my need and also be a compliment to my friends. Why didn't I ever ask anyone for help or for a favor? Why was I so damn self-reliant and independent? Did I perceive that only a weak man asked others for favors? But, didn't it really take strength, not weakness, to humble oneself in order to ask another for a favor?

Need?? I had needed my Father. Had I ever again needed anyone? It was there and put out into the open by Stuart. It was true. I had seldom if ever asked anyone to do me a favor or to ask anyone ever for help. I projected the hard tough image of a completely self-reliant man who did not need another person in the world. It certainly was the 'mask' that I wore.

It wasn't that I intentionally pushed people away; it was just that I didn't allow people within the walls that surrounded me and seemingly protected me. From what did they protect me? From what potential hurt did they keep me? All of this had the effect of pushing people away from me—an unintended effect.

In my daydreams I never got the girl as in all of those movies to which I related. I was always, as the movie heroes with which I seemed to have related, the hero who walked away alone. I was intelligent and perceptive enough to recognize that a woman desired a strong but vulnerable man who needed her. All women wanted a man who needed them. Perhaps it was their motherly instinct?

I often told friends what I recognized as my problem, (I am repeating myself) what seemed to be the reason I remained unmarried and alone. It seemed that the characteristics in my personality and character, which enabled me to survive alone, also kept me alone. I appeared to others to be too self-reliant, too independent, too strong, too aloof, as though I didn't need or want anyone. It was the 'mask' that I wore and the 'role', which I played, to my dismay. Again I feared that I had lost the ability to accept being loved by any woman.

While at college during my senior year in 1964 I had written the following poem:

A Man

Alone is he, who is a man,
Brave but lonely is his lot.
He walks straight, head up high.
Scorned and hated is he.

His heart is filled with courage.
His mind is filled with truth.
Yet he walks alone
For a man is he.

Had the poem revealed my inner self? Had the poem become prophetic and self-fulfilling? I wrote of being alone and wasn't I alone? Hadn't I always been alone, even during the 12 years I was married? From where in my heart and mind did such sentiments and words come? What even made me write such words? Did I not know how to be loved or how to accept being loved?

Wouldn't psychiatrists and psychologists have a field day with me? I joked that I was 'crazy' and that I would enjoy going to a psychiatrist just to drive the psychiatrists nuts. Ha! Ha! Couldn't I be 'healed' by a psychiatrist? What was there to know about me that psychoanalysis could reveal? Didn't I already know myself?

I had stated to a close friend that I had become the man I wanted to be, but that the results of my life had not turned out quite as desired.

The man had the same high ideals, principles, integrity, and moral values that the boy once had. Nothing within me had changed. I walked a very straight line. I strongly believed in all of my values and I did my best to live my life by a very strict code of honor. I did not lie, did not cheat, did not steal, was faithful, was loyal, and did all that I could to be good and to do good. I was highly disciplined. But wasn't my living by a strict code of honor a recipe for failure in this world? Isn't that what Machiavelli warned by saying the following?

> **"IF a man would live as men should amongst men who live, as men do, wouldn't such a man be ruined"**
> —Machiavelli

I really tried to live as men should live yet always recognized that most men did not live, as they should. More and more it disturbed me to see the liar, the cheat, and the whore seemingly blessed with success and prosperity. I often read Psalm 37 in the Bible, but it just did not seem to apply to the world about me. While I certainly was not a 'saint' I did always try to be good and to do good. I was a decent guy. I repeat I am no saint.

I bowed to no man. I was honest. I did not knife people in the back. I was outspoken. I did not 'kiss ass'—not for any reason! I was not afraid to cross swords with any man. It was when I stood on principle that I was most tenacious and most unyielding. In that I was a true 'Sicilian' willing to risk all on a matter of principle. I was not afraid to standalone. I often did. I accepted that as the price one paid for being a man. I was willing to pay the price, as I would remain as I was. I would continue to live by a strict code of honesty and integrity. As a friend had observed and remarked to me: "I respect you as you've lived your life on your own terms." And I have!

The first summer I worked for Johnson & Johnson the manufacturing plant was shut down for two weeks and virtually everyone was forced to take their vacation during the shutdown. Upon receiving my vacation pay envelope I discovered that the check was for an incorrect amount—it was for $3500 instead of the correct $350. I immediately went back to the Personnel Director and handed the check back to her explaining that it was incorrect. Years later this same Personnel Director met my mother at a political function and related to her how her son (me) had demonstrated such honesty.

When I bought my townhouse I actually moved in before the closing date with a handshake agreement with the builder that I would pay a certain amount for rent and for the appliances. Both of us forgot the arrangement. It was nearly two years later when I remembered that I had not paid him and I sent a check for the correct amount to the builder who was quite surprised, as he had completely forgotten our handshake agreement. He was quite thankful if not shocked!

I am proud of such actions. I do not—and it must be repeated—I do <u>not</u> feel any moral superiority because of such actions. I just feel good about being the man that I am. My word is my bond!

Upon calling on a major account with a Region Manager while I was still with Xerox in 1987 while selling the voice mail product, the account told the RM: "he does what he says he will do when he says he will do it." For all, of my sales career I had been an honest and ethical salesperson! It had been mentioned in the majority of my Xerox Performance Appraisals that: "his customers trusted him."

Restlessness, sleeplessness, anxiety about my future, and dreams that could not be remembered all plagued the darkness and night. Last night again I'd had several dreams but none of them had been vivid nor had been remembered. It was my daydreams that were most vivid in my mind. Can my mind tell the difference between my actual life experiences and my imagined daydreams? Did the power of my 'creative imagination' produce a warrior?

Didn't my self-image, which is an individual's mental and spiritual concept or picture of myself, create my warrior personality? Hadn't I 'pictured' myself as the lone fighter pilot flying my plane out of the glaring sun to attack the enemy as had the 'Red Baron' done in WWI? Wasn't I the lone gunfighter in the Old West out on the dusty street facing an opponent? Wasn't I the lone gladiator in the arena holding sword and shield? Wasn't I a knight with King Arthur? Wasn't I all of these because I thought that was who and what I was? And don't thoughts become things? How did such thoughts originate within me? That is the big question!

All that I was I had created in my mind—the warrior mentality and personality. I really was hard, tough, and a survivor. It was what I imagined myself to be and what I was!

I thought of my Son and my Daughter who were the loves of my life. How many other fathers had taken their children to see the movie The Great Santini as I had done in order to try to explain my own personality? How many other fathers had allowed their children to witness their crying and tears? Of course I wondered—how many other fathers were like me in personality and character? I truly loved my Son and my Daughter with my whole heart and soul, and as high as the sky and deep as the ocean, and so much more. I had sacrificed much for them—maybe too much?

Although there were thick impenetrable walls that surrounded this "warrior—man", they did not keep my Children out or later on, my Grandchildren. In many ways I had attempted to reveal more of myself and to share more of myself with my Children than with anyone else. I hoped that they would know and understand me better than would anyone else. I hoped that would be the case but I wasn't sure. Wasn't it a purpose of this book to reveal more of myself to my Children? Was this book a revelation to my Children or an apology to them? They would have to determine that! It was <u>not</u> meant to hurt my ex-wife in any manner—but the truth is the truth. In many ways and once upon a time she had been a good wife and a good mother. I would always remember that. I'll always wish that we had been able to share a lifetime of love together.

Although I could be aloof and distant, this seemed to be a trait which I exhibited only when people tried to get too close to me; when they tried to get inside those thick walls that surrounded me. Actually I was quite warm and friendly as I had a way of attracting people to myself. Therein lay the paradox! I was the lone wolf warrior who, despite drawing people to myself, kept them at a certain distance, sort of outside a perimeter of safety. Yet, I was <u>not</u> a 'loner.' My Granddaughter had observed and remarked to me: "Pop-Pop, you are very friendly towards people." I am!

I did not fear people and did not fear opening up to people, which I easily did to an extent. It was not fear that caused me to be a very private person. Perhaps I was just cautious, as I had learned that very, very few people could be trusted. I had been hurt too many times by people whom I had trusted.

Was it my 'Sicilian' nature or a learned trait, that I just did not have much trust in people? I had been hurt and the pain of hurt does destroy trust. I had been lied to and cheated on, deeply hurt by one whom I had deeply loved. That had much to do with my lack of trust in people. Could I really not help that way that I was and am?

Yet, it was really more than the hurt I had suffered. It was more of a warrior mentality, which caused me to be wary of people. As a gladiator in the arena, I knew there could be only one man standing at the end of battle. To survive the battle meant that I could not trust anyone—no one at all!

How much did my Father's death destroy my trust in people? How much did it destroy my ability to allow people to get close to me? Didn't I, as a twelve year-old boy, trust my Father to always be there for me, a trust that was broken by my Father's suicide, did that tragedy destroy my trust in everyone? The person closest to me, my Father, betrayed my trust and failed me.

That my Father was ill (<u>everyone</u> who takes his/her own life is obviously ill) did not abrogate the affect on me. A great part of the boy and later on the man died with my Father. Boyhood died with my Father and an unusually serious 12 year-old man was left in its stead. I became extremely quiet, withdrawn, very moody, and my ability to 'loosen up' and have fun just never seemed to have developed. I've often told my Children that I "never learned to have fun."

Right this moment, at age 66, I fully comprehended that I had never really outwardly cried over my Father's death. I'd been a "good soldier" and had held back my tears at the funeral and at the gravesite. For all of my life I had been crying on the inside. The concept of closure was a complete myth!! Did anyone bury a loved one and then go on with their lives without continuing to feel the hurt associated with such a loss? Closure? Who the hell came up with that stupid idea? When a parent buried a child did they ever get over such a loss? The idea of 'closure' was a complete myth!

TRUST? What about my trust, in the God to Whom, I had prayed that awful night to save my Father? I had envisioned visiting my Father in the hospital to tell him how much I loved him. I had envisioned my Father coming home and that everything would be okay. I had prayed to God and I trusted God, as I was an altar boy who served God at Mass and who trusted God. My Father had died instantly. Another person, in whom I trusted, God, had failed me and that continued to disturb me greatly.

Hadn't I prayed to God after my ex-wife and I had separated? Hadn't I really believed that she and I would reconcile? Hadn't I expected a miracle? I had had no doubts that the marriage would be saved. And then when it was apparent that God would not answer that prayer, didn't I firmly believe and expect that I would be awarded custody of my Children? Why had God not answered either of those particular prayers? Could I trust God for anything? And if God could not be trusted was there anyone who could be trusted? Why had even God failed me?

Is this the reason I did not trust people? Did I expect too much out of people? Were my expectations too high when it came to people, and even when it came to myself? Did I demand and expect too much of myself and of people? Would I never be happy with myself or satisfied with people? Like Nietzsche I had become a very cynical man when it came to God and to women! Could I ever trust either again?

I seem to have accepted that I would never be satisfied with myself no matter what I accomplished—it just would never be enough. Anything less than perfection was not enough. I was extremely hard on myself! I had mellowed somewhat when it came to others. I had come to accept that others could not be perfect. I had not mellowed much when it came to myself. I still demanded perfection of myself.

While I had difficulty in trusting others, could I trust myself? After my divorce I wondered IF I could ever trust myself to discern who might be truly a 'good' woman from a woman who had no value or values? I feared that I could not! Could I ever trust my ability to be able to distinguish between the image of a woman that I might foolishly create in my mind and the reality of her? I thought of Shirley. She and Tom had been married for 20+ years. That was proof to me that I had been correct in my observation that she was a truly good woman!

Had I experienced too much hurt to ever trust anyone again? It seemed that the people I loved the most failed me, people I trusted most failed me, even God seemingly failed me and that was the deepest hurt of all. It deeply depressed me. Heck—maybe I was not lovable?

In anger and disappointment, over the years, I would often quit attending Mass as I periodically 'gave up on God.' The 'loving Abba'—the 'loving Father in Heaven' about Whom the priests preached—that God just did not appear to exist, and if He did, appeared not to love me, or so I felt at times. Having faith in God was a major struggle for me. It was the ultimate 'contest' and I was losing it.

Jesus had even said that if we were to ask our earthly father for bread, would he give us a stone? No, our earthly father would surely give us bread. Jesus further stated that our Heavenly Father, Who loved us dearly, would give us what we ask for in His name. I asked God for much but felt that all I got in return was adversity, failure, evil done to me, and aloneness with unanswered prayers. And I wondered why?

Some men often claimed that, "God had blessed them with the desires of their hearts" as they enjoyed love, happiness, success, financial wealth. As Solomon in The Book of Ecclesiastes observed—"the race is not always won by the swift but time and chance happen to all men." Why did God greatly bless some men and not others? In all of my readings, I never could find an answer to the 'why' question. It seems that Solomon had no answer to that question either!

Of course the really big question was why do I think the way that I do, and why am I the way that I was/am? Did 'God' make me the way that I was? Or did some other 'force' cause me to think as I do? Was it due to the 'stars' and my being 'Taurus' as to the astrological calendar my having been born in May? Was it due to environment and due to what had happened to me as a boy and throughout my life?

I firmly believe that the mind experienced from the inside out, that the outer environment did not have such a great impact on a man, that it was how a man viewed his environment from the inside out that impacted him. It wasn't what happens to a man, but what thoughts a man gave to such events that mattered so believed the 'Stoic' philosophers. The question again was—why did I think the way that I did? Why does any man think the way that he does? How does any man get to be the man that he is?

How do other men think and feel? What makes other men think and feel as they do? Do all men think and feel the same way? IF some men had different thoughts and feeling—why did they? IF some men thought and felt in different ways from most men—did it bother them that they were not like other men? How alike were men? Again, I ask these questions seeking answers for myself and trying to find a connection with other men.

To combat and survive the deep depression that I suffered in my waking hours, I had envisioned and actually created the 'warrior' man that I'd become in my dreams. My defense mechanism was to enter what I called "another dimension of time and space" in which I acted out my role as a warrior and a hero. In that dimension it was best not to trust people, as one never knew who his enemy might be. Unfortunately, there was no definitive line to separate the different dimensions of time and space in which I existed, as I now always appeared to be the warrior. All I knew is that as a warrior I did not get depressed and that was a comfort to me.

In a recent issue of 'Money' magazine, I read the stories of highly successful people who had retired while still very young. It depressed me to read about these very young men who all made high six figure incomes and who planned to retire by the age of 55 with great wealth and significant pensions. I had neither. Here I was at age 51 (at the time) and I was out of work, I had no job prospects, I had no wife, I did not feel attached to anyone, and I was still trying to climb the mountain of success. Damn, I thought, I was starting all over in a career at the time most men had long ago achieved their career goals. I should be winding down at this stage of my life and looking forward to retirement instead of looking for a job. Of course there I was comparing myself to others!

I was alone and was reminded of a couple of sayings from songs: "You're no one until someone loves you"—and—"Everybody loves somebody sometime." Dean Martin sure did know how to sing about love! Deep depression set in, enveloped me, causing great sadness in my heart and soul. I did need love, I did need someone, I needed to love and I needed to be loved. I just wanted to cry as I deeply hurt. The adversity, failures, and aloneness I suffered made my life a horror of deep hurt. It was extremely painful for me to bear.

As I has previously remarked herein despite what Psalm 37 advised, I did 'fret', because I did witness 'evil' men and women being blessed with success and prosperity despite their lies, cheating, and stealing. It seemed that 'God' favored those who did evil, as He sure seemed to bless them? What the heck! Even Solomon wrote that he had observed: "I've seen the evil get what the good deserve and the good get what the evil deserve." Life was indeed unfair!! Was there no law of Karma?

I would read an article in a magazine, see a pretty woman in a television advertisement, hear a song on the radio, and those little things reminded me of my own current status, which depressed me. Despite my anguished cries and prayers to God, I was alone with my needs and desires unfulfilled as my prayers went unanswered.

As per the book Men are from Mars and Women are from Venus—didn't men withdraw and 'retreat' into a 'cave' when experiencing confrontation or stress? Isn't that what the majority of men did? I had my own cave. It was another dimension of time and space into which I withdrew and retreated. My depression subsided as I drifted off to sleep, drifted off to enter his world of dreams in which I was a warrior.

I suffered another restless and sleepless night with only brief moments of 'dreams', none of which were particularly vivid as they were fuzzy in my memory. I was physically tired, as I'd come to recognize that depression robbed me of my energy and physical strength, and also of my sexual virility.

Mine was very much a 'situational depression' or so I thought. After all I was out of work for the first time in my life and I was alone. I felt a hopelessness that came from the feeling that, perhaps, my hopes, dreams, and aspirations would never be fulfilled. Under such current circumstances as being age 51 and out of work, with no job prospects, cause depression in any man? There was the fear that I would never know true love, never know success, never experience financial wealth, and that God would never answer my prayers. The future was so uncertain.

Statistically five years after their divorce 80 percent of men and women married again. The other 20 percent who passed five years since their divorce seldom married again. At my then age of 51 twelve years had passed since my separation and divorce. When I reached age 66 I accepted that I would never again marry. It was not impossible that I would marry again but it sure as hell was not likely.

But, wasn't it true, that for nearly all of my life, I had suffered from some depression or was it just sadness? Had I ever been happy? Hadn't I suffered unhappiness even while I was employed? Had I suffered depression and unhappiness even while I was married? Wasn't it more than 'situational depression' from which I suffered? Hadn't I always been 'moody' even as a boy after my Father had died? What was the reason? Was it my 'Taurus' profile—the most melancholy of all of the star signs?

Family pictures of when I was a boy and while my Father was still alive, did show me with a smile. After the death of my Father, such photos did not show me to be smiling, but instead with a very serious look on my face. Even my ex-wife had complained to me that I did not smile enough. Was it because I thought that I looked better with a serious face instead of a smile? I didn't want to look like some big goofy clown with a clown smile on my face. Ha! Ha!

Wasn't I a true 'Taurus' personality? I certainly seemed to fit all of the personality traits generally associated with those born under the astrological sign of Taurus, some of them good and some of them not so good. And, as per being a Taurus, didn't that mean, according to the stars, that I had, like it or not, a 'melancholy' personality? It was certainly not anything to dismiss so easily. I had been melancholy as a boy, even more so as a teenager, and was so as a man. Had the 'stars' caused my dominant personality traits which further caused me to suffer from depression most of my life? Was I more 'melancholy' than depressed? Was I unique or just normal?

Of course 'Taurus' was the 'money sign' but somehow financial wealth, like love and happiness, had eluded me all of my life. Hadn't I had to give up playing high school football and all sports in order to work to save money for college? My Mother was working in a factory after the death of my Father and she seldom made even $2000 income per year. She was not able later on to provide any financial assistance to me as I paid for all of my college expenses myself. I worked summer job and even jobs during semesters.

Was my depression caused by my Taurus melancholy personality? Was my depression perhaps age related? How many men at age 51 do not suffer from depression? What IF the ambitions of their youth have not been realized, they have not achieved the success or prosperity for which they had hoped and strived, and there were so many dreams that would just never come true as time was beginning to run out on them—how would such men feel? Wouldn't such failures depress them? My failures depressed me.

It seemed that even those men of age 51 who had achieved and realized the ambitions and dreams of their youth were just as depressed, as they evaluated what they had sacrificed and lost in order to achieve their goals. Didn't the realization that they had paid too high a price for what that had achieved depress them deeply?

Both the 'winners' and the 'losers', it seemed, had ample reasons for their depression. Was it merely the lot of men to suffer from depression? With each passing year of age, didn't depression increase and become more serious for men? There were so many aspects of a man's life, at age 51, which could and did cause depression, especially the realization that he had pretty much passed 'mid life' as measured in years and was getting older with more time already passed than was in front of him. Entering the youth of old age—wow—old age—now that is depressing!

"Age forty is the old age of youth and age fifty is the youth of old age"

At age 31 I had weighed 198 pounds on a 5' 9" frame, as I was stocky and built like a bull. Heck, I was fat! At age 51 I weighed 178 pounds and looked good! I was in much better physical condition than I had been in a long time, doing sit ups, push ups, jogging, and walking nearly every day. But, the sexual virility of a man of age 31 was a thing of the past!

I did not look like a man whose age was 51, and later on at age 66, I looked like a man of much younger years. At both ages I was in much better shape, physical condition and health than the vast majority of men my age and I looked it. As my Granddaughter had observed, (when I was age 65 and she was age 9) "Pop-Pop, you live alone but you are not like most men who live alone. You cook for yourself and you eat healthy. You exercise, you jog and you walk. You take good care of yourself." As I told her: "I want to be around to dance with you at your wedding." I am fortunate not to have to take any prescription medication—yet!

Although at age 51 I did not look my age and at age 66 I did not look my age; I knew my real chronological age. I knew that time was getting short for me. I was fast approaching the September of my years. The deterioration of sexual virility was very depressing to me as it is to most if not all men as they age. Time did not respect men as it took its toll on ALL men.

Didn't the great football player, Bronco Nagurski, become a virtual recluse in his latter years? He did not want people to see him as he declined in strength and health, as he had been exceptionally strong as a football player when a younger man.

Each man was different and unique, yet in many ways alike. I certainly was much different from any man I had ever known. Yet, pain was the equalizer as I had learned while going through my divorce and while hearing other men articulate and share the pain that they had suffered in going through their divorces. It did seem that all men hurt in much the same way.

Often I heard friends, who were single as I was, reflect how they wanted to find a woman soon because they didn't want to be old and alone. I often reflected that I didn't want to be young and alone. I wished for a woman now while "my parts still worked." It wasn't to be. I had gotten to be 'old' as age 66 was considered and had been alone all the years since my divorce. Of course I always told myself, and my friends that: "no company was a lot better than bad company." And when I thought of so many other men who had gone through 'serial marriages' and who had gotten divorced after brief marriages—heck, I believed myself to be better off being alone. I did not need anyone to take care of me—I could care for myself!

Men at age 51 died! I read in the morning newspaper's obituary of a 51 year old man who was a college president who died while having heart surgery. Wow! The man had achieved great success in his profession. It didn't matter—he was dead anyway! What had caused that man to even have heart surgery? Did he have bad genes? Did he smoke and was obese? Did he pay a high price for his success? Or, was it just his time to go? Didn't the Bible even say that our "days were numbered?" Despite my failures, I would NOT change places with any man on Earth.

A high school classmate of mine, a JV football teammate, a successful attorney in our hometown, had recently died. The year was 1992. I was age 51 at the time. It again reminded me of the saying: "Time does not shout, it just runs out." Yet another classmate of mine, a freshman basketball teammate, who was one of the stars on the high school varsity basketball team, who married one of the prettiest girls in our class (one whom I had valued greatly from afar), died of a massive heart attack. Both classmates died at age 51—I was now age 66. What had I done with the extra 15 years?

How many more years would I have? My Godfather's wife had died at age 73—my Uncle was now age 86. John Wayne had died at age 72. Wow! Those ages were not so much older than I was now. Of course my maternal Grandmother's brother—my Uncle Louie—had died at age 97. Another Uncle was with him at the time. Uncle Louie just looked at him and said: "the hour has arrived"—he slumped over and died. My maternal Grandmother's youngest Sister, who had never left Sicily, was age 102. I believe that I will live to be age 100! Time would tell!

Ironically and sadly there were all too many tragic and violent deaths in my family such as: suicides, being shot to death, getting hit and killed by cars, boating accidents and drowning. Fortunately cancer and heart disease did not run in the family. Could it possibly be written in some 'big book' somewhere in the heavens as to when and how a person was to die?

At age 51 a man is supposedly into the youth of his old age, but it was not really youth, as young men know youth to be, and not really the youth that they once knew. At age 30 while still young, a man's view is mostly forward looking with the enthusiasm that their hope and dreams are yet to be fulfilled. At age 51 (even more so at age 66) a man's view becomes more backward looking with a view to all of the hopes and dreams that were not yet fulfilled and which may never be fulfilled. Now that was depressing!! My Son had accused me of "living in the past" and I was very guilty of doing just that. Indeed it seemed that I too often looked backward instead of looking forward. Was it due to a sense of emptiness in my life that I felt in the present? Did I have too many regrets over which I brooded? Surely I dwelled on too many could haves, would haves, and would haves.

Didn't the angel 'Monica' in the TV program 'Touched by an Angel' tell someone that: "the reason God put our eyes in the front of our heads and not in the back of our heads so that we could see where we were going and not look back at where we have been." The past is certainly the past! But the past can haunt a man.

"Though no one can go back and make a brand new start—anyone can start from now and make a brand new end"

Had time and opportunity already run out on me by the age of 51 (most certainly by the age of 66)? Had love, happiness, success, financial wealth, had all eluded me completely for my entire life with no chance left to ever grab onto the brass ring? That was the deep fear that I felt within. What did other men feel, suffer, and fear at the same age? Although I was 'unique' in many ways, was I really so different from other men? Were other men so different from me? Didn't all men bleed the same red blood?

As to that "grab the brass ring" phrase—from where did that term originate? It actually comes from the New Jersey Shore! Extended out towards the merry-go-rounds on the boardwalks at Point Pleasant and Seaside Heights on the New Jersey Shore was an arm with a brass ring in it. It was up to the riders of the merry-go-rounds to reach out and to "grab the brass ring" as they went by that extended arm. Perhaps only the Jersey people knew the origination of that term? I was still a Jersey guy! Unlike the guys in the Carolinas who '"went to the beach"—Jersey guys "went down the shore." I will always be a Jersey guy!

I was once asked the question: "Do you think that you have already experienced the happiest moments that you will ever experience in your life?" Wow!! At the time that question was asked of me, I would have said "yes" as what could compare to being in love, to getting married, to having a Son, to buying our first house, to having a Daughter? Oh, but that question was asked of me when I had been recently divorced in 1981 and when life sure looked awfully bleak for me. Years later, the birth of my Granddaughter and the joy she gives to me; the birth of my first Grandson and the joy he gives to me; and the birth of my twin Grandsons and the joy they give to me; <u>now</u> I could answer that question with a resounding '**no**' as I realized that there was more happiness for me to enjoy in my life with even more to come!

I felt 'guilt' over my own failures as I thought of those who died in the Viet Nam War, such as Ron, and I wondered what more would they have done with their lives than I had done with mine had they lived? Did other Viet Nam War veterans who had come close to dying in that war experience similar feelings of 'guilt' as did I? Was it a 'normal' feeling? Ron died at age 23. I was now age 66. What had I done with the extra years?

When I gave blood at the Red Cross I always stayed to spend time and share conversation with the Monday volunteer who was an Army combat veteran of the Viet Nam War. The eyes of this man had welled up with tears as he reflected on the guilt that he felt in having survived that war when so many he knew had been killed. Both of us felt guilt about being alive and as having come back alive from that awful war while 58,000+ had lost their lives. Was it a feeling from which other veterans of the Viet Nam War suffered? What about men from other wars, did they feel guilt in having survived when so many other were killed? Is it a feeling experienced by many other men? Yes it did indeed seem to be a feeling that was suffered by so many other war veterans as the program about the WWII Normandy invasion survivors indicated.

Was the feeling of guilt a demon that combat veterans of war, who had nearly lost their lives in war, experienced? Did other war veterans ask of themselves as I asked of myself: "did I earn having been given all of these extra years?" The more years that I have lived, as have other veterans of the Viet Nam War, the more years that those who had died have missed out on having lived. That was a disturbing thought. Wouldn't the dead trade places with me? Wouldn't the 44 who died in the Oriskany fire trade places with me?

Whenever I heard people say: "if they had their lives to live over again, they would make the same decisions and live their lives in the same way", I often kidded them that they must have led perfect lives with their every decision having resulted in a perfect outcome. The problem, as I saw it, was that if one could go back and make different decisions in their lives, it would result in different outcomes, NOT necessarily better outcomes as things could have turned out much worse! I really would not change anything?

I could NOT and would NOT give up my Children or my Grandchildren! So, like it or not, I accept my life the way it turned out, even with the sadness deep within my heart and soul. I had the Son and the Daughter that I wanted. I had the four Grandchildren that I wanted. I had the Daughter-in-Law that I wanted. NO others could take their places in my heart and in my life.

As to the sadness within my heart, I did have the great fear that I would die without ever having truly lived and that I would die without ever having been truly loved by a woman. I accepted that my wife of 12 years never really loved me. IF she had loved me, would she have lied to me and would she have cheated on me? Did wives who loved their husbands do such things to hurt their husbands? Maybe her actions had nothing to do with me?

And yet, I am thankful for our marriage that gave me a Son and Daughter, and four Grandchildren. Maybe that was God's 'plan' all along? Interestingly the very first words in the 'Memoirs' of General Ulysses S. Grant are:

"Man proposes and God disposes—there are but few important events in the affairs of men brought about by their own choice"

I was sad and depressed, angry at and with myself for my own failures. I was also angry at and with 'God' for seemingly abandoning me for I was truly alone this day. I wanted to cry but there were no tears, there was just the pain.

As I jogged and walked this Sunday morning, I could see couples in cars all dressed up and on their way to church. Couples! It sure did seem to me that it was a world of couples! I was alone and I felt very alone. I felt like the most alone man in the universe. Was there another man anywhere who felt as alone as I did this day? Was I so unique as to feel greater aloneness and pain than did any other man felt? Hadn't I always felt such aloneness and even isolation?

What did other men feel who were alone? Didn't every man desire to share love and happiness and passion with a good woman? After all God did instill in every man a sex drive? Didn't every man desire love, happiness, success, and financial wealth? Was I really so different from other men?

Vaguely I could remember being a very young toddler who still slept in a crib and seeing my body, or was it my spirit, floating above my crib as I looked up at myself. I vaguely remembered my body, or spirit, floating above my crib and seeing my body still in my crib. Simultaneously, I was in my crib and I was floating above my crib. It was an experience that I remember, about which I had never told anyone until recent years. It happened in the early 1940's. Today it would be referred to as "an out of body experience." I knew that it did indeed happen! It had not been a dream but it had been an actual experience. What had it meant?

When I related the event to my Granddaughter, she told me that it was the "angels that I saw looking after me." Perhaps she was correct? It was an experience that happened quite often while I was in my crib. It was such an experience that made me feel 'different' from others, not in a bad way, just different. When I thought of my frequent close brushes with Death, the Viet Nam War being only one of many, perhaps 'Angels' had been looking after me all of my life and had protected me?

Throughout my life, and especially after the death of my Father, I had always felt like I just was not a part of things. Although I had participated in all sports (football, baseball, basketball, track) on organized teams, I had the feeling of aloneness and isolation. Maybe it was a sign of depression that was not recognized by me as a boy, nor as a teenager. Since I never articulated such feelings to anyone, no one suspected or recognized my likely depression? I was merely a 'serious' and a 'moody' boy.

Right now, at age 66 while writing herein, the realization hit me hard that perhaps I had suffered from depression or sadness all of my life—<u>all</u> of my life?? Damn, my feelings of aloneness, of isolation, of deep sadness, had I always been depressed? Had it robbed me of the joy of living? I sure did not know how to have fun! But, was it depression or was it sadness, and is there a difference between the two, or does depression cause sadness? Were the two even connected? While I felt isolated, I really did not isolate myself from other people. While I felt alone, I did connect with other people, although I kept most people at arms length from myself. As I have already written herein and it bears repeating—my Granddaughter reflected when I was age 65 and she was age 9: "Pop-Pop, you are very friendly towards other people." And I am! Virtually ALL of the regulars at the jogging track know me and I know them because I engage just about everyone in friendly conversation. I don't see strangers.

Would truly depressed people even get out to jog and walk, to exercise, to cook for themselves and eat healthy, to take good care of themselves? I remain an avid reader, mostly of biographies, history, and current events. I have interests. I get out of my townhouse most every day. I travel to see each of my Grandchildren on their birthdays. I had even traveled (during 2006) to Pensacola, Florida to attend a reception for former crewmembers of the USS Oriskany CVA-34, the aircraft carrier on which I had served in the Viet Nam war and on which I had very, very nearly lost my life. IF I were truly depressed, would I do such things? I had hoped that by attending the Oriskany Reception I could have finally buried and rid myself of the demon that haunted me daily—the memory of the Oriskany fire. The demon remains alive!

Yet, (as previously commented within this book) a friend of mine had remarked that he sensed a deep sadness within me. It was an observation that my Daughter-in-Law had also expressed to me. I did not deny the sadness. Perhaps it was just that, sadness, as I didn't really act like a man who was depressed?

I could step out of my townhouse any morning, look up at the clear blue Carolina sky, feel the warmth of the sun, and I did feel glad to be alive. I actually felt enthusiasm for the day and for nearly every day. Other joggers often ran with anguished looks of pain on their faces, but I always ran with a smile on my face.

It really didn't make any sense. IF I was so depressed and deeply sad with a desire to just cry, how could I step out and look up at the clear sky with a feeling of joy and then jog with a smile on my face while enjoying each step? And I always 'rejoiced and thanked God' for, having given me the day, as a gift to enjoy. If I were suffering from deep depression would I be accepting the challenge of writing this memoir? Now that is a good question.

This day each passing car seemed to have a very pretty woman as a driver, or occupant with one especially pretty blond haired woman catching my eye. For a moment all of the love that was within me, and yearning to be shared was stirred as I thought of my unfulfilled needs and desires. I needed a woman to love and a woman to love me. It seemed that the need and desire to love was greater than even the need to be loved?

As a sexual lover I was tender, loving, caring, sensitive, giving, perhaps too tender, and certainly too controlled. I was uninhibited, certainly not kinky, just more free and uninhibited, more revealing of myself than, at any other time anywhere else. The bedroom was perhaps the one place that I could safely reveal myself. Perhaps it is the one place that every man reveals himself? For me, it was the one place in which I let my guard down, where I let go of my sword and shield. Lovemaking required great trust. It was the bedroom in which men were most trusting, most free, and most vulnerable to a woman. After our divorce my ex-wife did remark that: "at least we had had a good sex life."

Hadn't 'Samson' in the Bible succumbed to the charms of a woman whom he trusted as he had let his guard down to her? Sadly, it had cost Samson dearly and he had paid for her treachery with his life as she betrayed him!

Remembering a segment of the TV series 'Married with Children' made me laugh to myself. It was the one in which 'Peggy' is explaining to her next-door neighbor 'Marcie' that "in order for a man to function sexually all of the blood had to leave his brain and flow southward." While that is not really physiologically accurate—it does appear that a man in love is incapable of making reasonable decisions? Didn't Nietzsche say something similar: "One ought to hold onto one's heart for if one lets it go, one soon loses control of the head too." It is no wonder that Nietzsche was one of my favorite philosophers!

Perhaps there was no greater fear for a man than to be betrayed by the woman he loved and whom he trusted? For it was in loving a woman that a man becomes most vulnerable. NO 'enemy' could ever get, as close to a man as the woman he loved. NO 'enemy' knew how to hurt a man more deeply than the woman he loved.

The very cynical philosopher Nietzsche said it best when he declared:

"In revenge and in love, woman is more barbarous than man"
—Nietzsche

That is so true!! Ask any man who has been through a divorce the truth of that statement!! All men would agree to that statement's veracity! How many men have been taken to the cleaners—so to speak—by their wife in a divorce? It becomes a financial disaster for many a man. Sadly, in today's society a married woman can decide that she just no longer wants to be married to her husband and the man pays for it! The man loses his house and his children and is forced to pay!

A woman could hurt a man most deeply in the bedroom. What deeper hurt in the love marriage relationship between a husband and wife could a man experience than to hear his wife, in the throes of sex, cry out the name of the man with whom she was having an affair at the time? That is a hurt that cuts deeply to the heart and the soul of a man, and to his very being. When the name cried out is not that of a former lover but that of a man with whom the wife is currently having an adulterous affair, that cuts the heart out of a man, and it is a hurt that remains in the man's heart for the rest of his life. Even the Bible seemed to infer that there was nothing worse than a cheating wife, at least nothing worse in the love relationship shared between husband and wife. That was a hurt which I had experienced in 1970 and from which I still suffered pain. She had hurt me more deeply than I had ever imagined that it was possible to have been hurt. Sadly, that terrible hurt remains in my heart and still pains me.

I thought about my former wife with angry thoughts. In most respects she had been a good wife and mother, but, her 'flaws' were major as she <u>lied</u>, she <u>cheated</u>, and she exhibited a selfishness with a need to be the center of attention. I was better off without her. Her own Aunt had told me after the divorce: "you are better off without her." I wondered why was she the way that she was?

Having been totally betrayed by a woman I deeply loved and married—by my wife and the mother of my children—could I ever again allow myself to love and trust another woman? I discovered this about myself—I now had a greater capacity to love and a greater ability to express that love than ever before but I also had a greater reluctance and fear to love than ever before. Despite my need for love and I indeed wanted love yet I needed it less. As I remarked to a friend:

"A man wants out of strength and he needs out of weakness"

There were times when the desire was so great that I felt like I could not go on for even another minute. I wanted—I did not need? I often acted as if I did not need anyone in the world. That was my 'defense', the 'mask' that I wore in order to survive the aloneness that hurt me deeply and in order to survive the unsatisfied need and desire. It was in the dream like state of mind in which I imagined myself to be a warrior that my need was not felt. Didn't everyone wear a mask? What mask does my ex-wife now wear? Is she really happy now?

That is why I truly enjoyed being a warrior. As a warrior, I am whole, complete, satisfied, and without any unsatisfied needs. All of my attention is directed to executing battle plans; in defensive perimeters; and in attack strategies. It was exhilarating to me! It made me feel truly alive!

What about other men—how did they feel and how did they deal with their aloneness and unsatisfied needs? How did other men cope with their aloneness? I did not turn to drink nor to drugs as I valued my body and my health far too much to ever risk damage to either. How many other men did turn to drink and drugs in order to deaden their pain? I did not turn to promiscuous sex to satisfy needs—I was too much a moral man for such destructive behavior. Actually it has less to do with morality and more to do with my caring about my body. Didn't many other men turn to such destructive behavior? Didn't they regret such behavior later?

Really, it was a very redundant question and one, which is repeated many, many times herein—what did other men think and feel? Even the closest of friends among men just did not share their innermost personal thoughts and feelings with each other. Men could articulate for hours on end about sports, politics, even religion, but they seldom ever talked about their personal thoughts or feelings and they just NEVER talked about their fears to each other. After all, men were supposed to be strong and not have any fears—right? And who created that myth about how men should be?

Men at work; boys and men of all ages who participated in team sports together; men who just went out to drink together; especially men who shared the horrors of war together; they 'bonded." But they remained at arms length away from each other. All such endeavors brought men close to each other, but not too close as men kept their distance from even the closest of friends. Why are men as they are?

The actor, Peter Fonda, recalled how his Father, Henry Fonda, and Henry's close friend, actor, Jimmy Stewart, would work on models together for hours with nary a word spoken between them. Weren't all men the same? Didn't all men accept being together with a close friend or friends and words were not required to enjoy such company? It seems indeed to be a man thing. Women talked with each other, often about intimate subjects, which men would just NEVER discuss with each other. Men and women were indeed very different! Men sure were from Mars or from some other planet!

Although there were many activities during which men 'bonded', it was in sports (especially football) and at war, in such physical 'contest environments', in which men more readily bonded and became warriors. Perhaps football was the closest thing to combat in that a man's physical strength and endurance were tested plus his reliance on his teammates. Combat is the ultimate test of a man's strength and endurance plus his survival often depended on his fellow warriors.

I was most comfortable and even happy as a 'warrior', in combat so to speak, as I felt most alive as a warrior. All that I was; every inner strength; my courage; and my toughness; it was all felt by me when I was tested. Perhaps it was some connection to a primordial past when all that a man had on which to rely for his survival was his own strength. It was satisfying to be stronger than another man.

I had participated in all sports, but it was football that I'd loved the most. I loved the physical contact and the tackling, blocking, charging into another while I carried the ball as a halfback. Football allowed one to pit his physical strength against an opponent's strength. It was the closest thing to being a gladiator in the arena. It was the sport of warriors and I had loved it.

I had played softball for the company team. I had told my Son that I played softball because I enjoyed it and that I did not play it to make my Son proud of me. I had always told my Son to play sports only if he enjoyed playing and never for me, his Dad, that I was just as proud of my Son whether or not he played sports.

When I played softball it was as though nothing else in the world existed except for the game at hand, so great was my concentration and total involvement in the game. That is what I loved about sports, the 'escape' that sports provided into another realm. To play well one had to be totally immersed into the game and he did just that when he played at any sport. Heck, wasn't sex sort of like that?

On a recent trip to visit my Son and his family we all went out bowling one night. I had not bowled in several months. That night I bowled a 192, which was a high score for me. I did not have a single open frame, which is something that I've never done bowling before. I can remember that I'd gotten into a zone while bowling. Each time I picked up the ball I was in another place out on the ally with nothing else in the world existing for that moment. I had escaped into another world while out on that ally.

Did other men feel the same? It is a redundant question throughout this 'book'; one that I continually asked of myself and a question that I suspect that other men asked of themselves. Do all men think the same? Do all men feel and hurt the same? Do war veterans think and feel any differently than men who have never served in war? Do non-war veterans have different 'demons' that haunt them? Do all men—war veterans and non-war veterans—compare themselves and their lives to other men? Although I consistently fell into the 'trap'—and it is indeed a trap—of comparing myself and my failures to other men and their successes. I was very much the 'non-conformist' when it came to my actions. In this arena I compared myself to no one. And, in my lifelong outspokenness, I exhibited that I was not afraid to speak my mind despite the consequences. I was my own man—always!

My personal belief of 'manhood' was to always stand up for my beliefs, ideals, and principles. I did just that. I had always, in my own way, been much a non-conformist and sort of a 'maverick' even in grade school.

While in grade school in the 7th grade in May (my Father had died in September of the previous year at the start of the school year) my classroom Nun had asked for a 10 cents donation to the missions in return for a Mothers' Day card for each student in the class. Unfortunately the cards did not get distributed until the Monday after Mothers' Day. I refused to make the 10 cents donation to the missions; refused to accept the card; as I complained that it was too late to give my Mother the card as Mothers' Day has passed. I was the <u>only</u> one in the class who took such a stand!

It wasn't over the 10 cents, instead it was over the lateness of the card that caused me to make such a stand—and it was really over my personal principles. I received a red 'U' for unsatisfactory behavior during that 'marking period', which I did not regret. Perhaps I was still hurt and angry over the loss of my Father and such a stand was my way in expressing it? That school year, despite the loss of my

Father and as previously stated, I had the highest grade point average of any year in grade school.

What really caused me to take such a stand over an insignificant 10 cents and a seemingly unimportant principle? So what if the card was late? It was only 10 cents. Perhaps it was the developing nature of me, that once I took a firm stand on principle, I was steadfast and unyielding to the end no matter the consequences? Of course it was more likely that it may just have been an expression of anger over the loss of my Father?

Later on during that school year I got into a pushing match initiated by another classmate that resulted in a fistfight between us two boys. I 'exploded' on the other boy repeatedly punching him and 'winning' the fight. I could still hear a classmate's words in the background during the fight spoken about me: "I didn't know he had it in him." I was probably the mostly quiet boy in my class; I was the top academic student; and I was an altar boy—not a 'nerd' but no one would have suspected that I had such 'fight' within me. Perhaps it was just another display of anger over the loss of my Father earlier that school year that caused the fight within me?

A funny sidelight to that incident was that Paul, one of our classmates, then 'promoted' a rematch of the fight between me and the other boy. Paul took bets of 25 cents. Neither of us was angry with the other in the rematch fight. The other boy caught me in the eye with a punch and 'won' the rematch. Such was life in the poor Italian neighborhood in the 1950's! The fights had occurred outside the schoolyard grounds and fortunately were not observed by any of the nuns. There were no suspensions from school. The two of us remained friendly towards each other afterwards. It was just two boys having a fight—perhaps a ritual of growing up back then? It was the last fistfight that I would ever have.

At college I was required to take two years of physical education. Boxing was part of the program. The coach had questioned me one day after class, wanting to know where I had boxed before? The coach had gotten a little angry with me when I repeatedly stated that I had not boxed anywhere before. I explained to the coach that while growing up and while my Father had still been alive, that I had tailed along with my Father on Friday nights to watch televised boxing matches. I had seen just about all of the great boxers of the day on TV and had copied some of their moves. It was the Gillette sponsored live Friday night fights! The coach remarked to me: "with some coaching you might make a pretty good boxer." That was not for me!

Although I suffered greatly from the loss of my Father, unlike so many other about to be teenagers and teenagers who had suffered such a loss, I did not become rebellious and I never gave my now 'widowed Mother' any problems while growing up. The term 'single mom' didn't exist in the 1950's. I suppressed my feelings and buried them deep within my heart and soul. The anger I may have felt came out later in small doses. And I apparently 'escaped' into that 'warrior dimension' and into my daydreams.

I had mentioned the incident about the Mother's Day Card to a few friends many years later and I had speculated to them how it apparently had revealed much about my nature which was something that was never understood by so many of my managers at Xerox. I just was not a man to be challenged. I was too quick to pick up a sword and shield, to do battle, to remain steadfast and unyielding on principle to the bitter end. I was a 'Sicilian' in every way and to a fault! I often paid the price for such actions.

Ironically, as a boy, I had always pictured myself to be a great warrior and leader. I had always 'dreamed' of being a great leader who led my men into battle. Yet, as a man, in my personal ideals and principles, I never looked to sway the crowd and I was most comfortable standing alone. I was <u>not</u> a 'rabble rouser'; I was certainly not a 'rebel'; but I was definitely a 'maverick' who marched to the beat of my own drum. It was most important for me to come to terms with myself; to respect myself; to never bend to another man's will; and to never compromise myself nor my ideals and principles. I was not a follower.

I did not bend to other's wills and I strongly felt that a man, in order to be a true man, must not ever bend to another man's will. I prided myself for my iron will and nerves of steel, as I certainly was iron willed and highly disciplined. There was much the Sicilian within me; in my thought and feelings; and certainly in my warrior mentality. I had watched the movies, Godfather I, Godfather II, at every opportunity. In my own imagined world of daydreams I had transformed myself into 'Michael Corleone' as I could be just as icy cool while internally raging with furious anger. I could be just as controlled. I just was <u>not</u> ruthless like Michael was. I had not given myself over to 'the Dark Side.' I would not hurt anyone intentionally.

In all of my confrontations with managers at Xerox, I had never once raised my voice, nor shown any expression of my feelings or anger. During every confrontation, I had remained calm, controlled in both speech and demeanor, never revealing the anger I felt within. Some managers had even remarked how, under the circumstances, they would have expected me to be pounding my fists on the desk in anger and how they expected verbal outbursts of anger from me. There were none.

My control of my emotions was unsettling and even frightening to some. I was not like others. Even senior managers did not and could not intimidate me. How could I, a lowly sales representative, be stronger and more powerful than were they? By what 'rules of the game' did I play? What 'force' was within me?

It was a black and white movie that I had seen on television while still a teenager, which had left an indelible impression on my mind. I could not remember what the movie was about; who the actors were in that movie; or anything else about the movie. What I did remember, was a bit of advice given by an older man to a younger man:

"The trick to life is to survive the worst that happens to you and the worst that you do to yourself in your efforts to do and to be your best"

It was time for me to drift off into a <u>daydream</u> and into a world of imagination—into the dream world of the warrior. I drifted off into the Old West in which I was a gunfighter again writing the story in the second person as though I was observing myself in my daydream:

He had walked into the saloon quietly and slowly as if he was trying to avoid any attention to himself while at the same time observing everyone who was in the bar. Going to the far end of the bar he ordered a plain soda and not a beer. That seemed strange to the usually suspicious bartender who held his remarks to himself. This cowboy was a stranger to the bartender. His clothes were dusty from riding the trail. He looked like just an ordinary cowpoke. Yet, as the bartender observed, there was just something about this cowpoke. The bartender's sixth sense set off an alarm. He didn't know what it was, but this stranger just was not any ordinary cowpoke. And he was wearing—as in the Marty Robbins' song—"a big iron on his hip"—a Colt Walker 44. His holster was also tied down to his leg in the fashion of a gunfighter. The bartender took notice of that. It seemed that no one else in the bar took notice of that revealing 'sign.'

Zack Saunders was at the saloon near enough to the stranger and he heard him order a soda to drink. Now Zack was the town bully; a ruthless gunslinger; no one in the town ever messed with him; and many a stranger had wished that they had not as they lost their lives in a gunfight with him. He was mean and he was very fast on the draw with his Colt 45 six shooter. All too many men had found out too late how fast Zack was on the draw. He was also a deadly shot! He was a mean and troublesome man.

Moving over to where the stranger stood, Zack ordered a whiskey for himself and one for the stranger. While laughing out loud so that everyone in the bar could hear him—"have a real drink on me"—Zack challenged the stranger. He had been drinking all that afternoon and the excessive liquor had dulled Zack's senses while emboldening him to be all too brazen with the stranger. Zack had also failed to take notice that the cowpoke had had his holster tied down to his leg, which made drawing his firearm smooth and unhindered. It would prove to be a fatal oversight.

The stranger just looked at Zack, his brown eyes dull and expressionless, masking any anger or fury that might be boiling within him, while also hiding the danger to any challenger. The bartender, who was observing the challenge by Zack to this stranger, and the stranger's unemotional response, thought he got a glimpse of something in the stranger's eyes, and it frightened him. If Zack had caught that same hint of danger, in his alcohol-dulled senses, he had totally ignored it.

"I already have a drink, thanks anyway." The stranger politely responded to Zack with an expressionless stare from his brown eyes.

"You're drinking soda." Zack voiced his belligerence for all in the bar to hear. "Are you saying that you won't have a real drink with me?"

The stranger held his icy cool stare and again softly answered: "I have a drink, thanks anyway."

With a sweep of his right hand Zack swept the stranger's drink off the bar. "Now you don't have a drink. HA! HA!" he laughed.

The stranger just held his stare as the blank expression never changed on his face. He merely turned to the bartender and ordered another soda.

"Mister, please I don't want no trouble, please, just have a whiskey with Zack. You don't want to mess with him, please." The bartender pleaded with the stranger, as he didn't want to see the cowboy harmed like so, many others had been killed by Zack, after just such a confrontation. Yet, even then in his pleading with the cowboy, the bartender continued to sense that some great danger lurked within him, he sensed a hint of trouble that Zack's senses were missing.

"Bartender, thanks for the warning, but he seems to be messing with me." The stranger turned back to Zack with still an expressionless look on his face, but his eyes narrowed. There was a hint of warning in his comment, like the faint stirring of a coiled rattler that was getting ready to strike if disturbed any further.

"Damn you! Who are you to turn down a drink from me?" Zack hollered loudly at the stranger so that every man in the bar could hear his challenge.

"No one, I'm no one at all." The stranger responded.

"I see that you're wearing a gun." Zack spoke even more loudly to the attention of everyone in the bar. "You know how to use it, Mr. No One?" He mocked the stranger as he became even more belligerent.

The bartender was probably the only one to see that the facial muscles of the stranger had tightened ever so slightly. His whole body seemed to tense. It was more like a coil with a readiness to strike. Zack again missed the signs of danger to him.

The stranger just stared at him not saying a word to Zack, which infuriated the gunslinger even more. He had never encountered anyone like this Mr. No One. Everyone else he had ever challenged; whom he had outdrew, shot and killed; had responded to his taunting. This man had not yet stirred.

As the town bully, Zack could not allow this stranger to cause him to lose his grip on the town. He now had to challenge this stranger to a deadly gunfight, which Zack was confident would end the way they always ended, with him surviving and the other man dead. Many men had gone against him and all had died.

"I'm going to kill you right here and now, and pour damn soda on your dead body." Zack stepped back a few paces from the bar getting himself in position to draw on this stranger.

"Please, outside, please, not in here, please." Pleaded the bartender with both of the men, while still eyeing the stranger and sensing a real hint of deadly danger.

"Did you see the sun rise this morning?" The stranger asked Zack as he further commented: "The warrior who is willing to die makes a formidable opponent."

"What's that gibberish?" Zack laughed as he walked out towards the street. "Let's go out into the street. I don't want to mess up the floor with your blood."

As the two men slowly walked to the door, the bartender knew what the outcome of the gunfight would be even before the men had faced off against each other. He was the only man in the saloon who had heard the rattler give off its warning. He just knew that the strike of the rattler would be deadly! He knew that this would be the last gunfight for Zack Saunders. He intuitively knew that the stranger would win the gunfight.

Zack was an experienced gunslinger and he looked for every advantage in a gunfight. Stepping out into the street he walked a few paces into the sun and then turned around to face the stranger, expecting that the sun with would be in the stranger's eyes and that it would throw off the stranger's aim. Zack figured that he would have the advantage over the stranger.

The stranger's eyes surveyed the street for any hidden dangers lurking from the alleys or shadows. With his left hand he adjusted the brim of his hat slightly to shield his eyes from the glare of the sun. He appreciated the advantage that Zack had sought for himself and recognized the experience of the gunslinger.

It had unsettled Zack a little when the stranger, while they were both still in the saloon, had asked him if he had seen the sun rise this morning. Zack had answered that he did. Then he wondered why would the stranger ask him such a question just before they walked out on the street to draw their guns against each other?

The two men squarely faced each other in the dusty street. They were only a few paces apart. Zack looked into the soft brown eyes of the stranger and for the very first time in his life he felt a chill that reached into his bones. Looking into the eyes of the stranger was like looking into the eyes of a cobra that was poised to strike. He finally saw what the bartender had seemed to see in this stranger, but it was too late for Zack, as he could not back down now. Damn!

Zack's right hand reached for his Colt 45 as he had done so many times before in such gunfights in the past. But, everything seemed to be in slow motion for him. His hand just wasn't moving fast enough, as his gun was only halfway out of its holster when he felt the slug slam into his chest exploding in his heart and killing him.

The stranger's hand and draw had been fast as lightning, striking out like a deadly rattler. While drawing his own gun, the stranger had shifted his body sideways so as to give a narrower target to Zack and making a heart shot impossible. He had extended his right arm and his Colt Walker 44 had thundered out death to the gunslinger. He sighed a deep breath and his face remained expressionless. He just seemed to nod his head ever so slightly as though it was just another gunfight in which he had vanquished an opponent. He was a 'gunfighter', a true warrior as he had warned Zack!

The gunfighter would see the sun rise on the next morning. Zack Sanders would never again see the sun rise in the morning.

It had simply been a '<u>daydream</u>'—my escape into that other dimension of time and space in which I often exist. This time I was a gunfighter who wore a Colt Walker 44 on my hip; whose draw was lightening fast; and who acted only after being forced by a challenge from which I could not walk away.

For at least a brief moment, if only in the deep recesses of my mind, in my dream world, I acted out the role in which I was most comfortable and happy. I was a gunfighter this time in this daydream. I had been in the Old West for a brief moment. Ironically I still tell my Children and now my Grandchildren that when I grow up I want to be a cowboy.

It had all been very real to me. I could still feel the weight of the Colt Walker 44 in the palm of my right hand. It was a heavy firearm that weighed 4 ½ pounds. I could still smell the dust of the street in the Western town in which the gunfight had taken place. I could still hear the sound as my gun had thundered out death. It was real, or so it seemed to me, deep in my mind.

What of my mind? Was this imagined experience accepted by my mind as having been real? Did my mind accept this daydream, this visualization, as having actually happened? Remember the experiment with the basketball players, some who spent thirty minutes a day visualizing in their mind shooting foul shots with their scores having gotten better? Their minds seemed to have accepted the visualization as having actually happened. What of me? How had I 'selected' such a daydream? Could I possibly have been remembering and reliving an actual event from some past life? Had I actually lived in some previous life in the Old West of the 19th century and had actually once been a gunfighter? Had my 'daydream' been a memory from my subconscious mind brought to my conscious mind? I just don't know.

Could my mind have accepted my daydream and visualization as having once been physically experienced in the time and space of reality? IF the mind could improve basketball foul shooting scores through visualization, what affect did my visualization have on me?

Didn't the subconscious mind accept into its realm of experience all that the conscious mind fed into it? How does the conscious mind act in regards to the sub-conscious mind? In what part of my mind had I become a warrior? Where and when did it all start? More importantly, where was the separation between the real and the imagined? Was there any separation?

Then there is the question and theory of 'reincarnation'—was I the reincarnation of some warrior who had once actually existed in some other time and era? Were my daydreams merely the memory of so-called past lives? Didn't General George S. Patton believe that he was a reincarnated warrior who had actually fought in battles throughout Europe in past lives? Was I possibly remembering my own past lives and reliving them in my daydreams? Was I creating such daydreams or was my memory remembering what had once happened? Were my daydreams merging with my reality?

I sat back and propped up my feet. I noticed that my shoes were dusty, very dusty. I hadn't been anywhere all day. Everything around him was pavement and grass. How could my shoes have gotten dusty? Then I rubbed my left bicep remembering the gash I had suffered while in the arena. "No" I thought, "it couldn't be" … "it just couldn't be." I murmured aloud to myself. It had all been just a daydream. I had been a gunfighter only in my dreams. None of it had happened—had it?? The dust on my shoes must be there from another day? The gunfight had seemed real.

I did 2 sets of 50 pushups, 50 sit-ups, pressed a 55-pound barbell over my head for 3 sets of 15 repetitions, then went out to jog and walk 2 ½ miles. I felt very good physically. My weight at age 51 was 178 pounds. (At age 66 it was back up to 188 pounds.) I was in far better physical condition then I had been at age 30! I was thinner yet more muscular.

I'd had a very restless and mostly sleepless night, which had been disturbed by a deepening depression, and even an anger at God. I cried out to God to help me, an anguished cry born out of the pain and frustration of the hopelessness I felt. I felt helpless, hopeless, and there was despair and depression. God did not answer me, or so it seemed to me. I recognized that I needed God, but it appeared to me that God either could not or would not help me or even answer me. I further recognized that I needed to trust God. IF I trusted God and God was not there for me, could I trust anyone else? It did seem to me that everyone whom I trusted had failed me? Did God fall into the same category?

Perhaps it was out of this sense of abandonment by God, or perhaps a sense of abandonment by my own Father's suicide, that I chose not to really trust anyone? My reason told me that if the people I needed, God included, were not there for me and despite that I still survived, then, I did not really need anyone—did I? Couldn't I and didn't I survive alone?

While out jogging one day out on the street I passed a small store with the following sign in its window, which caused me to question whether or not I was really surviving?

"To change we must first survive; to survive we must change"

Had 'Life' hurt me so deeply that in a sense I'd even turned away from living? Had I turned away from love? Had I even turned away from life and reality to escape into an imagined world of daydreams of being a warrior and a hero? Was there any real danger to me associated with all of this daydreaming and imaginations?

I again rubbed my left bicep even though the gash had healed completely. It was just a dream, a daydream, and nothing more so I thought to myself. None of it had been real, had it? I still had no idea how I'd cut myself.

Once again I asked the very redundant question—how did other men think and feel? Was I the only man who escaped into another dimension of time and space? It was accepted that other men, if not all men 'escaped' into a cave from time to time. What was the nature of the cave into which other men escaped? Was it merely a quiet solitude? Was it a world of dreams? Was it a world of imagination? Into what kind of a cave did other men escape?

Did other men escape into what I referred to as that 'other dimension of time and space' in which I was a warrior? Did other men escape into a dream world? Could I be so unique that I was the only man on Earth to create such a fantasy world into which I escaped? Was there at least one other man on this Earth who did the same thing? And if reincarnation was a fact, were there other men on this Earth remembering past lives as perhaps I was remembering my possible past lives? How the heck did I even come up with such questions of myself and of others?

I had suffered through yet another restless and mostly sleepless night which left me very tired and I was later than usual in getting out of bed. Tired as I was, I still worked out then went out to jog and walk. I laughed at myself. I was getting stronger to face 'Charlie' in the jungle. In my daydreams I had served in the Army in the Viet Nam War and in combat 'in country' in the South. In reality I had served in the Navy and all that I saw was the coast of North Viet Nam. I had not served "in country" in the South. The only in country combat service I had experienced was all in my mind and in my daydreams.

The closest I may have gotten to being in country in Viet Nam was when I'd gotten a helicopter ride way up north to the USS King, the northern most positioned rescue destroyer that was just outside Haiphong Harbor in the Gulf. I was lowered by cable from the helicopter that normally delivered mail and personnel. I was there to deliver a communications code to their Communication Officer. That afternoon a helicopter circled above the King, lowered a cable, and I was pulled up to the helicopter. Upon climbing into the helicopter I saw three machine guns and several boxes of ammo on the deck of the helicopter. The pilot and copilot had flak vests on and were wearing side arms. The crewmember also had on a flak vest. I was wearing a short sleeve khaki shirt—no flak vest and no side arm! I remember nervously asking the crewmember "who are you guys?" He responded that, they were, the helicopter taking me back to the Oriskany. I said something like "you guys don't deliver mail dressed like that." He laughed at me and said that they were the 'rescue helicopter.' Very nervously I then asked him what happens if they get a call to rescue a downed pilot? He smiled at me and said: "welcome aboard, sir." That scared me greatly! All I could think of was that they would get a call and that possibly I was going to spend the rest of my life in North Viet Nam as a POW. This is all too vivid a memory!

I thought of a friend who was in "therapy" and who was going through a second bitter divorce at the time. I advised my friend to read the book—Psycho-Cybernetics written by Maxwell Maltz—and for him to write journals about his thoughts and feelings because it helped me through periods of especially deep depression and sadness. In fact, it seemed that it was only when depressed or sad that I best articulated my thoughts and feelings as I seldom wrote when I was happy and content.

This friend responded that he had many "toys" to keep himself "distracted" and that he had no inclination to write journals as I did. It was interesting how men found different ways to distract themselves, to amuse themselves, and to escape into their caves. Beyond sex, toys, and solitude, what more did a man need? At least it appeared to most women that the majority of men needed little more?

How many men escaped into a world of drugs, excessive alcohol, promiscuous sex, all in an attempt to escape their emotional pain? Of course, such activities generally caused even more pain for a man and often caused their premature deaths. Why did some men sink into such self-destructive behavior? Could such men just not survive being alone with their own thoughts and feelings, or with themselves? What causes men to do the things that they do? Am I not asking these same questions about my own behavior?

I have always been much of a Spartan. I've had few toys. Hell it seemed that I was stuck in the 20th century—not quite into the technology of the 21st century. I still had no cell phone; no DVD player; no CD player; and no cable TV—hell—I just might have been in the 19th century! Ha! Ha! I had never sunk into self-destructive behavior. I had never used any drugs; I had never been sexually promiscuous; I had never had a one-night stand; I drank moderately; and I continued to do all that I could to remain healthy by eating healthy, exercising, jogging and walking. My 'distraction' to escape my pain was to escape into another dimension of time and space in which I was a warrior and hero. Could any other man be like me?

I seldom even took any aspirin for a rare headache. It was almost as though I welcomed the physical pain and derived pleasure from being able to bear it, almost as though I was punishing myself.

I was really strong willed and even stubborn and hard headed with nerves of steel. The 'Taurus' astrological sign is of the bull! I was very tough mentally and emotionally. I had no doubts about this. IF it involved a test of my will and of all that I was, I knew that I could tough out a situation in my way and not ever succumb to the distractions of weaker men. I have always kept and continue to keep very tight control of myself. It is not easy for someone with a potentially quick temper.

Often I've wished that I could be different and that I could lose control and 'let my hair down', that I could allow myself to escape into the distractions of drugs, or excessive alcohol, or even promiscuous sexual activity. But I recognized that I derived all of my inner strength and toughness from the way that I was. I could not 'lose' myself in such distractions. IF I allowed myself such distractions then I would no longer be who and what I am. It would be like Sampson losing his hair and his strength. NO way—I really am forced to stick to my own path. I really have to keep on my path, as it was the only path for such a Spartan warrior.

I felt no moral superiority and it wasn't even a matter of morality for me. After all, I often wished that I could allow myself to succumb to such distractions while thinking that such moments of weakness would do me good as a temporary means of escape and release. I just could not let loose of myself.

I was/am all that I was/am and I could be no more and no less. It was a statement of mine, which seemed to put a restriction on me. I was 'trapped' within myself, within all who I was/am and what I was/am—or in all in who and what I perceived myself to be? It was like I was held by some invisible bond to all that I believed myself to be, and my distractions could never be drugs, excessive alcohol, or promiscuous sexual activity. I would continue to escape into an imagined world of warriors. Why—why was I the way that I was? Was there any other man like me anywhere? Could my escape into that dream world of the warrior perhaps be self-destructive? I really don't know?

Two of the brutal and constant criticisms of my ex-wife was that "you can't help it the way that you are", and "that it is not your fault for being the way that you are." I had heard this from her during our marriage and most often during the breakup of our marriage. It had cut me deeply and most likely she had meant for such criticisms to hurt me deeply. Was she absolving me of possessing traits and habits, which were incompatible with her? What disturbed me was that she had never really explained to me just what she meant by "the way that I was." She had left it up to me to speculate just what she meant by such criticism. But she always said it in such a way to make me feel bad about myself. It worked—I did feel bad about myself!

IF I could not help it the way that I was, then perhaps she could not help it the way that she was. Was that what she was really saying by her criticism of me? Was she really saying that she could not help it that she was a pathological liar, or that she cheated, or that she didn't love me, or that she later on after our divorce went on to lead a lifestyle of promiscuous sexual activity? Could neither of us help it the way that we were? Can anyone help it the way that they are? What forces beyond our control determine the man or the woman we turn out to be?

As I reminded myself again—people can be no more and no less than who and what they are. Such applied to me and to my ex-wife. I had loved her. At least I had loved the image of her that I had of her within my mind, even though the image contrasted with the reality of who and what she was. As I repeated to myself—love is often blind and stupid!

I recognized that I would indeed always love the image of the woman whom I thought I had married. Wouldn't she laugh at such!! I also recognized that the woman I had loved and still loved never really had existed. Although I had seen beauty and goodness within her—well—had it really been there? Had it all been just an act by her? Had she merely been an image in my mind, a false creation of what and who I had desired her to be. Would I ever know?

Ironically, my very smart and very perceptive Granddaughter had remarked to me: "Pop-Pop, you still like Nana, don't you?" Of course I denied it. I laughed to myself. My Granddaughter sure was perceptive for a nine year old—too darn perceptive! Ha! Ha! She was correct!

It was Christmas 2002 while my ex-wife was between marriages that our little family all had dinner at her house. She had invited me to come along with the Children as I was visiting them for the holidays and I did go not sure what to expect. My Children didn't know what to expect either! My ex-wife had stated: "the past is the past" and that seemed to eliminate any stress from the situation. Thereafter we have remained cordial with each other. The past was indeed the past. Sadly it was one of heartbreak for me and it had not turned out the way I had once hoped.

She was currently (2007) married and apparently very happy with her current husband. She even now had a decent relationship with our Children. Despite all of her previous mistakes she claimed that she was now greatly blessed. I wondered—did she ever think of me or of our twelve years together? I thought not! I still wished that we had been happy together—and—I was certain that she would get a really big laugh at that! She had never really loved me. It intrigued me that she was happy and I was sad! Her happiness was her happiness—my sadness was my sadness. Neither was cause of the other!

"Who made you?" "God made me."

"Why did God make you?" "God made me to know, and love, and serve Him in this world and to be happy with Him in the next world."

These were the first two questions asked in the Roman Catholic Baltimore Catechism into which every Catholic School child was indoctrinated, or brainwashed if one prefers, from the very first day of school.

Each child was taught that they were "made in the image and likeness of God" which is straight out of the book of Genesis in the Bible. Forget the 'New Age' philosophy, this seemed to be a statement about the general condition of the characteristics of mankind.

Left unsaid and unexplained is why was each individual man is as he was? What made each man think, feel, and imagine as he did? Why was I so much of a warrior? What made me that way? Could I not, as my ex-wife suggested, help it the way that I was? Does a man have but one destiny, as proposed by Vito Corleone in The Godfather? IF that is so, what determines a man's destiny? Was it the one true God? Was it the 'gods on Mount Olympus' in Athens, Greece? Was it the stars? Who or what determines a man's destiny?

I am very much a Taurus. Had my destiny been determined at birth? Was there anything to the stars? When I read a profile of the Taurus personality, I sure seemed to fit it completely. I did possess the characteristics of the Taurus man in nearly every way. Could the stars really determine a man's personality and destiny? Ironically Taurus is the 'money' sign. Now how did I miss out on that aspect of being a Taurus? Ha! Ha!

In a book that I was currently reading, the author who was a doctor, stated that: "50 % of emotional programming was received by age 5 and that by the age of 8 a person is 80 % programmed psychologically." Further it seems that: "all of 95 % of emotional programming took place by the age of 18."

Hadn't it always been said that: "the boy is father of the man." Hadn't the Communists believed that if they could have a child for the child's first 5 years, they could program them and brainwash them for life. After such programming and brainwashing the child would always be theirs. Of course the Church had that same objective! This did not give a satisfactory answer to the very important and so very redundant question of why was I the way I was as a man? Why was I a warrior in my thoughts and in my mind? Why was any man the way that he was? Did the memory of a past life determine a man's current life?

As I had once remarked to my best friend in New Jersey: "I became the man that I wanted to be, but my life has not turned out the way I had hoped it would." I was a 'knight in shining armor' when it came to values, ideals, and high principles. I had made many conscious choices about what kind of man I would be, or had I?

From birth to the age of 5, supposedly, I had already been 50 % emotionally and psychologically programmed. The Catholic Church had not yet gotten their hands on me. How many real choices did I make from birth to the age of 5, choices that determined the kind of man that I was? What other forces, outside of myself, had shaped me for the first 5 years? Again, was a past life a determining factor in how a man was in this life? I just don't know?

While I was growing up—what affect did my Father have on me? What affect did my Mother have on me? Which parent had the greater affect on me? My Father always told me (and my Sister) that: "I love you as high as the sky and deep as the ocean." My Mother had never told me that she loved me when I was a boy growing up. Despite often showing pride in me, my Father was extremely hard and tough on me.

I had always valued the expression of love by my Father. That my Mother had never expressed love for me in words did <u>not</u> seem to be a factor, as I had never really given it a thought until recent years. To be sure, I had asked my Sister: "did Mom ever tell us that she loved us when we were growing up?" My Sister confirmed my memory. I had never doubted that my Mother had loved me. I was a Daddy's boy and what my Father thought of me, and what my Father expressed to me is what mattered to me. What about other boys growing up—what had they experienced?

When I was growing up there were no birthday parties for any children, boys or girls. Parents just didn't seem to do such things back then. I could not remember ever having a birthday cake as a boy? I did remember turning age 12 (months before my Father's death) that my Father had bought his first car that day, a new car, and he had picked me up after school; drove me downtown to a sporting goods store; and bought me the expensive baseball fielder's glove that I had picked out. I even remembered the brand—it was a Reach brand of fielders' glove. Now that was a great birthday!

What did I even remember from birth to the age of 5? I did remember those 'out of body' experiences that I had experienced as a baby in a crib. I could not remember the birth of my Sister, nor could I remember her being in a crib. I remembered my Father showing my Sister and me the scar, from having his appendix removed. He had told us that it was from a war wound and of course, as little children, we had believed him. My Father had spent less than 90 days in the

Navy during WWII and had been medically discharged for having a heart murmur.

There just were not any recollections of any particularly traumatic events or experiences during my first five years that could explain why I was such a warrior. Try as hard as I did, I could not remember enough of my first five years or even of my first eight years that could have been the predominant programming of me.

What of my genes? Of course there was my Father. Could any credit or blame be attributed to him for the way I was? Certainly there were events from the twelve years that we shared which most likely had a profound affect on me, both for good and adversely. How much was in my repressed and suppressed memory? Did I possibly inherit genes from distant ancestors? What about my Great, Great Grandfathers? Had there been 'warriors' in my family tree? It had been only recently that I found out that my Paternal Grandfather had been in the Italian Army. Wow! And speaking of 'genes', my oldest Grandson is a Taurus like me, and he is very, very much like me in personality. Perhaps it is in the genes that we inherit so many of our traits? He is much like me.

The 'legacy' of my Father would always be in his expression of love for my Sister and me in the words: "I love you as high as the sky and deep as the ocean." I had loved my Father. I had also feared my Father those times when the man was angry. The man did have an awful temper! My own temper was none too mild! To a degree I've learned to control it.

How much is every boy affected by his Father? Isn't it the same sex parent who has the most affect on the child? Isn't every man's journey one in which he resolves himself to his father, or his father to himself, either directly with his father, or in a way through his own son? I was a boy of age 12 when my Father had died. I never got to know my Father man-to-man and we both really missed out on that experience. I also never got to see my Father get old, weaken, and deteriorate. My Father still had a full head of jet-black hair when he died at age 37. My own hair, at age 66, was thinning badly and was mostly gray. My own Son was getting to witness me getting old.

There was a tradition amongst men and boys in the South. It was: "that a boy wasn't a man until his father called him a man." Although I had gone to college in the South I was still a 'Yankee' as I had been born and raised in New Jersey. I was a second generation Sicilian. My Father had died at age 37 when I was just a 12 years old boy. My Father would never get to call me a man. Was it a 'release' that I was denied which affected me greatly, or even at all? I really do not know? I've always thought that it was a nice Southern tradition.

Another tradition in the South was for young men when they got married to have their fathers stand in to be the 'best man' at their wedding. I especially liked this tradition!! Virtually no one in the North practiced that tradition. Funny—but I like eating grits! Ha! Heck, they are high in iron!

Not only would my Father never get to call me a man, when he had gotten angry, with me while I was a boy, my Father had called me a "baby." Had I spent a lifetime trying to prove my Father wrong? Wasn't this the 'ghost' that most men chased, trying to live up to their father's expectations while trying to live down a father's criticisms? How much had my own Father shaped me? Did my Father even have anything to do with the way that I was?

Again, don't most men chase the ghost of their fathers in trying to succeed in their careers, in their endeavors, and in their lives? Whether the father is alive or dead, and it is most challenging when the father is dead, doesn't a son always want to 'best' his father by achieving more than his father had achieved? Doesn't a son always want to please his father and to make him proud of him? What affect does it have on a son when his father does not express pride in him?

I had recently, in August 2007, been in the film 'Ships' that had been shown on the History Channel on TV as part of the Bone Yard Treasures series. In the film edited portions of an interview of me that had been taken while I was at the Oriskany Reception in Pensacola in May 2006 were shown. I was poised, articulate, and gave an excellent representation of myself and of my fellow officers and crewmembers who, could not be at that Reception. Upon seeing the film on TV my Mother remarked to me: "your Father would have been proud of you." I was quite surprised by that compliment from my Mother and by her mention of my Father.

What affect does it have on a father as he ages and weakens while seeing his son get stronger? What affect does it have on a son when he witnesses his father age and weaken? Does the son look at his father with a fear that he is seeing his own future?

I had, when my own Son turned age 13, wrote the boy a long letter. In my letter to my Son, I predicted that my Son "would be more handsome, taller, more intelligent, more personable, more successful" than I had been. My Son had recently turned age 36 (I was now age 66) and I had complimented my Son for being and achieving all what I had predicted and desired for my Son. I was very proud of my Son for 'besting' me in all areas of his life and most happy for him that he had! I knew that he would be better than me and do better than me.

Were other fathers as proud of their sons as I was proud of my own Son? (I was also very proud of my Daughter) I recognized that men do not like to be 'beat' by other men in any aspect of their lives? How did other men feel about being 'surpassed' by their sons? I was proud and glad that my own Son had surpassed me! But in that letter I had also expressed the opinion that every man feared being bested by his son. Was that true? Did being bested by a man's son lesson the son's pride in the father?

Often I had stated that it was in their quiet hours of solitude and make—believe, away from parents or anyone, that children really became who and what they were. In solitude, in a private world of daydreams and imagination, children become the adults they became because as children they imagine themselves as being adults. And no one really knows what is in those childhood thoughts and imaginations.

I did remember often sitting as a boy at the little roll-top desk in my bedroom, which soon became the marshal's desk. In those imaginary playtimes, while alone in my room, I was the marshal or the Texas Ranger, champion of law, order, and righteous values, fast with a six-gun, and a straight shooter. I had very often 'played' at that desk the imaginary games which in adulthood became the other dimension of time and space into which I often escaped. Had other boys played such imaginary games? If they did what kind of imaginary games did they play and what affect did those boyhood games subsequently have on them as men? My games sure have affected me.

In grade school while studying ancient history, I loved to read about the Spartans of ancient Greece, about Alexander the Great, about the Romans, about ancient warriors. Wasn't History my favorite subject all throughout my schooling? It was the history and stories of warriors at battle which I had liked the best. I enjoyed reading about men who had exhibited courage, strength, and even sacrifice. They became my 'heroes' as they all were men of honor. I imagined myself one day leading a great army into battle. Ancient warriors and ancient battles intrigued me as a boy.

"Duty, honor, country"—it is the motto of the Army's West Point Military Academy. I had lived by that motto myself. Although my Father never got to tell me that I had become a 'man', I have never questioned my own manhood. I knew that I had become a man! I just didn't know why I was the man that I was?

I had often cried out in anguish: "why did God make me as I am?" Why couldn't I be different than the way I was? Why couldn't I be like other men? Why couldn't I be a weaker man? Yet, down deep I really liked the man that I was and I did not want to be any different than the way that I was. I just wished that my life had turned out different and better than it had become.

As a man I remembered being a boy. I remembered the daydreams that I had had as a boy. What daydreams did I have now that I was old? Were they the same daydreams or were they different daydreams? Where had my youth gone?

It was now time for me to escape into South Viet Nam; to be 'in country'; to be reporting for duty as a young Army Lieutenant ready for battle and war. I escaped once again into a <u>daydream</u> written, as usual, in a second person format as though I was observing some other person instead of myself in this dream:

He was introduced to them as their new platoon leader, a newly commissioned lieutenant 2nd Grade, fresh in from the States. The sergeant and the rest of the squad silently groaned as they thought to themselves—here he was, another fresh, wet-behind-the-ears, most likely gung-ho young Army officer. How many of them would he get killed in combat before they properly trained him?

As he warmly shook each man's hand he asked him about his wife, or his children, or his parents, or a specific loved one that the man had back home. He even knew each man's home city and state He also knew how many months each man had already served 'in country' in the Viet Nam War in which they served. He obviously had gone over each man's personnel file. That seemed to put the men just a little at ease with their new lieutenant.

There was something different about this 'LT' despite his being fresh in from the States and his being a sparkling new Army lieutenant. Each man seemed to sense a difference in this LT despite not being able to tell just what it was. The sergeant, who was battle tested and in his second tour of duty in the Viet Nam War, immediately sensed that this new LT was no ordinary green lieutenant. Like the other men in the platoon, he couldn't pout his finger on it, but this LT was different from all of the others under whom he had served.

The LT informed his platoon that they would all would report at 0600 hundred hours sharp the next morning for calisthenics. All of the men silently groaned, as their previous LT did not require such of them, He had been content to let the men sleep in as he did himself. The next morning at exactly 0545 hundred the new lieutenant was waiting for the men in his platoon. He led them through a series of pushups, sit-ups, calisthenics, and a one-mile jog with a one-mile walk to cool down. All of the men were exhausted except for the LT who informed them that this would be their daily ritual while they were in camp. He wanted them ready for Charlie, which is how the men referred to the Viet Cong, because, as he warned them, Charlie was getting ready for them.

Then he did a strange thing as he went with them to the enlisted men's chow hall to have breakfast with them. The sergeant had even asked him: "Sir, aren't all you officers suppose to eat in the officer's mess hall?" The LT responded: "Yes, but we need to all eat together as a platoon." His actions raised some eyebrows from a few other officers, but no one said a word to him about his eating in the enlisted men's chow hall with his men. No other officer did what he did. He did ask that the men reform at 0900 hundred hours for a strategy session.

At the strategy session the LT asked each of his men what their views were on combating the enemy, what seemed to have worked, what had not worked, and what they recommended. He listened intently to each man's comments and observations of combat while taking down notes. A couple of the men in the platoon remarked that they had not yet experienced any combat. So what he laughed, he hadn't experienced any combat either, but he still wanted to hear their views.

At first all of the men in the platoon, even the sergeant, became nervous about their LT questioning them as it apparently pointed out his own lack of combat experience. Initially they all thought that he was questioning them and taking notes because he had no idea what to do or to expect in combat. Was he asking them all of their views because he was so green? Then again, as all of the men thought, none of their former lieutenants had ever asked them what they thought or had asked any of them their views or opinions. Yes, this LT was indeed very different. But, was he any better than the others had been? How would he act in the face of the enemy?

The LT then asked each of them what they thought their enemy's thoughts were of them as they were <u>his</u> enemy in <u>his</u> country. They hadn't been asked that question before, not even the sergeant had ever been asked that question. For all that mattered to them, 'Charlie', which was the name they all gave to their Viet Cong enemy, was just some 'gook' that they had to go out and kill, or at least that was what they all had been led to believe. The LT was not asking for their views pro or con about the war in which they were fighting, but only what they considered might be their enemy's thoughts. Each man gave his view of Charlie.

The LT then explained how he wanted each and every man to get inside of the mind of Charlie, to think his thoughts, to feel his feelings, to try to figure out how he fought so that they could beat Charlie. He wanted them to think of Charlie all of the time. To survive combat against Charlie they needed to thoroughly know him, to get inside his skin. He reminded them that Charlie was out there in the jungle, getting ready for them and that they needed to be prepared for him!

IF they could get inside of Charlie and think like he did, perhaps they could then anticipate his battle strategy and better defend themselves against him. He wanted to predict what Charlie would do in any given combat situation so as to defeat him. IF they could predict what Charlie might do, then they could devise attack plans of their own that could surprise Charlie. He explained that the outcomes of battles were often predetermined in the minds of the combatants long before the first blow was struck.

He reminded them that football coaches often viewed hours of game film on their opponents in order to search for flaws in their offenses and defenses that they could exploit. Quarterbacks were trained to "read defenses" so that they could exploit weaknesses. Defensive coordinators were trained to look for weaknesses in the opponent's offense that could be exploited. The platoon's strategy sessions were meant to do the same thing, which was to look for weaknesses in Charlie that could be exploited. He suspected that Charlie was doing the same thing to them.

The men were surprised at the respect with which this LT talked about Charlie. He referred to the Viet Cong and North Vietnamese as a most formidable enemy and one of the very best that their country had ever fought against. He wanted them to have the highest respect for their enemy. Unlike other lieutenants, which they had had in the past, this LT had no fiery rhetoric about the enemy being 'gooks' or Communists. There was no hatred of the enemy. There was no talk of "body counts", or of defending democracy against the evils of Communism. This LT expressed no goals of killing more of Charlie than any other platoon, or of their making a reputation for themselves and for him, which would surely advance his career. Actually, he seemed to express a disdain for other officers who were all too willing to needlessly risk the lives of their men in order to advance their own personal careers. He was not into any fiery rhetoric or propaganda. He was into keeping his men alive.

He explained to his men that, as long as they wore the uniform of the United States Army, he expected them to act and fight like professional <u>warriors</u>. The expectations placed upon them, was that they would accomplish their assignments to the best of their abilities according to the highest standards of duty, honor, and country. He further explained that each man had an obligation to himself and to his loved ones back home to be the best damn warrior that he could be; and that he certainly had a great obligation to every man in the platoon as each man expected that all would watch each other's back. They would be like the 'Three Musketeers' and live by the motto: "All for one and one for all." The

LT smiled slightly as he told them that it was his responsibility to make them into an enemy worthy of Charlie and to be feared by Charlie.

He reached into his pocket and drew out a bundle of cloth patches, handing several to each man in the platoon while keeping several for himself. The patch was that of a fierce looking Apache Indian Warrior. He ordered each man to insure that these patches were sewn on the left shoulder of all of their outfits that they wore into combat and that it was mandatory that they wore these patches despite that they were not regulation. He handed out extra patches for all of their uniforms including their raingear. He explained that of all of the native-American Indian tribes, the Apaches had been the fiercest of warriors, and that he respected their heritage. Then he dismissed the men for the day without any explanation about why they were to wear the patches.

After being dismissed by their LT the men all asked their sergeant about the patches and why they were to wear them on their uniforms. The sergeant had no idea why their LT had ordered them to wear the patches. He was just as confused as were they. He remarked to the men that this he could tell the men, that this lieutenant was indeed different from any LT under which he had ever served, and he had served under many other lieutenants. There was something about this LT. He couldn't put his finger on it. The LT didn't refer to them as 'soldiers.' Instead he referred to them as 'warriors.' And he had a hell of a lot of respect for their enemy. As to the patches, that remained a mystery to the sergeant and to the men. The bigger mystery was how would this new LT act under fire in combat? That was a major concern of the men.

For the next week the men in the platoon with their LT continued with their physical workouts, strategy sessions, the diligent cleaning of their weapons, and generally getting ready for combat together. He also had them 'practice' being still for hours on end, which was something that he told them would possibly save their lives in the jungle. The LT called them 'skull sessions' not unlike the preparation of a football team before a game, except that combat was no 'game' and 'losing' had all too serious and fatal consequences. As curious as they all were about the patches that the LT had had them all sew onto their uniforms, none of the men asked him about the patches. What the heck were the patches all about? Viet Nam was not the Old West and they were not cowboys fighting Indians. What the heck were those patches all about?

They were scheduled to go out to the field in two days on a 'recon' mission. Helicopters would drop the men off at a 'landing zone' and then pick them up three days later at another designated 'LZ.' The LT instructed his men that they were not to take showers, not to shave, not to brush teeth with toothpaste, nothing that smelled good on their bodies for a full 24 hours before they were scheduled to go out into the field. Why not they asked? The LT explained that Charlie was out there in the jungle without such comforts and that he could possibly pick up the scent of freshly scrubbed Americans. The LT was not taking any chances. The sergeant remarked to the men that no other LT under which he had previously served had given thought to such matters and that such preparation made damn good sense to him.

The LT had studied the maps of the area to which they were to be dropped by two copters. He asked the sergeant for his opinion and advice regarding his plan. Again, the sergeant was somewhat stunned as this LT had a plan unlike any other officer who had taken him out to the field. The plan was for the copters to drop off the men to an area 5 miles away from the designated LZ. The designated LZ was a wide-open space, which would make it easy for the copters to land while the LZ to which the LT wanted the men to be dropped would be a difficult landing for the two copters. Further, the LT wanted the two copters after dropping off the men to then proceed to the designated LZ, to touch down, to wait 5 seconds, then to quickly take off and return to base camp.

Although the helicopter pilots first protested, they did follow the plan after the LT had explained to them that too many men had been dropped off to an LZ that very quickly became a 'hot zone' because Charlie was there waiting for the men because Charlie had recognized that the Americans tended to land in an LZ that was easy for the copters despite the potential danger to the men being dropped off. All too often such an LZ became a deadly trap for the men. Charlie had adapted to his enemy well. It was now time for the Americans to adapt to Charlie and to beat him by exploiting his weaknesses.

The plan was executed with the platoon dropped off 5 miles from the originally designated landing zone even though the copter pilots had protested that they barely had enough clearance between the jungle trees to make their landing. Proceeding to the designated landing zone, which was a large clearing, the two copters set down and immediately took on some small arms fire as they lifted off. Both helicopter pilots thought, the LT must have known something because it had been an ambush. In the future they would follow the plans of this LT without questions.

Meanwhile the LT had his men go only a few paces into the jungle in the direction of their originally designated LZ and then to stop all of their movements. He had them go to the ready, to not move, but to just quietly wait. IF Charlie had guessed that the men had been set down here then he'd be setting up an ambush for them just ahead, after all, the sound of copters gave warning to

Charlie that there were Americans in the area. The LT did not want his men to walk into an ambush, instead he wanted to be the one to set the ambush for Charlie and avoid having his men being caught in one.

Usually a platoon would move away from an LZ very quickly, but then a typical LZ would be a large clearing, which was just ripe for the men to be ambushed. When these men had been set down, there was barely enough clearing for the copters to land. Just a few paces and the men were in the thick jungle. Charlie would never have set up an ambush in such area as he never would have suspected that helicopters could make a landing there. How could copters even land there?

The hours passed and it was nearly 3 hours since the men had been dropped off and they had not advanced more than a few paces into the dense jungle. Could their LT have 'frozen' out of fear in his first mission into the field? Why didn't he have them advance to their assigned recon area? It was just what all of the men feared, a wet-behind-the-ears new LT who had no idea what to do in the field and who feared contact with the enemy and combat. They feared that the LT had been frozen by fear.

All of a sudden there were stirrings in the jungle and each man tensed as the LT again motioned them to remain very still with no movement and no noise. Then they saw them, four black pajama-clad Viet Cong all with AK47's. Had they seen the copters set down? The four men didn't appear to be especially alert to any danger. They appeared to be returning from a recon mission of their own. For the moment there was no other noise coming from the jungle around them and there seemed to be only four of the enemy. Capture of the enemy was virtually impossible and it was kill or be killed as the 'rule of war' in Viet Nam for both sides. In war there are no 'warning shots.'

After taking a very close look at the men through his binoculars and especially at their foot wear, the LT gave the order to his men to fire. The first burst from the sergeant's weapon got the lead Charlie right in the chest. His flesh exploded in an instant with blood spattering everywhere. The other three Viet Cong dove for cover as the squad fired at them. They got off a few bursts from their AK47's before all three were killed. It had not really been a 'fire fight' as it was more of an ambush by the Americans. It was too easy but that is exactly the way the LT had planned it and had hoped it would be. None of the men in the squad had as much as a scratch. The LT had especially looked at the footwear of the four Viet Cong soldiers. It was an observation that would serve the men well in another encounter with the enemy at a later date.

They searched the dead bodies, removed papers and maps, and anything that might provide intelligence on troop movements of the enemy. They started to strip the dead Viet Cong of their weapons as AK47's were a 'prize' to take back to camp but the LT ordered them to stop. He then ordered his men to prop up the dead bodies of each of the Viet Cong against a tree and to lay each enemy's AK47 in his lap. Then he pulled out four of those Apache Warrior patches from his pocket and instructed the men to pin a patch to the pajama tops of each of the dead men. They were the same patches that the men in the squad wore including the LT.

"Respect for the enemy" and "respect for a dead warrior" the LT, told his men were the reasons that he had them do what he had instructed with the dead Viet Cong. He wanted their comrades to find them this way, dead, with their weapons obviously left behind, no mutilations of their dead bodies, even personal belongings left behind, and with those strange Apache Warrior patches pinned to their pajama tops.

"Why" asked one of the men would they leave the dead men like that? Why leave their weapons behind and with one of those Apache Warrior patches? All of the men began to ask the LT why he had them do that? And why did he have all of them wear the same patches?

The LT explained how he wanted them to always follow this ritual, time permitting, with every Charlie or North Vietnamese soldier that they killed in combat. Leaving behind the patch was most important. There were several reasons why the patches would be left on the fallen enemy. It would indicate by whom they had been defeated and killed in combat; that their American enemies had shown great respect to their enemy; and as a warning that they were now facing an enemy as fierce as the ancient Apache Warriors had been. It was their identification as the men who had killed the enemy but who had shown respect to their dead bodies.

It was hoped that the platoon would develop a reputation amongst Charlie as being fierce fighters, these 'Apache Warriors' who wore such patches and who left them behind as a calling card, and whom to be avoided in combat. Further, and more importantly, that Charlie would recognize that these American warriors showed great respect to the enemy they killed. The LT also hoped that such respect by Charlie would be shown to any of his men who fell in combat and whose bodies could not be immediately retrieved as often did happen. The LT was looking out for their welfare.

In the Old West it was the practice of Apache Indian Warriors not to scalp the heads of fallen enemy soldiers who had fought bravely against them. It was their sign of respect to those who had exhibited bravery against them. The LT hoped that Charlie would show the same respect to his men that they were showing to Charlie.

He told his men that the enemy they had just killed, were not any different than were they. Charlie also had parents, wives, children, and loved ones who would mourn their deaths. They just wore a different uniform than the Americans wore, but they were all warriors. He asked the men to never forget this and to also remember that they were fighting a war in the country of Charlie who would fiercely defend his home against the Americans. He warned them not to underestimate their enemy. Heck, remember Sitting Bull defeated Custer at the Little Big Horn!! The Viet Cong were a most formidable enemy.

The men moved out slowly and cautiously with a lot more respect for their new LT. They'd seen their first action under their new platoon leader and it was successful. It may have been a 'turkey shoot' and not even a real 'fire fight' in which they had been involved, but it seemed that it had all fit into the lieutenant's strategy. They all had a sense of growing confidence in their LT despite his being green. He got them through their first combat together.

The sergeant especially reflected on how this new LT had contrasted with all previous platoon leaders under whom he had served. Although he was straight out of the Army's 'Officer's Training School' and had never seen combat before today, this new LT responded well. Could all of that book learning at 'OTS' have been so good that he had been properly prepared for combat? The sergeant thought about that and as he knew from experience, NOTHING prepared one for actual combat! Then there were those patches that he had the men sew onto their own uniforms and which he had left on the dead bodies of the enemy as a sort of calling card. Where in the heck did this LT come up with that idea? And the strategy sessions, which he put the men through again he reflected that none of the other platoon leaders had done that. His having the copters drop off the men at an alternative LZ, which the enemy would not have suspected, in order to avoid an ambush—that was good thinking by the LT!

Both sides often tended to mutilate the bodies of the enemy they killed and they always took each other's weapons as captured booty. The LT had them do neither. Hell, he damn near had them pray over the four dead enemy bodies. The sergeant gave thought about the possibility of his getting killed in combat—what would happen to his body if his comrades had to leave his body behind? Damn, he thought, he wished that damn VC squad leader was, as strange as his own LT. He feared having his body being mutilated. Hell, if he got killed he wanted to go home in a body bag with all of his parts to his loved ones for a proper funeral. He rubbed the patch on his right shoulder, damn, would Charlie even remember or recognize the patch? He hoped so!

It was days after the platoon had returned to their base camp when, the VC bodies were found by their comrades. To their amazement none of their fallen comrades had been mutilated and their weapons had been left behind with them. There was a strange patch pinned to their uniforms. They had no idea what to think of that, especially of the patches. It made no sense to them. It was as though the bodies of their fallen comrades had been left with a sort of reverence. Why would their enemy do this?

Their own leader picked up each of the patches and pocketed them. From having watched Western movies he recognized that the patches were of an American Indian Warrior. The fallen men would receive a proper burial and their spirits would be at rest. For that he grudgingly thanked his American enemy. It just was so strange and something that he had never before encountered in this war against the Americans. Why would these Americans who killed four of his comrades leave their bodies as they had? Would he encounter these Americans again? He would keep the patches.

As I awakened from my 'daydream' and 'returned' from the jungles of South Viet Nam there were no patches of an Apache Indian Warrior on my den floor. As real as it all seemed it had been just a daydream. I had escaped my deepening depression and sadness in my own unique way, not with drugs or alcohol or promiscuous sex, but by entering another dimension of time and space. This time I transported himself back many years to be an Army lieutenant who was a platoon leader serving in combat in the Viet Nam War. I was now 'back from it' for it had been only my daydream. But why had I selected such a daydream? Had I really selected it, or did it just occur because of some warrior mentality of mine? I would again return to this daydream and the war at a later date. Why did I escape into such a daydream?

I still had not answered the question of why was I as I was? Why did I think and feel as I did? What was it within me that made me the 'warrior' that I was? Why did this daydream have me escaping into the Viet Nam War? Damn, wouldn't a better escape be a daydream about being a photographer for Playboy magazine? Hell, I thought, I was selecting the damn wrong daydreams! Ha! Ha! Was it possible that the daydreams were selecting me?

Did God make me the way that I was? I remembered chastising my Granddaughter, when she was about 4 years of age that she needed to eat more vegetables, which she had told me that she didn't like. When I asked her why didn't she like vegetables her smart answer to me was: "I guess this is the way God made me." All I could do was laugh to myself over her smart answer to me!

God's answer to Job in the Bible story was that He was the Power behind everything and that He was responsible for all. Could my Granddaughter have been correct, that God made all of us to be as we are? Did God make each man as he is? Did God make each man to think and feel as he does? Didn't God tell Job that He knew him before he was even in his mother's womb? Was each man 'predestined' to think, to feel, to act, to live out his life as he does? What did other men think about these questions?

I thought about my warrior mentality, how my friendly smile masked the fury that was just under the surface within me and how I seemed always on guard and ready to strike out at an opponent. What made me this way? Did God make me this way? I wasn't blaming God. I was just wondering how did I get to be as I was? Was anyone to blame? Such questions taunted me!

Was there at least one other man who thought, felt, imagined as I did? Was there another man who demanded so much of himself as I did of myself? Was there another man who imagined himself, to be such a warrior as I did of myself? I had not ever personally met such a man. Surely Xerox had never encountered anyone quite like me! I doubted that there were 'mercenary soldiers' in the world who were as consumed with being a warrior as I was. I wasn't sure why I was such a warrior? Could there be others like me? Surely I wasn't that unique? No man is so unique is he?

Again I asked that redundant question which permeates this 'book'—what did other men think and feel? Wasn't there some kinship with men in general? Surely I was really like all other men and all other men were like me? Were not all men the same except for their habits, which separated them and made them different? Could I be so strangely unique that I stood alone?

IF all men were warriors why was I all warrior? Had I ever heard of any other man talk of battle plans, strategy, and tactics—no! Hadn't all, of my fellow sales representative in the division of Xerox for which we all worked asked me—"how do you get away with the letters you write?" That was in respect to my challenges to senior managers, my letter writing, and my battles. Yes, I was unique in many ways! Ha! Ha! Some thought that I bought ink by the barrel! I was the "mad letter writer." Was it a self-destructive nature?

Hell, I had turned down the offer of two different medical charges from the Navy in order to serve out my three years commitment after receiving my Commission as an Ensign in the Navy. Now how many men did that in the midst of the Viet Nam War? And I had served in the Viet Nam War, which had nearly cost me my life. That I had been on the early selection list for Full Lieutenant after only three years was something of which I was very proud, especially after having had those two Medical Boards for motion sickness on my record. I sure as hell was something! Ha! After the 9/11 terrorists attacked America I had written to the Secretary of the Navy volunteering to return to duty in the Navy. How many 60 year-old men did that? Others might have thought I was crazy? Perhaps I was? Of course as the saying goes:

"There are no crazy people, there are just people who do crazy things"

Deep depression and sadness descended upon me after a sleepless night and just leveled me completely. I had watched television until 5:00 AM yet couldn't remember any of the programs that I had watched. I remained in bed until 11:00 AM this morning. For the first time in a while I just wanted to cry as there was no escape from the hurt and pain I felt this morning. The full weight of adversity, failure, heartbreak, aloneness, and unanswered prayers crushed me, especially the aloneness.

There was no morning workout, no jogging or walking, no imagining that I was a warrior, and no distractions or escape from the pain. I just hurt and I felt all of the pain in my heart, my soul, and in every fiber within my body. It was awful pain!

I needed a hug. I needed to be with someone. I needed for someone to care. This day I was less than the hard tough warrior and more of the hurt little boy that existed within all men. I was less the lone wolf and more the wounded wolf having retreated into my lair to nurse my wounds.

This morning in 1992 I was a 51 year-old man who was out of work for the first time in my life. Once upon a time I had been someone's husband, but I was now divorced for as many years as I had been married. Once upon a time I had been a father and a daddy who lived in the same house with my children, but now my children lived in another state. Anyone who might care about me whether it was family or friends lived in other states far away from me too distant to help me this day. I was not connected to anyone here where I currently lived. I was alone!

I felt hopeless and helpless, unable to pick myself up, and just 'down', really, really down. The demons in my mind had denied me any sleep or rest last night. If only I could sleep or get some rest; if only I could shut down I mind; and if only I could somehow pick myself up out of the depression in which I was. Damn, I thought, where was God in all of my pain? I was then reminded of the saying:

"To be a man you have got to get up one more time than you've been knocked down"—John Wayne

It was Thursday and the rest of the world was working, contributing, being productive, earning a paycheck, and feeling worthwhile. I was still in bed, unshaven, depressed, and feeling lower than whale shit. Damn, what the hell good was I to anyone or even to myself? The brave warrior felt like a damn wimp!!

Did other men get so damn depressed as I was this day? Did other men feel so damn alone as I did this morning? If they did, what the hell did they do about it? Could I be suffering from 'situational' depression or from some 'manic' or 'bipolar' depression? Or was it just general depression from which I suffered this day? Hell, what did it matter to me what it was as I just felt awful pain this day. Of course it could also be a mild case of PTSD?

Wasn't a man measured by what he did for a living and by the size of his paycheck? Weren't all men valued by the success they achieved in their careers and by their titles? It was indeed in the arena of work in which men were judged to be winners or losers. The losers were certainly the men who were out of work. No one valued them, not employers or women.

Even the 'personals' written by women seeking men demanded "successful and financially secure" men. What woman would value a man who was out of work? What father would encourage his daughter to engage in a relationship with a man who was unemployed with no job prospects? Such a man was a loser. When the friends of a woman were told that she was dating—didn't all of her friends immediately ask what kind of a car does he drive?

Being out of work cut the heart and soul out of a man while destroying all of his feelings of self-worth. It made him less of a man in his own eyes and in the eyes of others. At my then age of 51 it was so damn depressing. It was 'HELL'!

I was at an age when men were being promoted to CEO's of companies and when men were achieving the pinnacle of success and peak income. That 'old trap', into which I all too often fell, was that of, comparing myself, and my failures, to other men and their successes. I did indeed buy into the idea that "a man is what he does" and it was what he did for a living that seemed to be the benchmark. Such thoughts and comparisons only caused me to sink deeper into depression and, yes, even self-pity. Damn, how had I grown so weak?

When a man falls into that stink hole, and it is a "stink hole" of self-pity, then he raises that old question of why were so many other men blessed with success while he was cursed with so much damn failure? Where the fairness to Life? It was really a stupid question because everyone already knew and accepted that life was _not_ fair!

What about God, was He fair? Didn't some men thank God for their blessings of success and happiness, which they enjoyed? Who then is to be blamed and cursed for the sufferings, which I suffered? Surely I accepted most of the blame for my failures, but there just seemed to be 'forces' beyond my control, which blessed and cursed. Could ALL be attributed to God?

The writer of the Book of Ecclesiastes in the Bible said it best:

> **"The race is not always to the swift**
> **or the battle always to the strong,**
> **nor does food always come to the wise,**
> **or wealth always to the brilliant,**
> **or favor always to the learned,**
> **but time and chance happen to**
> **them all".**

Is it God or Destiny that plays a hand in the blessings that a man receives? Could it just be a random stroke of good luck that blesses a man? Is there a pattern behind the apparent chaos that rules the world? IF a man is blessed by a stroke of good luck—what or who causes such good luck? Do we attract such good luck to ourselves by our thoughts? I sure cannot explain it. The following examples/stories defy explanation. I add them because they intrigue me and they certainly add to the questions I ask about life.

Earlier that year, in New Jersey, a man walked into a convenience store to purchase four computer picked lottery tickets. The store clerk, in error, ran off five quick pick tickets and the man decided to take all five of the tickets. It was with the fifth ticket, given to him in error and by 'chance', that he won a $17,000,000 jackpot. If the store clerk had run off only the four tickets asked for by the man—who else would have won that jackpot? Would the next person into that store, who bought a lottery ticket, have been the winner of that jackpot? Would the very next person who purchased a quick pick lottery ticket in New Jersey have won the $17,000,000 jackpot? Was the purchaser of that very next ticket just unlucky?

Scouts for both the New York Yankees and the Boston Red Sox had followed the high school and minor league career of Joe Dimaggio. But, Dimaggio while still a teenager suffered a knee injury which caused the Red Sox scout to back off from any further interest in him. The New York Yankee scout informed the team that Joe was still young and that his knee would heal properly and the team remained highly interested in Dimaggio. Again, the rest is history, as Joe Dimaggio became a 'Yankee Great' and not a member of the Red Sox. Was it 'fate' or 'destiny' which had intervened?

The story is actually true of how a college football recruiter got lost driving down a farm road in Minnesota while looking for someone to ask for directions to a candidate's house that he was looking to recruit. He noticed a burly young man pushing a plow across a field without a horse or a mule. The young man was Bronko Nagurski. The college recruiter stopped and then recruited Nagurski to play college football. Nagurski went on to become one of the greatest of all-time college and professional football players. What if that recruiter had not gotten lost? What if Nagurski had not been out plowing the field that day? What if? Again, had 'fate' or 'destiny' intervened?

Is life all a matter of 'chance', of 'fate' and of 'destiny'? And if so, how does one get chance—how does one get Chance, God, Lady Luck, Fate, Destiny, the stars, or, whatever, to shine down on a man and so bless him? I thought of how I, when I was just 45 years of age at the time, I selected 5 of 6 numbers in the New Jersey lottery only to miss out on winning a $3,000,000 jackpot by just one digit on one number. Had I changed that number while selecting the numbers to play? That thought haunts me. How would winning have changed my life—for better or for worse? I'll never know.

All of the pain and suffering of my currently being unemployed would be relieved if I had only picked that sixth number and won that jackpot. Damn, I often thought of all that might have been and all that I missed out on, because of one damn digit on one damn number! That sure was a stroke of 'bad luck' not to have won! Hell, for all of the times that I had gone to a casino I had not ever won anything. So much for Taurus being the sign for money—it had not yet been for me! Now why was that?

What the hell did a man have to do to get the 'fates' on his side? What special prayer or incantation would move 'God' or Destiny or Fate or Lady Luck to bless a man with success, happiness, prosperity, and financial wealth? How do the 'gods on Mount Olympus' decide whom to bless and whom to curse? I laughed at myself. Wasn't 'Luck' a 'Lady'? Didn't she like or love me? Ha! Ha!

WHY? Did every man ask the question—why am I not blessed with the success, happiness, prosperity, and financial wealth with which I see other men blessed? Every man seems to know at least one other man who seemed to "fall into everything"; for whom everything turned golden no matter what; and who enjoyed the fruits of love and money. What is it that determines such good fortune? Why didn't it happen to me is a question that I repeatedly asked. Didn't other men ask that same question?

My best friend had recently undergone an operation for colon cancer. He wondered why? I've told him that there was no answer to the why question—none that I have ever found.

To repeat it—it does say in the Bible for a man "not to get all puffed up" about the success and wealth that he enjoyed as though he had 'earned' it because it all really came from God? It was that 'time and chance' thing, wasn't it? Do we live in world that is ruled by 'chaos' or is there some 'pattern' to what happens in this world? It bears repeating that the Bible in the Book of Sirach states that:

"Human success comes from God"

Why was it so that for some men, despite their hard work and moral values, everything seemed to turn to shit for them? These were the men for whom it could be said that if not for bad luck they would have no luck at all. They didn't seem to get any breaks in life, certainly not any good breaks. Instead it seemed they got more than their share of bad breaks. Why was that? Do we draw such bad luck to ourselves by our negative thoughts? How many felt that you're born, shit happens, and then you die? Certainly during moments of self-pity each man felt that he had been cursed by the Fates, or by whatever curses a man's life. Again, why was that?

For all of the love that I had in my heart yearning to be shared, I was alone with no woman to love or by whom to be loved. Why had I been alone for so many nights these past 12 years, at age 51, (for 27 years at age 66) since my divorce? WHY? Why? Why? Damn that question!

Why the hell did I survive the Oriskany fire when Ron had died in it? Wasn't that the question that haunted me every day? Why? Damn it! Why! Why had 44 other officers and sailors died when I had survived? Damn! I had been in the midst of it all. Why had I survived the Oriskany fire?

The writer of Ecclesiastes was correct to declare perhaps in his own frustration that:

"For with much wisdom comes much sorrow; The more knowledge, the more grief."

It was better for a man **not** to ask the 'why' questions for which there are no answers. Each man's life was a mystery as was all of life as there was just no figuring life out. Wasn't it foolish for a man to be asking God the reasons why He did things? All came from God and it just wasn't for a man to ask why.

I once again thought of the college president's obituary I had recently read in the newspaper; a man of 51 years of age who was successful but who was now dead. I thought of a close friend from high school; who had been age 51 and planning to remarry but who died from cancer. I thought of two other high school classmates; of Tom who had been a lineman on the high school football team and Bruce who had been a star on the high school basketball team—both had died at age 51. For al of my perceived failures I was still alive!

I had recently dreamt of my high school classmate Bruce's ex-wife. In the dream we were still in high school. Still in the dream I had wanted to tell her that I would always remember her and would always be a friend to her. Ironically two years ago in 2005 I actually sent her a birthday card with a note enclosed telling her that she had been fondly remembered and that she remained in my daily prayers. She never responded back to me. I felt very foolish for having done that. It was that 'little voice within' that had 'prompted' me, or so I thought! Heck if I knew what I would have done if she had responded? What if she had responded back to me? What a dumb thing for me to do!

And there was the 'Wall', 'The Viet Nam War Memorial' in Washington, DC, that somber black granite wall on which were etched the names of 58,000+ men who, had died in that war. I could point to the spot on which my name very nearly got etched. I personally knew all too many men whose names were on that wall, officers and sailors who died in 1966 in the fire aboard the USS Oriskany and during its deployment. I thought of Ron, the A-4 pilot who slept in the bunk below mine in the 'O-I Junior Officer's Bunk Room.' I could still see Ron zipping up his flight suit after having awakened me to tell me: "it's really bad, you have to get up." Then Ron was gone out of the bunkroom; having gone 'aft' unknowingly towards the fire. Had I gotten up more quickly I too would have gone aft and would have died in that fire.

I came so very, very close to dying in Viet Nam in 1966 while I was only 25 years of age. Ron died at age 23. Why had I lived while 44 others had died in that fire? Did God, Fate, Luck, Destiny, or the Stars 'save' me? Who or what determines when it is time for a man to die? Was it the same 'force', which blessed one man with success while seemingly cursing another man with failure, which also determines when a man is to die? Did these same 'forces' decree how short or how long a man's life is to be? Is all of a man's life and death predestined?

A young woman was fired from her job in the New York Twin Towers on the Friday before the '9/11 attack.' Surely she went home that Friday somewhat depressed over the loss of her job. Quite possibly/probably she would have died in that attack if she had still been at work? Another man decided to drive his young son to school that morning making him late for work. He was not in the Towers when the attack occurred which saved his life. Here in the town in which I live a couple was driving home after viewing a Fourth of July fireworks display when a random shot fired hit the woman and killed her instantly. IF her husband had been driving one mile an hour slower or faster; if they had stopped to talk with someone before leaving the display; if the display had taken just one minute longer; if—if—if—and maybe she is still alive?

I was born 'premature' and weighed barely 4 pounds; nearly dying at birth and then again just a few months later. There had been other serious brushes with 'Death' throughout my life, so many that if I was a 'cat, I would have been well into my second set of 'nine lives.' Why had I survived all of them? I did not 'earn' being still alive. I did not feel like I 'deserved' to still be alive. That I had survived so many close brushes with death haunts me. Did I use up all of my 'good luck' in just staying alive and escaping death?

While in the Boy Scouts the troop spent a couple of days out on a field trip and we all slept in a large cabin at night. I slept in a top bunk directly facing the large fireplace. One night I reached for my blanket when my hand touched something very hot. I had grasped a few still hot shell casings from 22 caliber bullets that someone had stupidly thrown into the fireplace. Some of the 'crackling' of the fire had been the 22 caliber bullets actually firing off. The shell casings ended up in my bunk. What if the front ends of those bullets had been pointed at my bunk? Would I have been shot to death?

But it is memories of Viet Nam that especially haunt me. Why was I alive? Why did the others die? Why was I spared when I had been so close to getting killed? One of the most persistent 'demons' in my mind, which haunts me when I was alone in bed in the dark of night, is the memory of the shipboard fire aboard the Oriskany that had killed 44 of my fellow officers and sailors, and in which I barely escaped death. Damn but it tortures me!

IF I had not had a 'mid-watch' the night before the fire would I'd have gotten up more quickly upon hearing the fire alarm? And if I had gotten up more quickly wouldn't I have run aft towards the fire, as Ron had done? And wouldn't I have gotten killed in that fire? That I had survived the fire and had been granted an extra 40+ years haunts me. What had I done with all of the 'borrowed time?'

And as Private Ryan in that movie asks at the end, and at the gravesite of the officer who had lost his own life while having saved Private Ryan's life: "did I earn it?" Had my life been lived with any purpose in which to have 'earned' having been spared? Isn't that what I was asking myself every day? What purpose was there to my life having been saved aboard the Oriskany? Wasn't that question, a real 'demon' in my mind that tortured me every day? At age 66 I was haunted by that question, as I did not feel like I had 'earned' having been spared. I wondered if my life had been wasted? What meaningful thing had I done for the past 40+ years since the fire? Have I had any positive affect on all of the lives with which my own life had intersected during all of these years? I surely hoped so! But I just was not sure?

Was the Viet Nam War a 'demon' in the minds of other men who were veterans and survivors of that horrible war? Did other men feel often feel 'guilty' that they had come back alive when friends had died? Did other men, at times, feel that it would have been better if they hadn't come back alive? How had other men been affected by being 'Viet Nam War veterans?' Did those men who had come close to getting killed even ask the question—had they earned having been spared by the lives that they had lived? What did other war veterans think when they had seen the movie Saving Private Ryan? Did the movie remind them of their own experiences, thoughts, and feelings as it did to me?

A haunting statistic for all was that, since the end of the Viet Nam War, nearly three times (over 150,000+) as many war veterans had committed suicide as were killed (58,000+) in that war. Damn! Although they had survived the war by coming back alive, the 'enemy within' had eventually killed them. What a sad and very terrible legacy of that war.

Why had suicide taken the lives of so many Viet Nam War veterans? It is the highest rate of suicide among any group on planet Earth. Why? Why had they sunk into such a bottomless pit of hopelessness and despair that they committed suicide? Had anyone done any studies as to why these men had taken their own lives? What were the gory statistics? How many had been officers and how many had been enlisted men? How many had been Army, or Marines, or Navy, or Air Force, or even Coast Guard? How many had seen actual combat? How many were disabled from war wounds? How many were divorced? How many had been unemployed at the time of their suicide? What was the 'profile' of the Viet Nam War veteran who had taken his own life?

Did anyone even care that so many veterans of the Viet Nam War had committed suicide since its end? It appeared that no one in America cared. Even the veterans of other wars, such as WWII veterans and Korean War veterans, seemed to look down on the veterans of "the only war America lost", or at least abandoned. No one wanted to hear their stories as they were considered only to be "whiners."

Unlike previous wars in which units were trained together and reported to war together, in the Viet Nam War each man reported to his unit alone, served, and then came home alone. Afterwards, most if not all veterans of that war carried the horror he carried within his mind alone. It was a war, as are all wars in which it is worth repeating the saying in the bold letters:

"Some gave all and all gave some"

Veterans of the Korean War and WWII were not cautioned, when they came home, not to wear their uniforms in public for fear of what their own countrymen might do to them, as were Viet Nam War veterans. Thus, each veteran came home, suppressed the memories of his military experiences deep within his mind, at least, for several years. They did not talk about their experiences to anyone, not even to best friends or their wife. They allowed the memories to become a 'demon' in their mind that would have to be dealt with one day. I've done this. Have others?

I had not really talked about my own experiences for all of the years that I was married. It was only after my divorce, and after my age of 40, that I had opened up about having served in the Viet Nam War. For all of those previous years I had not acknowledged my thoughts or feelings about the war, or how it had affected me, even to myself, and certainly not to anyone else.

I remember attending a Xerox sales meeting in Dallas and, on the last day after the meeting was over, how a group of us, just guys, were sitting in the lobby and swapping funny stories while waiting for transportation to the airport. One of the guys, Tom from Upstate New York, who was a Ron Guidry look-alike, had us all rolling in laughter as he was telling how he and his family had been to Disney World and people were coming up to him asking for his autograph thinking that he was Guidry who pitched for the New York Yankees at the time. The year was 1981. We were all laughing so hard that we were all in tears.

Everyone seemed to have a funny story to tell, a fun experience to share with the other guys. We were all loose, relaxed, and just rolling in laughter. A woman might have observed: "so that is what is known as male bonding." It was just great story telling, loud laughter and no one wanted to break it up.

Then, one of the guys started to tell a story about when he "had been in the service." Another guy asked him: "had he served over there, you know, in Nam?" Yes, he had served 'over there' in the Army. Yet another guy said that he too had 'served over there' in the Air Force. Still another said the Marines, and that he too had served 'over there.' I had severed in the Navy. We had all served 'over there' in Nam in that awful war.

All of a sudden the smiles disappeared, the laughter stopped immediately, and everyone turned very serious. Each man had a pained expression on his face and one of deep sadness. There were memories there, stories held deep within each man's mind and heart, burdens, which we all silently carried.

It was as though someone had thrown cold water on the group, as almost in unison, we all got up and silently walked away from each other. We had all served in the Viet Nam War, we had all been there, we all had painful memories of it, and no one wanted to share their experiences with the group. We all knew what it had been to be there. It just wasn't the right time yet to begin to unburden our pain to each other.

Unfortunately each one of us probably had a need to reveal our own individual experience and to come face-to-face with the affect it had had on us and on our life. As I would discuss at a later date, when I myself began to talk about my thoughts and feelings to other friends who had been there, we all shared a certain pain deep within us that seemed to be common to all of us.

What of the men who had committed suicide? Had their memories of the war become so vivid that it created demons in their minds that they could not bear? Had they just never come to recognize the demons within, or had they never discussed their experiences with another, and had they never revealed the pain from which they suffered? What made these 150,000+ men commit suicide after the war and after they had survived being in the war?

I thought of myself and of how I had often asked myself the question: "why do you not commit suicide?" Why hadn't I? Had I ever really seriously considered such an act? After all there had been very painful nights that were restless and mostly sleepless when from the bottomless pit of hopelessness and despair that I truly wished that I had died in the fire aboard the Oriskany in Viet Nam. There were even worse nights when I had cried out to God to "send the Angel of Death" to take me so that my pain would end. I understood that those who commit suicide really do not want to die they just want their pain to end.

I even 'reasoned' that knowing that although my ex-wife would get the last laugh on me if I committed suicide that it was not reason enough not to do it. This was merely a mental game that I played with, debating within my mind the option of suicide—and no more. It was previously written about herein but worth repeating again just for emphasis. Heck, hadn't my ex-wife even told my best friend's wife in New Jersey that she feared that I was going to commit suicide like my Father had done. My perceptive friend, telling me years after the divorce that he knew then that she was "running around" again on me, cheating on me again! My friend had recognized this as her smokescreen to hide her affair at the time. The marriage did end months afterwards.

It was that same best friend who knew how devastated I was over my own Father's suicide and how because of my love for my Children that <u>no</u> matter what the pain I would <u>never</u> commit suicide. I could never and would never do to my Children what my Father had done to me. Anyway, I liked the saying by Nietzsche:

> **"The thought of suicide is a powerful comfort; it helps one through many a dreadful night"**—Nietzsche

I could accept my Father's suicide as the act of a man in the depths of hopelessness and despair; even as a man who had felt abandoned by God; but also by a man who was mentally ill. Suicide was the act of a man who had lost all faith, all hope, especially all reason; who had lost sight of the self preserving 'life force' within him; and who had lost his will to survive the worst that could happen to him,

In that I was far different than my Father. I was very tough with a strong will to survive. I never doubted my own toughness nor did anyone else doubt it. I was indeed a survivor! I had always believed that it was the duty of a man, and yes it was what made a man to be a man, that he would survive the worst that could and did happen to him. I'll repeat what John Wayne had said in a Western movie: "what made a man is that he got up one more time than he was knocked down." The great football coach, Vince Lombardi, had also spoken those words. I did not know if my Father had ever had any "heroes" but I did and I wanted to be just like them!

Then there was the saying:

> **"Within every adversity are the seeds of an equal or greater opportunity"**—Denis Waitley

Art Linkletter was to have said it a little differently: "Things work out best for those who make the best out of how things work out." It was an absolute requirement that a man face and survive adversity. There was 'victory' in survival. As long as there was a 'reason' to survive a man could endure any pain and suffering. My Children and then my Grandchildren were more than reasons to survive whatever pain I suffered. I planned to be there for them for many, many years to come. I wasn't spared from death in the Oriskany fire only to end my life years later. NO way! Churchill said: "never, never, never, never give up!"

I am an avid reader. I read the biographies of great men, leaders, and warriors, many who were warriors in various wars. I am an avid reader of motivational books, of philosophy, of history, and especially of military history. I also read about athletes and sports, and of champions. All such reading I find to be motivational for me as I try to pattern myself after my heroes.

Again, why did I not ever commit suicide especially when it seemed that my hopes, dreams, and fondest aspirations were all destroyed at my then age of 51; when it seemed that my needs and desires would never be fulfilled; and especially since it appeared that even whatever God there was refused to answer my prayers and had abandoned me? Well, it was merely a rhetorical question that I had asked, one, which I had <u>never</u> taken seriously, and nothing more. I laughed! Hell, true warriors might die in battle but they damn never committed suicide and I was indeed a warrior!! Heck I looked forward to eating the next pizza!

I had an iron will and nerves of steel. I was a gladiator, a knight in shining armor, a gunfighter, a fighter pilot, and a lone wolf. I was tough and I was strong. I hadn't been called "The G. Gordon Liddy of Xerox" for nothing. It was because of my recognized toughness. Besides, I dearly loved my Son and my Daughter and my Grandchildren and I would never do anything intentionally to hurt them. Suicide was never an option for me. It made me very angry while hurting me deeply that people thought that I might be suicidal because of my serious nature and because of what my Father had done. Damn! I was not my Father. I was a warrior and a survivor! I had strengths not possessed by my Father.

I again asked the question why had so many veterans of the Viet Nam War committed suicide? Why did they just seemingly quit and give up on life? Did they not know "the rules of the game", of the game of life?

Al Bundy, a favorite TV character from the program Married with Children, knew the 'rules of the game', of the game of life. In one of the segments of that TV series, the old librarian of his grade school called 'Al' a "loser"; she had also told him when he was a boy that he would never amount to anything; and that he would be a loser all of his life. But Al responds to her by telling her how he gets up every morning and goes to a job he hates; how he comes home to a family that doesn't appreciate him; how he will never know what it is like to make love to a beautiful woman; how he hates his life and accepts the loss of his dreams; that he knows that he'll never be what he had once hoped to be and that he'll never have what he had once hoped to have; yet he is not a 'loser' because he hasn't quit. He still gets up every morning and still goes to work. As he tells her: "quitters are the only losers and he is no quitter."

Al may not be a 'winner' but he also is not a 'loser.' He is not a quitter. He is a survivor. Every survivor knows and understands, as does Al, that the principle 'rule of the game of life' is to survive no matter what happens to you. Sometimes surviving is the best that a man can do, and that is okay! In a sense surviving is winning! Not every man is a survivor—that is what makes the survivors winners.

No matter what is happening to him in his life, a man just cannot give up and he cannot quit. He has got to stay in the game always. No one knows what tomorrow brings. I have often kidded people that it was a good idea for people down on their luck; for people who were depressed; for people to buy lottery tickets because it would give them enthusiasm for tomorrow—one could be a winner in the next lottery drawing! Didn't it say in the Bible, in the Book of Sirach: "in an instant God can make a poor man wealthy." Hell—six numbers on a little sheet of paper could change everything for a man! I continue to buy lottery tickets. Hadn't my Granddaughter told me: "Pop-Pop, don't give up, keep buying lottery tickets." Yes, I do continue to buy lotto tickets. The odds of winning are not very good, but the winner does have to have a ticket!

Why is the sky blue? Little boys often ask that question of their parents, and there is actually an answer to that question. But there are 'why' questions for which, there appears to be no answers. Why do some men return home alive from war while others come home in a body bag? Why do some men, who have no history of cancer in their family, end up with cancer and they die from that dreadful disease? Why do some men have 'mentors' in their career jobs while other men have almost a different manager for every year they have worked? I had worked for 18 different managers during the 21+ years that I had worked for Xerox and many of them were somewhat less than competent.

Many men had enjoyed successful careers having worked for only one or two managers in their careers, managers who had become their mentors. With each promotion of their manager/mentor these fortunate men went up the ladder of success with their manager/mentor. I had had no such 'luck' in my career.

Why was one man blessed with success, prosperity, financial wealth, even with a good woman with whom to share love, happiness, and his life? Why was the next man seemingly cursed with adversity, failure, and aloneness? To say that "time and chance happen to all men" just does not satisfactorily answer the 'why' question, even if it is the only answer. Why is there no answer to the question of 'why'? Are there any answers to the questions about life?

I wondered why I had been spared from death in Viet Nam and why my shipmates had died? Perhaps the real question was would those who had died done more with their lives had they lived than I had? More importantly would they have been men who had lived their lives with purpose? Would they have 'made their mark' in life? I felt that I had failed and that I had not made my mark in life. Maybe the best was yet to be?

Was I the only man who asked myself such questions? Did other veterans ask such questions of themselves as they looked back at their lives with a sense of failure and a lack of fulfillment or purpose? Was it a question that all men asked of themselves whether or not they were war veterans? Men are men. If they are fortunate enough, they grow 'old'; they then come to the end of their working careers; they then reflect on what they did and on what they did not accomplish in their lives.

There were many others like I was, age 51 at the time and unemployed with no job prospects, and wondering what the hell went wrong in our careers? I was not the only victim of a corporate 'reduction in force' as corporations referred to it when they 'downsized' long-term employees out of the corporation. Some men went on to find better jobs while others suffered financial disaster for them and their families. There was no 'fairness' to any of it. Damn it all anyway!

It intrigued me to think about all of those Viet Nam War veterans who had ended their own lives. What drove them to give up so completely and with such finality? After all, suicide is indeed a long-term solution to a short-term problem. Did they not know, as my best friend in New Jersey had advised me after my divorce, that: "the worm always turns."

Was it an accumulation of pain caused by failed marriages, failed careers, sad aloneness, broken and lost dreams that caused any man to just quit and give up? I was reminded of a saying given to me by another friend: "you can't win the game; you can't break even; and you can't even quit the game." I laughed at that saying! You can't quit the game!! I often reminded myself of that. Ha! Ha!

Did the men who did 'quit the game' of life fail to grasp that they were not alone in how they thought and felt? Had they lost their kinship with all other men, with men in general? Had they failed to recognize that no matter how unique a man may be, all men really hurt the same way and all men bleed red blood. There really is no 'uniqueness' of thoughts and feelings when a man is hurting no matter what the cause of his pain. Again, had these ultimate victims lost sight of their kinship with all men?

It was the philosopher Henry Thoreau who said it best:

"Most men lead lives of quiet desperation"

How true that statement really was and what wisdom for surviving was contained in those words. Every survivor comprehended the truth of the wisdom spoken by Thoreau and how those words connected all men to each other. Didn't the TV character 'Al Bundy' live by those words? He lived a life of desperation but he was also very proud that he was surviving.

Every man wants to be a 'winner' at the game of life. No man wants to be a 'loser.' Most, if not all men are competitive who play to win and to survive their losses. A man is not supposed to ever quit the game no matter what even if he is losing. A man just does not quit competing. It is the nature of a man to keep on keeping on always! EVERY mention of 'other men' is really about me!

I did not think of any man, certainly not of my own Father who had committed suicide; certainly not any of those Viet Nam War veterans who had taken their own lives; I did not perceive of them as 'quitters' or as less of a man for what they had done to themselves. I could not and would not believe that any man, or even any woman, would rationally quit the game of life by committing suicide. To me it was the act of a mentally ill person whose reason and mind had shut down completely. No 'thinking' man or woman would try to resolve a short-term problem with a permanent solution. After all, the worm always turns no matter what the problem, things do get better and even if they don't a man can survive today for there is always tomorrow.

The why question of what caused some men to commit suicide then became the why question—why did some men become mentally ill? Why did some men become ill while others remained healthy? Was it in their genes; or in their experiences; or in some weakness; or was it just their destiny? IF my Father was mentally ill when he committed suicide—what of my own mental condition?

Dwelling on such philosophical questions provided a short-term escape from my own situation and depression if only for a little while. The seriousness of my then unemployment with its very adverse financial implications concerned me greatly while also depressing me. I'd been out of work for four months already and had no job prospects. At the time I feared that I would never find another job.

Damn, I was a man, how could I not solve this problem of being out of work? Wasn't a man, suppose to be able to solve all of his problems? My feelings of hopelessness and despair were making me angry. The sense of failure was overwhelming. I felt like a damn failure at my then age of 51 and being out of work at the time. Damn! How did this shit happen to me? Why me? Isn't that the question men ask—why me? I didn't deserve this shit! Of course I often remarked:

"no one gets what, they deserve in life, not the good and not the bad." Life just seems to happen! I felt like I needed a swift kick in the ass.

I tried to take a nap. Sleep could be a respite from the pain from which I suffered. But I couldn't sleep and there would be no respite for me this day. I called my friend Danny who was also a Viet Nam War veteran. My friend had been depressed due to suffering from high blood pressure. He was really down. Even my friend's wife had cautioned him to take better care of himself. My friend was extremely blessed to have such a truly good woman for his wife. As I often told my friend—his wife was the 'benchmark' against whom I measured all women. She was special in every way. I, myself, did not want less of a woman.

We discussed a mutual friend of ours who, at the time, was going through a second divorce but who was already hot and heavy into another new relationship. We agreed that it was good for our friend that he was in a relationship as he was not one to be alone. Was it good that our friend had a woman, or was it not? They were both in agreement that perhaps our friend needed some breathing space; that maybe it would be good if he took some time alone to get comfortable with himself?

My own opinion was that a man needed to be able to standalone and that he only learned that by being alone. Yet, I remarked that perhaps I myself had taken that to the extreme by being alone for far too long. I wanted to love a woman and to need her because I loved her; and not to love her because I needed her. I wanted to love out of strength and not to need out of weakness.

It would not be weakness or need that would drive me into a relationship. I knew that I could standalone. I was alone and had been alone for many years. I found some comfort in my aloneness. Yes, I wanted love and a good woman, but in a sense I didn't really need anyone.

From when I first discovered girls and started dating I had come to recognize that, girls and women didn't like men, who were too strong to need them. Girls and women didn't like 'wimpy' men but they did want men who needed them and they really did not go for the strong hero type of man who appeared not to need anyone. Such is the way the cookie crumbles! Ha! Ha!

Weaker men had their sexual needs satisfied by having a woman there for them even if it was not the spiritual, mental, emotional, and physical sexual relationship that I desired. It seemed that warriors who were strong men kept searching for that one good woman who was a gift from God with whom they could share a complete relationship and sharing of love. Would I ever be blessed with finding 'my woman, my lady, my lover, my friend?'

I recognized that it was very tough on me to be alone. It was a world of 'couples' and not of 'singles.' No one should ever be so alone. Would I be alone for the rest of my life? There were men and women who, by coincidence met their soul mates—why hadn't I been so blessed?

A previous co-worker, who was divorced, had agreed to meet a blind date at a restaurant. He arrived early for his date. A very attractive woman also arrived early at the restaurant to meet her blind date. Neither was the other's blind date. They got to talking, with each other, found each other to be attractive, and exchanged names and phone numbers before their designated blind dates arrived. And, as Paul Harvey would say, the rest of the story is that they fell in love with each other and married!

What were the odds that each of them would have a blind date on the same night and to be scheduled to meet their blind date at the same restaurant? What were the odds that each of them would arrive at the restaurant early? Had it been a coincidence?

"Coincidence is God's way of remaining anonymous"

A couple had recently won $10,000 with a lottery ticket that they had bought in Arizona after having driven over from New Mexico to buy scratch off lottery tickets. They drove back over to Arizona to claim their winnings and they bought a Power Ball lottery ticket and they won a $15,000,000 jackpot. Was it just a 'coincidence' that they won such a jackpot? Was it perhaps their destiny to win? Or was it just time and chance happening to them?

Several years ago Donald Trump was to board a helicopter from Atlantic City back to New York. He got delayed and told the copter to go on without him. The helicopter crashed taking the lives of a few of his younger managers. Had it just been a coincidence that he had gotten delayed which saved his life?

The Notre Dame women's basketball coach was supposed to have boarded flight 93 on the morning of 11 September 2001. She was on a recruiting trip and decided to extend her stay while canceling her departure that day. It saved her life. Had it been just a coincidence or fate or destiny?

Is a man's life predestined by God? Does all come from God? What of 'free will' that is a gift to all men? Do not all men make decisions that end up having profound affects on the man and on his life? I was reminded of how I ended up in a long career with Xerox. Was it via a coincidence?

My wife and I had traveled to the state in which I had attended college to visit my Uncle and family. During the visit I interviewed with Xerox and actually received a job offer. My wife was expecting our first child and not having been informed that the Company would have picked up the medical costs I declined the job offer. One year later I received a phone call from my Uncle in that state telling me that Xerox was trying to contact me. The sales team had a new sales manager who was hiring new sales reps in building his team. The previous sales manager, with whom I had interviewed the previous year, was still with the company at the time and was asked about me by the new sales manager—would he still hire me today? The previous sales manager said yes! I was contacted; I interviewed again with Xerox; was again offered a job; and I accepted it. I made the decision to leave my home state to build a career in sales and to build a life for my little family in another region of the country. I felt that to have received such a call was 'destiny' and thus I accepted it! The year was 1971 when I moved to the South.

What if the new sales manager had not gone through the old resumes on file and expressed interest in me? What if the previous sales manager had not given me a good recommendation? What if Xerox had never called me? What if there had been no sales openings on that sales team to fill? What if there had not been a new sales manager? How many companies extend a second job offer to a candidate who had previously turned down their first job offer? Was it all a matter of 'coincidence' that I went to work for Xerox, or was a matter of 'my' decision? Everything had to come together in order for a second job offer to be extended to me, but in the end it was left up to me to make a career and life changing decision.

I have often remarked that: "people are like strands of spaghetti in a bowl; every strand of spaghetti is touching at least one other strand." Aren't people much like spaghetti in a bowl—all touching each other in some way or another and affecting each other's lives?

I thought of my Uncle—my Father's youngest Brother—of the story about how my Uncle had gone to college and about how he entered a career in sales. He had been an excellent football player in high school as was his best friend from the Italian neighborhood in which both lived. His friend had received a college football scholarship to a southern university. His friend encouraged the university to then offer my Uncle a football scholarship too and they did.

Think about all of the events that had to first occur for that to happen. The parents of both young men had to be born, to marry whom they did, to decide to move from Italy and to come to America. They then had to decide to locate in the same neighborhood in the same town in the same state. The Uncle's friend had to be born. The two young men then had to become best friends, which they did. Each then had to be gifted with athletic abilities and an interest in playing football in high school. Each also had to be allowed by their parents to attend high school when their siblings were forced to work instead of attending school.

A lot of events had to occur for my Uncle to attend college initially on a football scholarship—events that were not in his control. Then again, the Uncle had to make a conscious decision to accept the offered football scholarship and to attend college with his best friend. Was everything arranged by 'coincidence' or was it all the result of free will decisions? Isn't life interesting?

My Uncle is as good and decent man as I have ever known throughout my entire life and highly respected! The Uncle had great faith in God and a tremendous positive attitude. Had the Uncle 'attracted' the positive events into his life? Or was it just all coincidence or predestined?

After a stint in the Navy during WWII during which he never left the states, my Uncle had returned to the university. His senior year while working in a liquor store he successfully demonstrated his sales ability to a customer who then offered him a job in sales. The Uncle had a lifelong and successful career in sales and sales management having worked for just one company. He remained in the southern state in which he had attended college. He was blessed with marrying as good a woman as there ever was and to have three sons. He's had a good life!

It was during a trip to his home state to visit family—the same state in which I was also born and raised and in which I still lived—that my Uncle offered to take me back with him on a visit. I accepted the offer; spent a good part of the summer with my Uncle and his family; and then enrolled in the same southern university that my Uncle had attended.

Wow! Although a man's life is greatly affected by the decisions that he makes—the opportunities that are presented are generally not of his making. Look at all of the events that had to occur for me to attend the college that I did. Yes, I made the decision to go back with my Uncle—but—if my Uncle's friend had not gotten a football scholarship which then led to my Uncle getting a football scholarship—and if my Uncle had not gotten a job offer and if he had not remained in the South—if not for this and if not for that—one life does greatly affect another's life!

Are we actually in control of our own lives? Was I right now where 'God' wanted and 'predestined' me to be at this moment in time? Would I be writing this book right now if all the other events in my life had not happened? A very interesting book titled—The Impersonal Life—seems to suggest that <u>all</u> that happens to a man or a woman is in God's Hands and in God's appointed time.

Is the woman that a man marries really 'his' choice or does 'God' predestine that also for a man? Neither is in control of being born; neither is in control to whom they are born; neither is in control of in what city and in what state and in what country both are born; nor in what year, decade, and century. Do we have control over any of the events of our lives? Does God predestine all of the events of our lives? Again, is Vito Corleone correct when he stated that: "A man has but one destiny?" The thought that a man's life is determined by destiny is a constant theme throughout this book!

Ruth Graham, the wife of Evangelist Billy Graham, had recently died in June 2007. She had been born in China to missionary parents. When they returned to the United States she enrolled at Wheaton College. Billy Graham had been raised on a farm in the North Carolina Mountains. He eventually was awarded a scholarship and he attended Wheaton College at the same time that Ruth attended. As Paul Harvey would probably say—and the rest of the story is that they met, fell in love, and married! Did 'God' bring these two people together? How does a woman born in China and a man born in the mountains of NC come together at the same college and marry? Surely it was much more than 'coincidence?' It bears repeating: "coincidence is God's way of remaining anonymous."

I often think of Nancy the Navy nurse I dated and with whom I fell in love while still in the Navy in San Francisco. While in Pensacola for the Oriskany Reception I checked the local telephone directory for such a name as hers. There was a name listed. I almost called the number. Instead I waited until I returned home to do a 'personal search' for the name in Pensacola—it was not the Nancy I once knew. Had I not been so serious would she have married me? Just about the time that I was going to ask her to marry me—she broke up with me—I was just too serious for her. I remember her every day in my prayers—hoping that she has enjoyed a life blessed with much love and happiness. There was no rewarding 'coincidence' resulting out of my trip to Pensacola! What the heck—such is life! What is meant to be will be—what is not meant to be will not be! That I was so serious had cost me a relationship with a very, very special woman—one who remains in my daily prayers.

I went to shower. Stripped I turned my back to the large bathroom mirror and with a hand held mirror I checked the length of my hair to see whether or not I needed to trim my hair. I noticed four deep scratches, about six inches in length, in the middle of my back just beneath my shoulders. There were two sets of scratches evenly spaced and parallel almost like claw marks running down my back. I was stunned. How, where, what—I certainly did not remember nor did I know how I had suffered such scratches? They were very deep scratches. I thought—wouldn't I have been very aware of suffering such wounds? I even went downstairs and pulled the undershirt that I had worn yesterday out of the dirty clothes bin to check it for dried blood. There was no blood on the undershirt.

How had I received the scratches? I thought for the longest time. I had not fallen down or brushed against anything while out jogging or at home. I had not made love to a woman in a long time. The scratches were running down my back and were not in a pattern to reflect a woman's passionate embrace while having sex. These scratches looked more like claw marks.

Using the hand held mirror and with my back to the bathroom mirror, I checked my buttocks and the back of my legs for other scratches. There were none. I had no other scratches on any other part of my body other than what looked like claw marks on my back. I had no idea of how I had been scratched?

I rubbed my left bicep. The cut seemingly caused by the slash of my opponent's sword was healed. Wait a minute I thought—I still had no idea of how I had suffered that injury to my left arm. Wasn't it just a dream that I had suffered the injury while doing battle in the area for gladiators? I could have gotten that injury anywhere—couldn't I? And the scratches with their claw like pattern—couldn't he have gotten them anywhere? Or, did I suffer them in yet some other dream that I could not remember? That thought was very disturbing to me.

At least with the cut on my left bicep I'd awakened to it bleeding. Although I did not know how I'd been cut at least I knew when. These scratches—when did I suffer them? I had not awakened from some vivid dream in which I had been scratched or clawed. Of course I could not remember any dreams from last night. I had awakened so very tired despite a rare long night's sleep. It was as if I had had a night of activity but couldn't remember any of it?

Often after a night of dreams, which I could remember, I would awaken the next morning exhausted as though I had actually physically done everything that I had dreamed of doing. I felt that way this morning although I had only a blurred memory of a dream from last night.

All that I could remember was a behemoth of man threatening me. We were face to face as if in a football player's down stance. I just could not remember any more of the dream other than the warning I had given to the man in the dream. I had warned the man that I was a "Sicilian." I could not remember any more about the dream. My memory was drawing a complete blank.

In the dream had we grappled each other in a fight? I just could not remember. The scratches or claw marks, hell I thought, a man just does not wake up with cuts he got in a dream. It's just not possible I thought to myself. Then I rubbed my left bicep again. NO! A dream was just that, a dream. I had no idea of how I'd suffered the scratches anymore than I knew how I had suffered the cut on my arm. I was very disturbed and concerned—first the cut on my bicep then the scratches on my back—what the hell was happening to me? Damn!

While out jogging and walking I was extremely vigilant and alert to all of the sounds around me. I was constantly turning my head, looking all around, and making sure that there was no danger lurking near me. It was when the street was most quiet and in the absence of any car traffic, that I was especially vigilant as I listened for any out of the ordinary sounds around me. I never wore radio headphones while out jogging or walking.

When I went out to lunch with friends I always sought to sit with my back to a wall and never in front of a window, and preferably at a table overlooking the entrance to the restaurant. I often joked with my friends, kidding them that "Sicilians always sat with their backs to a wall." I had watched the movie The Godfather too many times and had read the book too many times. Ha! Ha!

I did not live in fear of danger, I was just cautious while driving, jogging, walking, always! I always locked my car doors. While driving I constantly scanned the rear view and side mirrors. I was on constant guard!

While still with Xerox in 1991 I attended a region meeting in New Orleans. While I was out walking around the French Quarter with a few other sales reps, one of the female reps noticed that whenever someone passed them on the street going in the opposite direction that I often turned my head and looked back at them. She asked me about that and I responded that I was just checking, just making sure, and just being alert to any potential dangers as the French Quarter of New Orleans could be a dangerous place for visitors.

Although I was very cautious, I seemed to be without any fear. There seemed to be some intimidating power that I seemed to subtly express.

"The man who fears nothing is as powerful as the man who is feared by everyone"

I was once very surprised when someone at Xerox had remarked to me that I came across to people as being "very intimidating." I did not seek to intimidate anyone but I was not a man to be intimidated by anyone. Later I thought about that comment by a co-worker and reflected on it for quite some time. Was that how I came across to people—as intimidating to them? I found that observation to be interesting. Did others feel intimidated by me and thus fear me? While I certainly did not try to intimidate anyone—I was certainly one not to be intimidated by anyone.

The previous night I had watched a TV movie about a wife-beater and I reflected that a real man would just <u>never</u> raise his hand to strike a woman. It just was not something a real man would ever do and not anything that I would or could do. A man just would not strike a woman for any reason.

Even when my ex-wife had cheated on me while we were married, which was a deep hurt that I still felt in my heart and mind, I never thought of raising a hand to her. My ex-wife had been very fortunate with me. Another man would possibly and probably have killed her for all that she had done to me and to my Children. I would not and could not ever physically hurt her.

In the movie the wife speaks to her husband of the raging anger that he has boiling within him and of that anger which explodes and causes him to beat her. I reflected on that a lot. Did <u>I</u> feel a raging anger within me? Was there just beneath my surface a furious anger that had the potential to explode at any time? If so, I recognized it and controlled it well. In his autobiography, 'Will', G. Gordon Liddy tells how a man once observed and told Liddy that: "you have a lot of anger within you." Gordon responded by telling the man: "I control it."

<u>Control</u>! I was a man under control. I did have a lot of hurt and anger within me. I hid the hurt and controlled the anger. The more anger that I felt, given a particular situation or confrontation; the greater control that I exerted over that anger. I was indeed like Michael Corleone from 'the Godfather'—I was most under control when most angry. I turned to ice when most angry. When attacked it seemed that all of my senses went under control of my warrior mentality and I quickly became poised for a counterattack. It all became a reflex of my nerves. It was almost some animal instinct.

Upon further reflection I accepted that the reason I so enjoyed confrontation and being a warrior was that sense of being in control of my emotions and that sense of being able to master other men who lost control of their emotions and senses. It was a strange feeling that others might not understand. There was a great sense and feeling of power that I experienced by being able to control my anger.

I again thought of the gash on my left bicep, which had healed completely and of the scratches on my back, which were now barely visible. I thought of those vivid dreams, of both the night dreams and the daydreams, into which I escaped to that other dimension of time and space. It was a warrior existence that I created with my mental imagery. Yet it seemed all so very real to me!

I worked another one-day 'consulting job' for Xerox. It was such a laughable irony! They tried so hard to get rid of me, having downsized me out of the company, only to have to call upon me because there was no one left in the District who knew anything about the facsimile product line. I had been an "expert" having sold fax equipment during my entire Xerox career. I had quietly told them that they would not be able to find anyone else with the 20 years of experience selling fax equipment that I had. Despite the District interviewing several candidates for the position, the job was unfilled and they needed some help. So much for the wisdom of Corporate America!

Although I was tempted to tell them to "stick it" when they first called asking for I help, I felt that the more complete and savory vengeance was for me to answer their call for help and I did. I was sure that such a helpful response by me was a big surprise to many still with the company, especially after how poorly I had been treated. It was part of my armor to be so unpredictable and to insure that no one could ever figure me out. I liked to keep people guessing about me! I laughed at that! I also took some pride in having done the right thing in helping out as I did.

When asked by the Personnel Manager of a company with which I had interviewed for a management job if I was angry over having been downsized by Xerox—I honestly answered that I was not angry and that I had felt that I had done all that I was going to be allowed to do at Xerox and it was the proper time to move on to something else. I really felt that. I prided myself in having worked and survived at Xerox for 21 years. I had <u>no</u> anger towards the company. I was thankful for the friends that I had made while with Xerox—lifelong friends.

It was only after I had completed the day's work and during the drive back home that I got very quiet and sad with my thoughts focusing on my out of work dilemma. It was putting a financial and emotional burden on me. Damn! A complete sense of failure overwhelmed me. For a moment—for a very long moment—I just wanted to cry from the intense pain from which I suffered.

I sought escape, some distraction, I stopped at a truck stop for an orange juice and snack crackers. It was the same truck stop I had been to before. I recognized the same attractive young woman I'd seen the last time I had stopped there. She still looked very attractive, very sweet looking, and with the same friendly smile, on her face. She sure was pretty! Some young guy will be blessed to have her as his wife—if all that I thought I saw in her was really there?

What joy I would feel if I had a special woman at home waiting for me; a good woman with whom I could share love. Well, I didn't have anyone waiting for me to come home. I was alone and I was feeling my aloneness too much this day. It would pass.

There was currently no woman who held my interest and no woman I wanted to date. It had been far too long for me that I could not remember when I last met an available woman with whom I wanted to be? Hell, I could not remember!

It seemed that the only attractive faces that I saw all seemed to be actresses or models on TV in programs or commercials and they were all too young for me anyway. The last time that I had attended Mass there was not one woman I found to be attractive. I prayed thanking God that I didn't have to go home with any of the rather chubby and even obese married woman I saw. I was thankful that I was not their husband. Of course if I'd ever had a wife who had gotten so obese, I would probably still love her but I'd also miss her because I'd be gone! Ha! Ha!

The desire and the need were more intense than ever; the ability to love and share love were more developed than ever; yet I was alone. Would there ever be anyone for me? I looked at the graying hairs on my head and I thought, could it be too late for me? What a dreadful thought—that I might remain alone.

Could I be the only man who was alone this night? Was there even one other man anywhere in the universe who was as alone as I was this night? Did any other man suffer such intense yet unsatisfied need and desire as I did?

Once again the question is asked—how do other men think and feel. How do other men deal with their thoughts and feelings? How do other men deal with their failures? How did other men deal with their aloneness? How do other men deal with all of their could haves, should haves, would haves of their lives?

It seemed to be a statistical fact to which the majority of wives and girlfriends could attest—if while driving a man got lost he would continue to drive for hours without stopping to ask for any directions. The male species seemed to have a most difficult time with asking for help. Wasn't it only after extreme frustration and in total desperation that a man would ever refer to the 'how to' directions in putting something together or in trying to operate some gadget? I had often been guilty of this.

This 'flaw' in the male species extended to an inability or great reluctance to 'open up' and to reveal thoughts and feelings to another, especially to another male. It seemed to be a fear among men that to do so would be some sign of weakness and to be less of a man. No man wanted to appear to be weak to another man. Thus most men suffered alone and with the mistaken belief that they were alone in their feelings and thoughts. Ignored by men is that while each man is somewhat unique all men are ultimately alike—they are all human beings!

Men and women are indeed very different. Although women can be more vicious and barbarous than men—ask any man who has ever gone through a divorce about that—it is men who are designated to be the 'warriors' in society. It is in their role as a warrior that men develop the characteristics that cause them to be private, introspective, and like it or not, to be self-reliant loners.

A man is supposed to be self-reliant and independent. A man is supposed to be strong. A man is supposed to be silent and long suffering. A man is supposed to be able to overcome adversity. A man is supposed to be the provider and protector of his wife and children. A man is supposed to be a good soldier. A man is supposed to be a lot of things—isn't he? Who says what a man is supposed to be—society? Or is all that a man is supposed to be inherent and instinctive within a man?

The squirrel that is born in the spring knows to gather nuts in the fall for the upcoming winter even though it has never before experienced a winter. Some 'instinct' within the squirrel tells the young squirrel what it is supposed to do. Its role is 'predetermined' for it.

Does a bird get taught how to build its nest? Or is it some Creator instilled 'instinct' within the bird that tells it what to do and how to do it? Would it be possible for a lion to be a vegetarian? What 'instinct' within the lion predetermines that it must be a predator that eats only meat? A bird is supposed to do what a bird does and a lion is supposed to do what a lion does—each must be and do what they are supposed to be and do. Their 'roles' appear to have been predetermined for them?

How do the swallows know when to leave South America for the long flight home so that they can arrive on the feast day of Saint Joseph at the monastery of San Juan Capistrano? What even draws them back to that monastery? Is 'God' the cause of their annual ritual? Is it 'instinct?' Is it their 'role?'

What of men? Certainly much of the role identity of a man is taught to man by family and society, but is there some primordial instinct within every man that has predetermined his role as a warrior? What is it in the psyche of men that causes them to be a warrior in personality and character despite thousands of years removed from primitive man's environment?

Of course in looking at the History of the twentieth century and at all of the wars fought it would seem that man is reverting back to some other time as war has become a way of life for man almost as though men enjoyed the killing and destruction. Isn't that the damn problem? Men do enjoy war! Isn't it only when men are at war with other men that each man can then ignore the battle that takes place within each man—the battle between Good and Evil, the battle between the Dark Side and the Light? Does war allow a man to ignore the basic question of who is he, why was he born, what is his purpose, and what will he leave behind as his legacy?

In ancient 'hunter' societies a boy became a man after his 'first kill' of an animal. The tribe could then award 'manhood' on the boy and everyone in the tribe now knew him to be a man, a hunter, and a warrior. In a sense it was a wonderful ritual. If a boy passed the 'test' he became a man.

There is no such 'test' for a boy today, certainly no simple test. While men are trying to be like ancient warriors they never really know if they have passed the test to prove their manhood. There is no 'final test.' It appears to be a never ending test for which there is no final score. At the then age of 51 I felt like I had failed the 'test' and even wondered if I was still in the game? It seemed to me at the time that most of the tests should be behind me yet I found myself to be out of work with no job prospects and I was alone. I was questioning my own manhood. The overwhelming sense of failure made me feel like a boy out on his first hunt; like a boy who failed to make his first kill; and still a boy who had not earned manhood.

Damn! How can a man of age 51 properly verbalize his personnel sense of failure and shame due to being out of work and his feeling like a complete failure as a man? It is just not something that he wants to reveal to anyone and certainly not to the tribe of men who have been successful and not to any woman. Wouldn't it be too much of a sign of his weakness for a man to admit to anyone the deep emotional hurt that he is suffering due to his being out of work and the sense of failure that it brings? So what does he do? He holds all of the hurt within and suffers silently as he is supposed to be because he is a man. Is it any wonder why so many men die of heart attacks? Again, every mention of 'other men' is a question about myself.

I decided to eat a dish of pasta with red sauce this night. In the refrigerator was a tall glass of sliced peaches in red wine—what my Father referred to as a "peach cocktail." Often during summer months when I was a young boy and my Father was still alive—my Father would ask me if I wanted a peach cocktail. It would be a fresh peach that was peeled and sliced with the slices put into a tall glass that was then filled with the homemade red wine that our family made each winter. It was allowed to chill in the refrigerator for a few hours. Then we would eat the peach slices and then drink the wine. Italians have the lowest rate of alcoholism because alcohol was not the forbidden fruit that it was in some other ethnics. Red wine is good for a person—in moderation.

I remember meeting a fellow sales representative at the first Xerox District meeting that I attended. I went up the sales rep and told him that I recognized him from college. The sales rep protested that he had graduated from a different college. I looked again at him and then told him that I recognized him from our freshman year; that I remembered this fellow as always having a cup in his hand; and that I suspected that there was more than just a soft drink in the cup. Embarrassed the fellow then admitted that he was indeed at the same college as me but for only one semester. He had partied and drank and flunked his way out of that college after only one semester. The forbidden fruit had gotten to him!

My drinking of peach cocktails during summer months was a ritual that I continue to follow as another way of remembering my Father. Sadly I had all too vivid memories of the night that my Father died. It had been a Friday night in September 1953. I was just a young boy of age 12 and my Father was a still young man of 37 years of age. My Sister and I were in the living room watching TV. The program "Life of Riley" with William Bendix was on TV. Not long into the program we heard our Uncle's voice cry out: "NO, Joe, don't do it" with the sound of a gun going off. It was just past 7:30 pm.

The death of my Father was one of the great 'demons' in my mind—as has been previously mentioned herein. I had loved my Father and felt that each had failed the other—me by not going to my Father that night to tell him that I loved him. I wondered all of these years if I could have made a difference and if I could have 'saved' my Father? Would have going to my Father have made a difference in the events of that awful night? Of course my Father had failed me by taking his own life and by not being there for me all of these years when I needed a father's guidance.

I had not seen my Father that day; not in the morning nor even that night. I would forever hear my Father's accusation against his Mother that "she had turned his own Son against him"—something which was <u>not</u> true and which was evidence of the mental illness that obviously gripped him. But, I suffered from the thought—would my Father be alive today if at that moment I had gone to my Father and told him that I loved him? Did I suffer from an unreasonable sense of guilt that my inaction doomed my Father to death that night? What a terrible burden for a boy of age 12 to have mistakenly developed within himself and to have carried all of his years.

That question was perhaps the worst of the 'demons' in my mind and the one that troubled me the most. It was the one that I had never been able to shake free from its grip on my psyche. I felt that I had failed my own Father, the man for whom I had so much love. For me to even ask myself if I could have saved my

Father that night was to put a tremendous burden and misplaced responsibility on myself.

Sadly no one in the family had any 'counseling' after that night's events—not my Sister who was nine years old at the time; not me; and not my Mother. We just all went on with our lives with no discussion about the tragedy that had taken place.

Perhaps, just perhaps, I could have saved my Father from himself that night? But what about the next night and the next night and the night after that—was there any way that anyone could have saved my Father?

I have often wondered what had driven my Father to do such a thing? It seemed that the man had not gotten any 'breaks' in life. It seemed that he had been cheated by life. Although he had been the most intelligent in his family of six brothers and sisters he had not been allowed to attend high school but instead was forced into a job that he hated yet was very good at doing. I once remarked to an older cousin of mine—"how good would my Father have been at a job that he enjoyed?"

I feared that I had been cursed by life much as my Father had been. I seemed to have not had any 'breaks' either in my life and I sure did not seem to have any 'good luck' in any aspects of my life. I wondered what hopes, dreams, and aspirations did my Father once have that seemed to not ever have been realized? Would I also fail to realize my own hopes, dreams, and aspirations?

It seemed strange to me that in all of the years since the death of my Father, despite how often I thought of him and missed him, I had dreamt of him only 2-3 times. I thought it very strange that someone whom I loved so much was so seldom in my dreams? I hoped that it reflected that my Father's soul had found peace and rest in some other dimension of time and space that he had not found during his life. Despite a night of remembering my Father by drinking a peach cocktail I again did not dream of him. Hopefully his soul was truly at rest.

In writing of my Father and of the night that he died, I reflected that the feelings expressed herein had not ever been revealed to anyone during all of these years. The sense of guilt and the mistaken burden that I had carried all of these years was one that I had always kept to myself until writing of it herein. In many ways I was a very private man who kept most of my thoughts and feelings buried deep within my heart and mind. It was a flaw in my character and personality.

How much influence had my Father had on me and on the way that I was? My Father had been very tough on me yet I was much tougher on myself than my Father had ever been on me. I suspected that my being tough on myself was more of a conscious choice than any influence from anyone else. Then again I may have inherited his negative attitudes towards life.

I chose to admire and respect coaches like the late Vince Lombardi of the Green Bay Packers of the 1960's. I chose to admire baseball players like the late Mickey Mantle of the New York Yankees who had been extremely hard on and demanding of himself. I grew up watching the great New York Yankee teams of the 1950's and players like the late Hank Bauer who had served in the Marines in WWII. It was my choice to admire and respect tough coaches in all sports, men who were demanding of themselves and of their players—also such players.

It was Sergeant Stryker—the John Wayne role in the movie Sands of Iwo Jima—a favorite and the reason it is so often mentioned herein. It was how I wanted to be—tough, demanding—and I was! I reflected on the way that I was; on the man that I'd become—wasn't it all a matter of conscious choice and decision made by me when I was still a boy? Again it is worth repeating: "the boy is father of the man."

I questioned how much influence had my Father really had on me? That I loved current events and history was due in large part to my always being around my Father when he was involved in a group of men discussing WWII and politics. History was my favorite subject in school. Even my Navy 'Fitness Reports' reflected my knowledge of current world affairs and my senior officers remarked how rare that was for such a young junior officer. I would attribute that more to being around my Father as a young boy than to something that my Father had fostered in me. I remembered watching the TV program, Crusade in Europe narrated by then General Eisenhower, with my Father. I later watched the TV series Victory at Sea. I felt that my Father was responsible for my love of history and for my avid interest in current events.

In grade school during my 8th year the Nun had each student once every week on a Friday stand in front of the class to give a ten minutes report on any subject on which the student selected. I avidly followed the French—Indo China War and each week I would give the class an update of that war. Never in my wild imaginations would I have ever thought at the time that I would one day serve in the American—Viet Nam War! I then had and always have had an avid interest in current events, politics, and in History.

Part of my training at Naval Officer Candidates' School was to stand in front of the class and to give a 'talk' much like I had done while in 8th grade in grade school. I had recently read the book 'Guerilla' and I briefly discussed how the Viet Nam War could not be won militarily—that there were the religious, social, economic, and cultural aspects of the war that had to also be won. Little did I know at the time how prophetic my brief talk and analysis of that war turned out to be!

Perhaps more than any visible personality trait of mine that could be attributed to the influence of my Father was that of my tendency to seriousness. I was quite serious as a boy and all too serious as a man. I was comfortable in being serious. I was also highly responsible. And I have a control and calmness about me. I am also highly disciplined.

Once in recent years and before her current marriage, my ex-wife called me in regards our Daughter. She couldn't contact the Daughter and didn't know where the girl was. She had feared that the girl had run away with her own daughter, our Granddaughter. She called me and expressed "you always remained calm" and that "you would know what to do." Wasn't that damn ironic! Our Daughter had taken ill and had traveled out of town to see a doctor—her own daughter was being cared for by her other grandmother. Yes, it was damn ironic that my ex-wife had called me in that situation!

Yes, I did wonder—did my ex-wife ever think of me? And if she did—what thoughts of me did she have? Did she remember that we were once married? How did she remember those years that we were together? Hell—with all of her other husbands and with all of her other lovers—I doubt that she ever thought of me! Why would she ever think of me?

Even while I was a boy and as a young man my friends often took their problems to me for my help. My seriousness seemed to demonstrate a level of maturity and responsibility that others the same age lacked. I never panicked no matter what the circumstances. I seemed to possess the calm seriousness that I could handle things especially the ability to provide solutions to my friend's problems. A younger Cousin of mine once remarked that I would make a good priest. We were still young boys at the time.

I was not one to back off from responsibility and to me friendship was one responsibility that I always gladly fulfilled. That was indeed the 'Sicilian' heritage within me that family and friendship were everything, with "friendship the near equal to family" as claimed by 'Vito Corleone' in 'The Godfather.'

Was that something that I had learned from my Father? Was it the influence of books that I had read and of movies I had seen? Or was it the Sicilian blood that coursed through my veins and a heritage that just came natural to any man of Sicilian heritage? Obviously 'The Godfather' is one of my favorite books and movies.

Who or what is responsible for the man that each boy becomes? Do we credit external forces for the man the boy becomes? Is it all in the boy's genes? What about parents, grandparents, teachers, friends, books, and movies? What about a boy's experiences and those tragedies such as the loss of a parent?

If 50% of our emotional programming takes place before the age of 5, it seemed that it is difficult for a man to reflect on why he is the way that he is when so little of a person's existence from birth to age 5 is even remembered. IF "the boy is father of the man" at what age does the boy 'father' the man? Does it happen before the age of 5 or after the age of 5 or during all of the years of boyhood?

Could it be that the problem that each man encounters is that he is subject to forces during his first five years that then become unseen and undetected influences over him for the rest of his life? Is that why my ex-wife seemed to give me the benefit of the doubt when she stated to me: "it's not your fault for being the way that you are?" Was it my fault? Was it the fault of unseen and undetected 'forces?' Heck if I know?

Whose fault was it for the way each man is? How much, if any, could be attributed to subconscious and conscious decisions? Did a boy 'decide' to be the man that he became? What about all of those hours when a boy was alone; quiet hours when he was left with his own imagination by which to create himself; hours when as a boy he imagined himself acting as a man; hours during which to create his character and personality? Does a boy become the man that he becomes out of choice? IF reincarnation is a fact, does a man carry into each life the personality and character from previous lives? Is part of who a man is today that which he was in a previous life?

I am of the strong opinion that it was indeed during those private moments spent alone in a world of make believe and imagination that a boy is most influenced to become the man that he does become. Hadn't I always been the warrior in my own private world as a boy? Hadn't I always been a knight, a gunfighter, a lone fighter pilot, and a hero always. Had the books that I had read and the movies I had seen been a major influence on me or had they been merely a reinforcement of what I was already? What had influenced me most? What influences other men? Does each man really 'choose' the books that he reads, or does some unseen 'Source' choose them for him? Who chooses the movies that a man sees?

Perhaps little if anything during my first five years affected me to have been responsible for the warrior I eventually created out of myself. It appears more likely that I made some very conscious decisions as I chose to emulate so many John Wayne movie roles. It seems that I chose to adapt to a character and personality that reflected the ideals and principles of fictional heroes. I chose to be a man of character and integrity—a man of very strong character.

Still, the question remains—what within me prompted or caused me to make such choices? Why did I have such high ideals and principles while so many other men did not? What made me so much of a warrior? Did I actually make such 'free will' choices to become the man that I was?

Other men are presented 'opportunities' and moments of decision in their lives—what college to attend; what job to take; who to marry; where to live; and other such moments of decision. How do other men arrive at the decisions that they make about their lives? What causes other men to make the decisions that they do make about their lives? Do other man take control over the events in their lives or does the tide of events just take them along? Does any man have any real control over his life? How many opportunities were presented to me in which, I made the wrong or no decision?

A friend from college had recently told me of how he had ended up at the same Southern university as I did—we had met and become friends while at college. The fellow had not yet made a decision as to what college to attend when his mother had taken him to a men's clothing store to buy him some new clothes for college. The sales rep who, attended to them was presently attending a Southern University—and—he talked this fellow into attending that same college. What if his friend's mother had taken him to a different men's clothing store? What if that sales rep had not worked that day? Was it all just a 'coincidence' that led him to that particular university?

One generation grows up facing the Viet Nam War and a draft that, like it or not, causes them to enter the military and go off to war. The subsequent generation faces no military draft. Again the question is asked—do events control our lives or does our response to such events control our lives? What is it within a man that causes him to think as he does; what causes him to feel as he does; and what causes him to make the decisions that he does and to act as he does? Is it all predestined? I never received a draft notice—I volunteered to join the Navy. Is it possible that I would never have been drafted and could have avoided the war?

These were all questions that both plagued and intrigued me for years. Did other men ask such questions? Obviously there are philosophers who over the centuries have asked such questions. But what of ordinary men—do they ask such questions? The advice of most philosophers was "to know thyself". Is it the never-ending quest of each man to know who he is? And if he can determine who he is, does a man ever get to know why he is?

It was time for our warrior to escape such questions and to return in his <u>daydreams</u> to the jungles of Viet Nam again writing a narrative in a second person format because it was as though I was viewing a movie of myself:

While in base camp the lieutenant continued to run the men through a series of drills in preparation for their next recon mission. They kept up with their calisthenics, jogging, exercising to maintain peak physical conditioning. The LT also put them through an unusual drill, that of sitting still and completely quiet in full battle gear, remaining motionless, hardly breathing, often for hours at a time. Even the sergeant wondered about that drill although he gave the LT his full support.

The next morning they were scheduled for another recon mission. The platoon was told to shower the night before; to not use any soap; not to shave; and no body lotions of any kind. As before there previous mission out in the field, the LT reminded the men that the 'Viet Cong' could possibly pick up any scents that were foreign to their jungle habitat. Only the Americans used body lotions.

At 0500 hours the next day the platoon boarded their choppers for the hour ride north to the designated landing zone. Once again, as a precaution and as he had done on their last mission out into the jungle, the LT made the chopper pilots drop them off in another area a few miles away from the designated LZ. The choppers barely squeezed down between trees damn near hitting the trees with their rotating blades. The chopper pilots appreciated the strategy of the LT but damn it sure made it difficult on them trying to land their choppers down in such tight spaces.

The LT asked that the chopper pilots then fly over to the designated LZ, fly around as though they had just made a landing with a drop off of troops and then to return to base camp. This time, to the relief of the pilots, the choppers did not draw any ground fire. Perhaps there was no VC in the area?

Quietly the platoon moved into the jungle with the 12 men careful in their steps fearful of the many booby traps that were set by the Viet Cong. The LT had them travel for thirty minutes then they would go into their silent still practice for thirty minutes more before resuming their trek. Each time that they stopped the LT seemed to be listening to the jungle noises very carefully for any unusual sounds; for any movement around the men; and for the enemy. He was being extremely careful and not wanting to have his men get caught in some ambush by Charlie—the Viet Cong enemy.

There was supposedly no North Vietnamese Army activity in the area as per military 'intelligence' reports. The platoon was on a recon mission out looking for VC base camps or suspected VC concentrations. They had been out all morning without any enemy contact. The LT stopped the men and had them sit quietly but on full alert. They remained in the jungle away from any clearing so that they would remain hidden.

Movement! Suddenly from a small clearing in front of them came noises and movement. The LT signaled the men to remain very still, completely silent, and ready for battle. Every man in the platoon tensed up in anticipation of action.

A few hundred yards away from the men in the clearing moving in a direction away from the squad were what looked like six black pajama clad Viet Cong soldiers. The suspected VC came just a short way into the clearing almost carelessly and seemingly inviting attack. The men in the American platoon all trained their weapons on them anxious for the signal to take the VC out. It would a 'turkey shoot' much like the last recon mission that the LT and his men had out on the field. The VC generally was a lot more careful than these men were being—maybe they were new recruits? How could the men in the platoon again be so lucky to catch their enemy in an ambush?

The sergeant looked at the LT for the signal to fire on the six enemy soldiers but the LT just stared at the enemy and he seemed to be overly cautious. The LT again gave the all-still and all-quiet order to his men to their consternation, as they were anxious to fire their weapons on the enemy. Even the sergeant was wondering why was the LT so damn cautious—why had he not given the order to fire?

The LT seemed to be looking for something. He took out his field glasses and scanned the six suspected VC and all of the area around the clearing from where they had emerged. The he just waited while his men became even more anxious and restless although they remained still and quiet. Then the LT saw something. It was just what he was looking for and it seemed that his sixth sense had alerted him about.

He quietly passed the field glasses to the sergeant and asked him to take a really good look at the suspected VC soldiers. For a long while the sergeant looked through the field glasses at the enemy. What the hell did the LT want him to see? He then turned to the LT with a puzzled look on his face.

"Their shoes, sergeant, look at their shoes"—responded the LT.

Again the sergeant scanned the six pajama clad enemy while taking a closer look at their shoes which were now visible in the short grass of the clearing. All six enemy soldiers were wearing full combat boots.

"NVA" whispered the LT "NVA combat boots."

"LT, you thinking what I'm thinking?" the sergeant whispered back.

"It's a trap, sergeant, they're not VC but NVA in pajamas to look like VC."

It was whispered down the line to each man in the platoon "NVA" and for them to remain very still and very quiet with absolutely no movement. Each man was grateful for the patience exercises, as the LT called them that he had them practice while in base camp. They all quietly looked out at the clearing at the enemy. A shiver went down the spine of each of the men as they wondered and feared upon what had they stumbled? How many more NVA troops were there in the area? Would they engage them in battle? DAMN! Each man hoped not!

A full two hours passed after the six pajama clad NVA troops moved on when a great deal of movement was heard coming from beyond the clearing from the same area from which the six enemy had emerged from the jungle. All of a sudden the area and the clearing came alive with hundreds of full uniform clad NVA troops. They seemed to all pop out of thin air like they had been there all the time!

It had indeed been a trap! The six men had been decoys dressed in black pajamas and made to look like Viet Cong who were just careless enough to have looked like sitting ducks and easy prey for any Americans in the area. A platoon of less than cautious Americans would have quickly fired on those 'decoys' not aware that NVA troops were just beyond the clearing waiting for just such an attack on the decoys. If the platoon had attacked they would have most probably all been killed by the NVA.

Army intelligence had been wrong about there being no NVA activity in the area. The LT was wise not to have trusted the so-called intelligence but, instead to have trusted his instincts. He probably saved the men in his platoon from certain death. It seemed that the NVA was in the area conducting its own recon missions and its own 'search and destroy' missions against the Americans.

The NVA had prepared an excellent trap by dressing up six of its own troops in black pajamas, which was the normal garb of the Viet Cong troops. It was a great disguise except for the combat boots that the decoys had worn. The NVA commander who had set up the trap must have forgotten that the VC generally wore sandals and not combat boots. Charlie always wore sandals. It seemed that only the sixth sense of the LT and some special alertness of his caused him to notice the combat boots and to recognize that they were NVA troops. The platoon had narrowly avoided the trap this time!

The NVA troops passed but the LT had the men remain still and silent for another hour before the Americans slipped away into the jungle away from the NVA. He wanted to insure that there were no NVA stragglers setting yet another ambush for his men. The men in the platoon moved even more cautiously than before. They all marveled at their LT. Damn! He had sniffed out a trap and an ambush. Damn! Who the hell would have noticed combat boots instead of sandals recognizing that the six enemy troops were NVA instead of VC? Who would have noticed? The LT noticed!

To the sergeant it seemed that the LT was in his element in the jungle. He just seemed to become one with the jungle, a part of it, like some jungle predator whose home was the jungle. He sensed that beneath the calm exterior of the LT was indeed some predator, a warrior, yes, that was it, a warrior. All that the sergeant knew is that this LT was unlike any other LT he had ever known and he was keeping them all alive.

As the sergeant thought more about the LT it just seemed to him that the LT had been to war in some other time and place. It seemed that he was the reincarnation of some jungle warrior who had gained extensive experience in fighting a similar enemy in some other war. How could a newly commissioned wet behind the ears lieutenant with absolutely no previous battle experience be so damn good at what this LT was at?

Just when it appeared that the LT was timid, overly cautious, and lacked aggressiveness, it turned out that he was merely being patient and that some sixth sense possessed only by this LT had warned the platoon of some perilous traps. Somehow this LT was able to do what he had wanted all of the men to be able to do—to get inside the mind of the enemy and to be able to anticipate what the enemy was doing. How did he know what traps the enemy had set for them and how to avoid them?

That night the LT had explained to all of the men how he'd spotted the combat boots on the pajama clad enemy and that the VC wore only sandals always, and how he had sniffed out that it had been a trap and a potential ambush. When the enemy was first sighted he further explained how they were being too careless; how it appeared to him that they were almost inviting an attack; and of course they were! His patience and alertness had avoided their trap.

How, his men asked the LT, did he figure out that it had been a trap? He then asked them to be quiet and still and to listen to the sounds of the jungle. What did they hear around them? There were no noises from the animals; no sounds from birds; nothing! The animals knew that there were intruders in the jungle. It was more than that.

The LT reminded the men that they were always the prey and the hunted when they entered the jungle. It was always the enemy that was the hunter despite what Army propaganda may have told them. The Viet Cong, the enemy owned the jungle. It was their home. They were like the spider inviting the fly into its web. They had to learn how to think like both the hunter and the hunted to be able to set traps and to be able to avoid traps. The more that they thought like the VC the better off they would be. Again the LT stressed how it was necessary to their survival to get inside the mind of the enemy; to think and feel like him; to be able to anticipate the VC's actions and traps.

They had to become as unpredictable as was their enemy in order to keep their enemy off balance so that the VC could not determine what they thought and felt and how these Americans would act. Heck, their enemy was out there trying to do to them what they were trying to do to the enemy. Didn't this morning's enemy of NVA figure out how to set a trap for their American enemy who was always too eager for battle? Wouldn't the typical American platoon have quickly jumped the six apparent VC in the clearing by firing their weapons as soon as they saw them? Unfortunately they would have stepped into the trap and most likely would have been wiped out. Their enemy was good! Their enemy knew to work the American's impatience against them.

"Don't you hate them, Sir?" asked one of the younger men in the platoon. The LT answered: "No, I don't personally know any of them to really hate them." Once again he reminded the men that their enemy were guys just like them who were given a mission to kill their enemy. Once again he reminded the men that their enemy had parents, wives, children, loved ones back home just as they did.

The LT further told his men that not only did he not hate the enemy but that he respected them for their professional talent. Despite that respect he was there to kill them and he would do just that because it was his mission to do so. The LT reminded them that even in the fiercest of sports rivalries in college and pro that the players may go at each other pretty hard but that they tend to shake hands with each other after the game. There was no shaking of hands in war—just a lot of body bags.

War was no 'game.' Men died in war, killed by their enemy. They needed to respect their opposing enemy; scout their tactics; evaluate their strengths; and find weaknesses that could be exploited. They needed to constantly adjust their own tactics in face of their enemy's strengths; always to be patient; and always to be very wary of their enemy. If there was one tactic that their enemy did not expect out of them; did not expect out of them because it was so uncharacteristic of American soldiers; was for them to exercise patience. It had saved them this morning and it would save them again!

The sergeant and all of the men in the platoon were mystified as to just how this young Army lieutenant had acquired the combat skills that he continued to exhibit. The sergeant rubbed the Apache Warrior patch on his shoulder and he wondered—was this LT the reincarnation of an Apache Warrior? Was that the reason this LT had given them all such patches to wear? Was this LT some Apache Warrior from the past?

"Sir, do you mind if I ask you a question?" The sergeant asked his LT.

"Yeah, sure, sergeant, what is it?" The LT responded.

"I know that you're straight out of Officers' Training School, Sir, but you seem to have been at war before?" Asked the sergeant of his lieutenant.

"Perhaps, sergeant, in another time and place." Answered the lieutenant.

The sergeant just walked away wondering and wondering about this young lieutenant who just seemed to be battle tested and possessing some sixth animal sense that came alive when they were in the jungle hunting for 'Charlie.' Maybe he really was some reincarnated Apache Warrior?

In my dark depression I had drifted off into a 'daydream.' I was not really asleep. I was merely allowing my mind to escape into an imagined world of the warrior; once again I was a young lieutenant serving 'in country' in the Viet Nam War. Why did my mind make such a choice of such an imagination?

I had served in the Viet Nam War, in the Navy, on an attack aircraft carrier (USS Oriskany CVA-34), and off of the coast of North Viet Nam. I had not seen any of the very popular movies about the ground war that was fought in South Viet Nam. I had not even read any of the books detailing the ground war that had been fought by the Marines and Army against the Viet Cong and North Viet Nam Army.

Yet somehow my imagination was able to create in my mind a full range of combat experiences as a platoon leader in the South against the VC and NVA. I often escaped into that imagined world and the imagined experiences were very vivid to me. I had 'been there' if only in my mind! Had I ever been in such combat in another life? Was I like Patton reliving experiences from another incarnation? I don't know?

How did these 'daydreams; affect me? In my 'battles' with Xerox I had imagined myself to be at war with an enemy that was the 'hunter' while I was the 'hunted.' To me in my imagination it was all jungle warfare; hunter, hunted, traps and ambushes, tactics, battle plans, and survival. Within my mind I worked out a battle plan and strategy that anticipated and countered the enemy's every attack. And I counter attacked my enemy in unpredictable ways that were never anticipated by my enemies. Yes, I thought of the managers with whom I had had confrontations as the enemy and I fought as though it was all jungle warfare in country against the VC and NVA.

In this imagined world I was what I loved being—a warrior in battle! All too often this imagined world was brought into my life in such a way that it was difficult for me separate the two or even distinguish between the two. What was real and what was imagined? Did it even matter to me?

Was I like no other man in the world? Was I like no other Viet Nam War veteran in America? Although I had actually submitted, in 2001, a written application for Post Traumatic Stress Disease benefits—I had been turned down. I had never sought treatment by any doctor for PTSD. Prior to 2007 I had never visited any VA facility to submit to an examination by doctors or had I sought treatment for PSTD. I never appealed the ruling of the VA—I'd continue to exist in that other dimension of time and space. And I continued to suffer from restless and mostly sleepless nights.

What made me think and feel as I did? What about the other 3300 officers and sailors who had survived the tragic fire aboard the USS Oriskany—what did they think and feel all of these years since the fire? How had they dealt with the memory of that tragedy all of these subsequent years? How had they been and how had their lives been affected by that war experience? Were there other men and other war veterans who thought and felt as I did? Could I be so unique and so alone that I was the only man and the only war veteran to have the thoughts and feelings that I did?

I felt so very alone and isolated as I had no connection to anyone or to anything. Recently while sitting in the lobby of a business I acutely felt this lack of connection to anything. Employees of the business passed me by; employees who were connected to other employees; and who were also connected to that business. They worked for and with each other; had others working for them. Monday through Friday they had a job to go to and the weekends meant something special to them.

For me while I was still out of work every day was the same; empty, without work, without accomplishment, with days and nights of aloneness, stress, and depression. There were those periods of time for me that caused me to seek escape into a world of daydreams and imagined experiences as a dream warrior.

The problems seemed to be that these imagined experiences were becoming more enjoyable than the reality I was suffering and they were becoming more frequent. My escapes into what I referred to as "another dimension of time and space" were becoming more vivid and real to me. If I had the power to decide in which realm I could permanently exist I consciously would choose my imagined world. Did I have mental problems as claimed by my ex-wife?

Wow! What was the line between reality and my imagined world? Hadn't the two merged into one? What world would take over the other? Would I permanently disappear into one or the other? Was I losing my grasp on what was real and on what I merely imagined within my mind?

Again it could be said that the mind takes into itself as reality anything vividly experienced or imagined to have experienced. The mind just does not distinguish between the two. Again, remember the experiment with the three groups of basketball players trying to improve their percentage of shots mad verses those taken? Hadn't the group that imagined taking foul shots improved their percentages of shots made? The imagined experience became real in their minds! Is this happening to me?

It seems that the mind draws no line between what is actually experienced and what is vividly imagined as having been experienced. Doesn't the mind take into it own deep consciousness both the real and the imagined equally? The jungles of Viet Nam and combat were 'real' to my mind. They were real to my consciousness. My mind made no distinction or evaluation of the experiences. I was in the realm of my mind and consciousness a 'warrior' and a combat veteran.

The 'gunfighter' within me had vividly experienced facing down a dangerous gunslinger in the Old West. I had looked into the eyes of the gunslinger; I detected my opponent's movement to draw his six-gun; and with a lightening reaction I drew my own firearm, shot first, and survived the challenge.

Was it an accumulation of such vividly imagined experiences that made me so hard, so tough, and as a man who would not back down to another man? Others had often asked me: "who do you think you are?" This question was in reference to my never backing down to managers no matter what their titles. Others did back down; others did bow down; who was I to not do the same? Oh, if only they knew who I thought and imagined myself to be!

I was all that I imagined myself to be! The sum total of what and who I was—was that of a fierce warrior-man. It seemed to fit in well in my mind's world of battle. I had never fit in very well in the corporate world of apparent lies, deception, politics, and ass kissing. It had never been my world despite a long work career in the corporate world. I had survived in that world only because of my toughness and because of all of my warrior attributes that protected me in that world. Again—hadn't I always felt that I have belonged to another place and time? Hadn't I often expressed that I felt that I should have been born in another century? Had I once existed in another century in another once lived life?

Was I like any other man that I had ever known during all of my years working in the corporate world? No! During my 21+ years working for Xerox had I met any other man like myself? No! It seems that I was truly 'one of a kind.'

It is no wonder that even my closest friends had never really figured me out; they had never determined what motivated me; and they had never determined what had caused all of my 'battles' with the company. I had been called a "legend" in the company. There was not another one like me anywhere. I felt that many of my peers laughed at me for all of the troubles and battles I seem to have brought upon myself.

I reflected on that evaluation of me by others; that I had become a legend in the company for all of his battles and confrontations with so many managers in my career; and that there was not another like me who had ever worked for Xerox. Was I really so 'different' from my peers? The thought that I was different added to my sense of isolation and aloneness. Others thought I was different. I always felt that I was different. Why was I different? Why?

The haunting words of my ex-wife often reverberated in my mind: "you can't help it the way that you are." Damn! Damn! What made me the way that I was? It was a deep philosophical question that I asked of myself every day! I cried out to whatever 'God' that there was—why am I the way that I am? How the hell did I become such a true and pure warrior? Why and how? Why?

Did other men even question what influences on them shaped their characters and personalities? Did other men question how and why they became the men that they are? Did the asking of such questions of myself isolate me from other men? Just how unique and different was I from other men? I felt even more alone. I felt even more separated from other men. I felt disconnected from all and connected to no one. Hadn't I always had these thoughts and feelings? Why?

It bears repeating: A long time ago when I was just a little boy (my Father was still alive) I wanted to be just like Superman from the old black and white TV program. I had even prayed to God to make a deal—for God to grant me Superman powers so that I too could "fight for truth, justice, and the American way." If God would make that 'deal' with me, my part of the agreement would be a willingness to forfeit the opportunity for love, companionship, a wife, all that other men needed and desired. As a little boy I was willing to make that deal with God. Why would I have felt like that at such a young age?

Of course God had never cut such a deal with me. But, how much had my even praying such a prayer affected my personality and character? Why would a boy of 8 or 9 years of age even pray such a prayer? Why would such a young boy even consider making such a 'deal' and such a sacrifice? What was it within such a young boy that made him want to be the champion of truth and justice? I could not have understood the personal sacrifice that I would have made as part of such a deal. I sure did not understand what I was praying!

After having read the book—The Prince—the words of Machiavelli haunted me thereafter:

"For the manner in which men live is so different from the way in which they ought to live, that he who leaves the common course for that which he ought to follow will find that it leads him to ruin rather than to safety".

Again, I am <u>no</u> 'saint' but I am a decent guy. I considered, what good had ever come to me by my good actions? Had I brought ruin upon my life due to my having high ideals and principles, and by actually living by them? I wondered if I had just been dumb and stupid to have, lived my life as I had? I sure in hell was damn hardheaded! Surely I was intelligent enough to understand that to recognize that my stand on principle had often brought me adversity and difficulties? Why did I persist in always seemingly trying to swim upstream instead of just going with the flow? Was it some self-destructive instinct within me? I suspect than many of my peers thought me to be stupid!

Were there any other men like me? Surely there were! Young men still join the military for reasons of duty, honor, country, and true patriotism. There were men <u>and</u> women in the business world who did do the right thing. There were corporate leaders who did value their employees as well as their customers, and who treated both fairly and with respect. I wondered about a lot of things!

I wondered if 'knights in shining armor' were valued by anyone? There didn't even seem to be any 'maidens' to be rescued and none that valued 'knights' anymore? Heck, I was alone. I existed in some other dimension of time and space while wondering if I truly belonged to another time; to another century and era?

It had been over six months since I had last heard from the woman to whom I had thought I had only 'loaned' $1500. At the time I loaned her the money I had been out of work and really needed the money for my own living expenses. But in trying to be a friend, and against that little voice within me that raised a 'red flag' of warning, I ended up getting 'stiffed.'

That which made me honorable; that I greatly valued friends and friendship; ended up being used against me by someone who was not really a friend to me. Hadn't I been warned by Machiavelli: "No good comes to the man who tries to be good and do good in a world where men are evil and do evil; in a world where the greater evils are done by women." Damn! I could laugh at myself when I thought of how I seemed to gravitate to such cynical philosophers such as Machiavelli and Nietzsche. Now why was that I laughed to myself?

I tried to live under a philosophy where I would be the very best friend in the world that a person could have. But the experience had shaken me as well as it had cost me. Once again, a woman had betrayed me. I certainly was vulnerable to the lies of a woman. When would I ever learn that lesson? Were not the days of men trying to be a knight in shining armor way past? What the heck, it was only money!

For six months, at the time in late 1992, I had been deeply sad and depressed; in great emotional pain; unable to even escape into that other dimension of time and space in which I was, as a true warrior, most comfortable. There had been very few dreams that I could remember over the past six months. There had been no daydreams into which I escaped from the pain I suffered due to adversity, failures, and especially aloneness. I just hurt and all of my 'defense mechanisms' were failing me at the time. I was hurting badly and others became concerned for me.

I received a telephone call from a cousin in Florida. She expressed the concern that all of the family seemed to have; that I would "do something foolish"; she further expressed the concern because of "what my Father had done." I appreciated the telephone call and the concern expressed. I valued this cousin and her concern.

In a long letter to my cousin I revealed much of myself to her. I wrote a lot of my relationship with my Father; and how I had been terribly affected by the tragedy of my Father's suicide. I wrote of incidents that had occurred as a boy that reflected how hard my Father had been on me, but how from my perspective I valued the lessons taught by my Father. I wrote that my Father had made me into a very tough man and for that I was very thankful.

I knew that there were family members whose view of my Father was not kind. I understood that. I wrote that they were not there when my Father spoke of his love for my Sister and I with the words: "I love you as high as the sky and deep as the ocean." They were not there!

Once I wrote a poem while still a very young boy. My Father took it down to the barbershop where he worked, pinned it on the wall, and told all of his customers that the poem had been written by his son. I'd always heard my Father tell me that: "You're going to go to Princeton University and be a doctor". Those who may have thought ill of my Father had not been there to witness these events that were treasured memories of my Father.

Yes, my Father had been very tough on me, but I knew that my Father had also loved me. No one really seemed to understand how much I loved my Father; how much I had missed him all of the years since his death; how I felt such deep pain for my Father and for myself. No one really knew how devastating my Father's suicide had been to me—no one knew! I felt great pain for my Father. I felt all of my Father's hurts and disappointments. If only the man had gotten a 'break' in life. Damn!

It seemed that I sort of lived under the potential curse: "Like father, like son." There was the constant fear my family felt that I would also, in my current depression, commit suicide as my Father had done. I had also feared such a weakness! But as much as I was like my Father, I was also very different. My Father had seen to that by having been so hard and tough on me. I wrote to my cousin that it was precisely because my own Father had committed suicide that I would never take my life. As I wrote to my cousin, I had the "benefit" denied to my Father, that of having been raised by him; that of knowing the adverse affect my Father's suicide had on me.

I could not, would not do to my Children what my Father had done to me. My Father had raised me to be tougher and stronger than he had been. I had succeeded because I was indeed very different than my Father in that regard. I indeed loved my own Children: "As high as the sky and deep as the ocean." I made every attempt to be a "consigliori" to my Son and Daughter.

Warriors just do not commit suicide. There is no honor in such an act. I was a warrior who was fiercely determined to survive the very worst that 'Life' inflicted on me. Besides, as I wrote to my cousin, I had already survived so much hurt in my life; being out of work wasn't even near the worst of it! Being out of work sure did not compare to the death of my Father; did not compare to serving in the Viet Nam War and my nearly getting killed in the Oriskany fire; did not compare to my divorce; and did not compare to separation from my Children. Hell, I'd find another job! I eventually did!

Had people held it against _me_ because my Father had committed suicide? My Mother, in recent years, had told me that the father of one of the nice Italian neighborhood girls that I liked as a teenager had discouraged her from dating me because of my Father's suicide. That was cruel! Having had a Father who had committed suicide appeared to have been a burden that I had to carry with me all of his life. I was _not_ my Father!

I had revealed quite a lot of my thoughts and feelings in my letter to my cousin. Did other men do such? Were other men willing to reveal their deep thoughts and feelings to another? I often revealed my own thoughts and feelings in letters to my Son and to my Daughter. I had the ability to write down in a letter what I was unable to verbally articulate. I wrote in my 'journals' what I was unable to articulate to others. That's just the way I was! I could write much better than I could talk!

The nephew of my high school football coach had committed suicide. The nephew's teenage son had found his father. I wrote a long letter from my heart to the boy trying to prepare him for how his life would be without his father and the 'battles' that he would face—the principle battle against those who would think "like father like son." I stressed to the boy that he was <u>not</u> his father. I sent the letter to the coach who approved of it and who then sent it to the boy. I wished that I had made a copy of the letter—that my Mother had read the letter.

Remember the time that I had taken my Son and my Daughter to see the movie: The Great Santini? It was because of my inability to express in words what I wanted to tell my Children that I took them to see that movie. I had hoped that their seeing the movie together would somehow say to them what I needed to tell them—that I was much like 'Bull Durham' and that I was sorry for that!

I had now in 1993, at the time, been out of work for nearly eleven months and that did depress me greatly as I felt so helpless and hopeless. I had no idea what to do? I felt like I had failed my Father who was to send me to Princeton to be a doctor. What would my Father think of me now that I was out of work? More importantly I felt like I had failed my Children. Both worked nearly full time while attending college. I was certainly feeling much like a complete failure!

Being single, unattached, and alone was probably an advantage to me now emotionally as there was no wife to criticize me for my failures. There was no woman to make me feel impotent as a woman had the power to do even if it was done unintentionally. Woman did have such power over men. How does it go: "the hand that rocks the cradle holds the power" and that is generally if not always the woman!

Perhaps what women least understood about men is that a man has got to be a man; a man has got to feel like a man; and a man has got to act like a man. It is especially to his wife and to his children that a man has got to be a man. Rightly or wrongly being out of work does not make a man feel like a man. Being unemployed is a failure that diminishes a man greatly, certainly in his own eyes. It robs him of all value. It makes him feel impotent, helpless and hopeless, a complete failure in his own eyes and in the eyes of his wife if married. And he feels weak! It has all these affects on me!

A man does not value another man who is weak. Why would a woman value a man who is weak? Women are drawn to successful, strong, powerful, wealthy men and there is nothing wrong with that. After all don't men strive to be the strong 'knight in shining armor' in order to earn the attention of a 'fair maiden?' Men strive to be 'winners' in order to 'win' a woman!

Does it all sound 'chauvinistic' and offensive to women readers of this book? I sincerely hope not! That is not the intention of such comments. It just appears to be the way things are for men and for women. Perhaps we just all need to admit that this is the way it is and to deal with it?

What of the 'fair maiden?' In order to 'win' the affection of the 'knight in shining armor' she must be a 'winner' emotionally, physically, mentally, spiritually, and in all that she is and does. Isn't it generally the pretty cheerleader who gets the star football player? Isn't it the star football player who gets the pretty cheerleader?

My encouragement to my Daughter and to my Son was that they were both very intelligent and that they were both capable of being and doing whatever they set their minds to be and do. There were no limits on either, and certainly not on my Daughter because she was a woman. There were no gender limits on either. Yes, I always told my Son that women were different from men! Ha! Ha!

If, in their partnership agreement and marriage, it was agreed upon that the woman/wife would work outside of the home and that the man/husband would be a 'house husband' that is okay! When the roles and responsibilities were defined, agreed upon, acceptable to both, they generally did not diminish either in the eyes of the other. The man is not made impotent in such an agreed upon partnership and working arrangement or is he?

I was alone and I had no such partnership; I had no wife; I had no helpmate; it was up to me to work, to earn a livelihood, and to put bread on the table. It was up to me alone to be and act as a man and to feel worthy of being a man. At the time I felt like I was failing everyone, especially myself, and it tore at my very being! I just hate to lose. I have always hated to lose.

Ironically I felt the urge to write to my ex-wife to apologize for being such a failure. Wasn't I a failure during our twelve years of marriage? Hadn't she been correct in her stated expectation that I would never be a success in my career? Hadn't she been correct in her criticism of me that I lacked self-confidence and was not aggressive enough to be a success?

Of course she had always been attracted to 'successful' men. Her affair very early in our marriage had been with her boss who was a very successful and wealthy businessman. After our divorce hadn't she sought out successful and wealthy men? Yet, interestingly, she had also had affairs with and marriages to men of rather dubious character. A few of her failed marriages were to men who were much less than 'winners.' That I still thought about her was evidence of the power she still had over me, at least at that time in my life. I still had love for the woman I thought and wanted her to be; for the illusion of her I held in my mind.

Despite the pain in the right side of my head from which I continued to suffer—it was due to a cranial nerve apparently injured during a dental procedure—I did exercise this morning; doing some push-ups, sit-ups, weight press and weight curl. Because of the rain I could not get out to jog and walk.

When I food shopped I carefully read virtually all of the labels for fat content and often putting back on the store shelf anything with too high a fat or even a sodium content. I very seldom ate red meat and I tried to stay away from snack foods that were too high in fat content. I ate a lot of fresh fruits, vegetables, tuna fish, salmon, and mostly oatmeal for breakfast. I often made lentil soup.

I seldom drank soft drinks or even alcohol. It had been many years since I even had a bottle of any kind of whiskey in the house. I did drink an occasional beer and I often had a glass of red wine with supper—to cut down on cholesterol.

Actually when I had last had my cholesterol checked it had been high; perhaps a result of stress and depressions? I had since read that stress, depression, and negative thoughts all adversely affected cholesterol readings. Wouldn't a job and an income all lower my cholesterol?

As my Granddaughter had correctly observed—I did eat healthy and for a single guy who lived alone I did take good care of myself. In that I might have been the exception instead of the rule? Was I?

What about other men who were unemployed and living alone with no family within the state in which they lived? Did such men carefully shop for food; did they cook for themselves on a regular basis; did they eat healthy and get some exercise? Were they healthy? I had read somewhere that the average age of death for a former National Football Lineman was at age 56. Former Pittsburgh Steeler and Hall of Fame center, Mike Webster, died at near age 51. He had been divorced, broke, and homeless after having suffered from mental illness due to too many and undetected concussions suffered during his playing career.

But what of all of the other players who died young—were there any meaningful statistics as to why former NFL linemen died at an average age of 56? Were they overweight at the age of death? Were they suffering from old football injuries? Were they married or divorced? Had they gone on to successful careers after the end of their football playing days were over, or not? Had they used steroids during their playing careers? Why had these former highly conditioned athletes died at an average age of 56?

One former NFL football player who had used steroids in both college and while playing professional football was killed while cutting down a tree in the front yard of his house. The tree fell on him. How the hell did that happen? Was it his destiny to die in such a freak accident? Is there some 'book' with all of our names written in it that records the day that we are to be born and the day that we are to die? Did other men think on these things? What did other men think and feel? All of these stories had a profound affect on me. I continue to question to wonder if destiny controls our lives including when and how we die?

I did have some muscle aches and pains; more at age 66 than I had suffered at age 51. I continued to suffer head and neck pain down to my shoulder that was all on my right side due to the injured cranial nerve. My left arm hurt but I had felt a 'pop' when I had injured it. I had recently strained my left leg and knee. When I went up the stairs in my townhouse there were noises that came from the knee that echoed throughout the house. I was able to do knee bends and to jog on it, but it stiffened badly when I sat for any length of time. It is hell getting 'old'. It is a hell of a lot worse dying young. Once again the Oriskany fire put things in proper perspective for me.

Most nights were restless and sleepless. I suspected that it was the demon of the fire aboard the USS Oriskany that kept me awake nights. Once again I was reminded that there was no one to watch my back. I had watched the TV program Vegas one night. It was the segment in which one of the young staff members, who was a Marine reservist, had returned from having been called up and after having served recently in Afghanistan—or so the story line went. He had nearly been killed in Afghanistan. A fellow Marine had saved his life. In the story line he was experiencing sleepless nights. When asked why he couldn't sleep he responded: "there is no one to watch my back" and that: "while in Afghanistan he had fellow Marines to watch my back." I sure related to that!

Again and again the question is asked—what about the other 3300 officers and sailors who had survived the Oriskany fire, did any of them have any trouble sleeping at night because of their memories of that fire? Was the memory of that fire a demon in their mind? How vivid was their memory of that fire? Had any of them been able to get past that experience and to bury it so deep in their minds that it did not affect them consciously? Surely men other than me were affected by the memory of that tragic fire and by the memory of those who had died in it?

One of my fellow junior officers had died late last year of cancer. Had the cancer been caused by asbestos aboard the ship? I had remained aboard the ship all during the stay in the shipyard while the ship was undergoing repairs after the fire. What had I been exposed to that would come back to haunt me by destroying my health? The sad legacy of war never ends, does it?

When the Oriskany was sunk in 2006 to be an artificial reef it seems that none of my demons went down with it. They remained above the surface in my mind and most likely in the mind of every officer and sailor who had served aboard the 'Mighty O.' Memories of war just get more vivid with the passing of time! They just do not fade and go away.

I lay back on the sofa—it was 2006—and my mind drifted off into yet another '<u>daydream</u>' as I sought temporary escape into my imagined dream world. It was like I was seeing myself in a movie. The narrative always in the second person although it was another person's daydream:

It was a hot afternoon and he decided to go out to jog and walk. When he got to the local college's track that was around the football field he was alone. Perhaps it was too hot and humid for anyone else to jog that day? Perhaps all of the 'regulars' had gotten out earlier and were done for the day? In any event he was the only one out on the track; dressed in jogging shorts and his tee shirt that simply had "NAVY" across the chest. He often wore it as a reminder to him that he was alive.

He looked down at his lap counter. He had jogged two miles and had just one more mile of jogging to go before he would walk one mile to cool down. He listened to the sounds around him; it seemed pretty quiet. Then he heard what sounded like a cry or a moan; he couldn't make out the sound or from where it was coming? He stopped in his tracks; stood still; and listened for more sounds. The sounds were coming from the wooded area beside the jogging track. He quickly ran to that area. He came upon two young men holding down a young woman. One held her arms while the other straddled her legs. They had pulled her tee shirt up over her bra.

"Please, sir, please help me." The young woman pleaded with him.

"Gentlemen, the party is over, let her go." He ordered the two men.

"Hey, old man, who the hell are you?" One of the men asked him, as they were a little stunned and surprised by his arrival. They were college age, young, each about his height, and perhaps weighing 170 pounds each. He was a pretty solid 190 pounds. The jogging shorts showed off his thick thighs and calves.

"Navy veteran of the Viet Nam War, that's who I am." He responded. "Served up North, way up North, sort of on special assignment."

"What the hell do we care, old man?" Said the man holding the young woman's arms. Both young men were in a kneeling position looking up him.

"Well, gentlemen, maybe you ought to care about what I've done while in the war and since then. Either of you ever terminate anyone with extreme prejudice?"

"Huh, what the hell?" The one straddling her legs looked up at him.

"You know, like put a round between a target's eyes. You know, like slipping up behind someone with a garrote, quickly getting it around their neck and terminating them; you know like hitting an enemy with such a hard karate blow to their neck that it killed them; either of you ever do that, gentlemen?"

The two men looked up at him beginning to get a little nervous. What could he be talking about? What would he do to them?

"Hey, look, old man, we don't want any trouble with you, why don't you just go on your way." The young man holding the girl's arms pinned said to him.

"Well, gentlemen, trouble has found you, very, very serious trouble if you know what I mean." He sort of flexed his chest muscles. He raised his right arm to sort of scratch behind his head, flexing his bicep. It wasn't that he was very muscular. He was doing all that he could to intimidate the two young men.

"What do you mean, mister, what are you going to do to us?" The tone of voice of the two young men changed as they each felt a certain fear of this 'old man' who was standing over them.

"Guys, after I left the Navy I went to work for what was 'the Company' to work for at the time and I got even better at the things I did. Either of you prepared to be terminated with extreme prejudice?" He further intimidated the two men.

"Wait, hey we weren't going to hurt the girl. How about if you just let us go. We won't cause anymore trouble." The one young man straddling the girl's legs asked. Each of the two men was getting nervous and very frightened.

"Can't do that guys, I can't allow you to just walk away." He answered them with a real hardness to his voice.

"Please don't hurt us, what are you going to do to us?" Both asked him.

"Let the girl up. Then I am making a citizen's arrest of you both or I can." He just let the 'or I can' just hang out there as a further intimidation. The look on his face got very, very serious and stern as he stared at both of the young men.

"Shit, man, look, please, we didn't really do anything, can't you let us go?" Again they both pleaded with him as they released their hold on the girl.

She got up, pulled her tee shirt back over her bra, and stood close to him for further protection not knowing what he was going to do to the two men.

"I want you both to take off your shoes and remove the shoe strings. Then I want you each to take off your trousers. I'm going to tie your hands and then we're all going to march up to the campus to find a policeman."

"Please, sir, please." The two men continued to plead.

"Guys, its either that or." He again left it at "or."

The two young men complied with his orders. He tied their hands behind their backs. All four then left the wooded area for the campus. He flagged down a College employee who had a cell phone and had them call the police.

"Thank you, sir, thank you. I don't what they would have done to me if you hadn't come along." The girl gave him a hug and a peck on his cheek.

Two police squad cars and an EMT truck arrived shortly thereafter on campus. The girl was put in the EMT after explaining to the police what had happened to her at the hands of the two young men. The police did a brief interview with the two young men and then arrested them.

"Sir, the girl told us what happened. The two guys said that you were some kind of trained assassin and killer. They were really afraid of you. What did you do to them?" One of the police officers asked him?

Upon hearing that he just burst out laughing.

"Who are you?" asked the Officer.

"Officer, I'm just a regular jogger here on campus. I heard some noises and ran to them to find the two guys holding down the girl. I just told them that I had served in the Navy way up North on sort of special assignment; that I then went to work for what was the Company; and that I had gotten very good at the things that I did."

"They were afraid that you were going to kill them, or as one of them said, to terminate them." Further stated the police officer. "Did you serve in the Viet Nam War as you told them that you did?"

"Officer, I did serve in that war on a aircraft carrier off the coast of North Viet Nam. I guess it was sort of a special assignment in that I had had a medical board written up on me for motion sickness suffered on a small ship and I was assigned to the carrier as sort of a trial. The 'Company' I worked for was Xerox as a copier and fax sales rep. In the early 1970's it was 'the Company' for which to work. I got pretty good as a sales rep. Hell, I've never hurt a fly." He told the officer.

"Sir, why were they so frightened of you?"

"I asked them if they had ever terminated anyone with extreme prejudice. That had the effect of bringing all of their fears to the surface, which was my intention. I never said that I had actually terminated anyone. Their own fears made them believe that I was really a trained assassin and that I was capable of doing great harm to them." He then laughed again. "Hell, if they both together had taken me on they probably would have kicked my ass—I haven't been in a fight since I was twelve years old."

"One hell of a bluff, sir, you were bluffing them weren't you?"

"Yeah, officer, it was just all a bluff." He answered the police officer with that sort of half grin on his face and with a sort of twinkle in his eyes.

The police officer began to walk away then he looked back wondering—was it really all just a bluff by that Navy veteran?

I awakened out of my <u>daydream</u> and that is all that it was, just a daydream and no more. The entire incident had never taken place except in my mind. None of it had ever happened. It had all been imagined. Yet, was the script sort of a preparation for just such an event if I had ever encountered it? Had it all been a 'role play' in my mind? What would I do if I ever encountered such a situation? How would I respond? Did I even know? I hoped that I would respond as a warrior!

I hoped that all of my daydreams were indeed a preparation for just what I would do in such a dangerous encounter. I hoped that if and when faced with life threatening danger I would respond as a warrior. I believed that proper self-defense required a man to accept the worst that could happen to him. Once there was such an acceptance a man was basically free to defend himself in any and every way that he could. G. Gordon Liddy was correct in his phrase:

"Defeat the fear of death and welcome the death of all fear"

Once a man accepted that his life might be lost there was nothing else to lose and he could fight with complete abandon and no fear. There is just no way possible to know what a man, including I, would do in a life-threatening situation? How would I act if my life were threatened? I could only hope that I would act in my waking world how I acted in my dream world—as a warrior and a hero! Could I carryover into my waking hours the bravery shown in my daydreams? I hope that I would never have to find out.

What about other men, how would they respond if they found themselves in a dangerous situation? Would they meekly submit to a knife attack? What would they do if facing a gunman? Does any man know beforehand how he would respond when faced with a dangerous and life threatening situation? Who knows? No one ever really knows unless they find themselves in just such a situation and perhaps their reaction would be a surprise to everyone.

I thought of the 32 students who had recently, in March 2007, been murdered at VPI. What would I have done in that situation? Would I have tried to hide only to be found, shot, and murdered? Would I have risen up and tried to attack the gunman with the acceptance that I could be shot and killed? I had no idea how I would respond in such a situation? But, perhaps my daydreams were a 'role playing' that I hoped would prepare me if I ever found myself in a life threatening situation—I hoped that I would respond with complete abandon as a warrior!

I remained sad and depressed, no doubt about that. My depression was reflected in my feelings of hopelessness, helplessness, negativity, and even in my temporary withdrawal from any social activity. I felt a desire to date but no great need. My sadness and depression robbed me of all self-confidence. I felt weak.

When I read magazine articles on the affect that depression has on people, well it seemed to be taking its toll on me. Yet I had not turned to alcohol or to drugs, or to promiscuous sexual activity, and I had not gained or lost any excessive weight. I continued to keep my townhouse relatively clean and I continued to shower, shave, and wear clean clothes. I did not abandon my neat personal appearance. I continued to exercise, jog, walk, and to cook and eat healthy foods. Most importantly I had not become susceptible to any physical illnesses such as the flu, colds, etc.

My stance was still upright, my walk very strong and powerful, and I had a presence about me that exuded power and not the weakness associated with depression. I had excellent muscle definition for a man my age due to my strength exercises. Oh, I was indeed depressed but the affect on me was not quite that it was on most men. I remained a warrior!

Would a man who took such good physical care of himself, ever seriously contemplate committing suicide? Of course *not*! Yes, I was deeply depressed but I was also a warrior yearning for the next battle. I was a warrior, a man, and I knew that I had to get up one more time than I was knocked down. Although I was down at this time I knew that I would get up again. I always had!

I had just finished reading a book titled: 'Who Needs God? in which the author concludes that we all need God. No one is really ever all alone because there is a God Who is with us always even in the shadow of death. An inmate at one of the Nazi concentration camps during WWII wrote the following profound statement of faith:

> **"I believe in the sun even when it isn't shining;**
> **I believe in love even when I don't feel it;**
> **I believe in God even when He is silent."**

Since the religious Easter season of 'Lent' began, I'd been faithfully attending Mass every Sunday having missed just one Sunday due to snow and ice on the roads. The year was 1993. Why had I returned to Mass when I felt so abandoned by God? I continued to reach out to God and I continued to struggle with my faith. It was a lifelong struggle for me! Attending Mass then neglecting to attend—that seemed to be something that occurred every few years for me. I desired to have a stronger faith in God—for whatever reasons it just was not within me and that struggle caused much disturbance in my mind. Sadly by Easter 2007 once again I had stopped attending Mass. Ironically, I continued to pray daily—I just seemed to have lost interest in going to Church. I had gotten tired of the meaningless sermons that were read by the deacons. It just appeared that the pastor and associate pastor at church had no passion about their beliefs? I continued to struggle with my faith.

What evil and darkness lurks in the hearts and minds of men? What is it that releases the darkness that is within? Is there a different measure of darkness within each man or is the measure of darkness the same in all men? What of me? Is the measure of darkness and evil within me the same, less, or more than in other men? I wondered.

It was 1990 when my Son was beaten and robbed by four young Black gunmen. He was badly bruised. He was fortunate that he was not shot. IF worse had happened; if worse than being beaten and robbed by the gunmen; if worse than the serious injuries that he had sustained at the hands of his attackers; what darkness within me would have been unleashed?

A week after the incident I remained stunned, numb, deeply sad, and very, very disturbed that such a terrible attack had been experienced by my only Son, who with my only Daughter, were the "loves of my life" from the title of a song by Carley Simon about her own children.

Beneath the surface of my sad, quiet demeanor, were the faint stirrings of anger. It was the darkness that stirred deep within me, a darkness I kept under tight control because I greatly feared it. At all costs I kept the dark side under control because its release would allow it to gain control over me and I really feared that! I felt it at times when in an instant all that darkness and potential violence seemed to come to the surface. I did not want to ever discover what I might be capable of doing.

"Either a great priest or a great Mafia hit man"—I joked with friends that I recognized the capacity to be either was within me. My 'good side' was better than that of most men. Didn't I live by the highest ideals, principles, and moral standards? But I suspected that deep within me was a 'dark side' that may be darker than that of most men? I just never wanted to find out what evil I may be capable of doing—never! That potential dark side frightened me greatly.

Would I have, as I told my Mother, made a pact with the Devil to sell my soul in return for the total vengeance I would have exacted on my Son's attackers IF worse had happened? Even such a thought frightened me! That I had such a thought made me feel very remorseful.

I thanked God for saving my Son's life and for sparing my own soul from damnation. I prayed to God for forgiveness, for the awful evil I toyed with in my mind, and for my reaching deep within to the darkness that is within me. That I would even consider unleashing the darkness within me frightened me and shamed me. I asked for God's forgiveness! I praised God for preserving my Son's life. My daily prayer to God was for Him to always bless my Son and Daughter—and my Family of loved ones—with perfect health, safety, and welfare; and to always keep them safe from all evil, harm, accidents, etc.

I renewed my 'pact' with God—asking that my Children always be spared; that I would rather take upon myself any harm, evil, etc. instead of my Children. I would bear all for my Children. I asked God to always spare my Children—I would rather that I bear whatever 'crosses' sent by God.

As a boy I had suffered what may have been the greatest hurt—the loss of my Father. As a man the loss of either of my Children would be a hurt from which there would not be any recovery. Heck, I had not really recovered from my divorce and the resulting hurt—I no longer tucked my Children in bed at night or was there every day to watch them growing up. I remembered that I should have won custody of my Children. I was reminded that not even an all-powerful God could give me back any of the yesterdays in which I missed out on so very much.

The year was now 2007 and I was age 66. All too many of my dreams had not been realized and they never would. As it was too late! That was the 'rub'—that it was too late for so many of my dreams to ever come true. Damn!

1992 had turned into 1993 and I had remained unemployed. It had been a full eighteen months of unemployment. Each day was excruciatingly long. Yet the weeks and the months passed by all too quickly without mercy. Despite my efforts I had no job and no job prospects at the time.

I was overwhelmed by a sense of complete failure. Hell, I felt like the family failure because no one in my family was out of work and no one seemed to be the career failure that I felt that I was. Damn that feeling depressed me greatly!

What did my Children think of me? How did they value me? This greatly concerned me for I felt that I was letting my Children down badly for my failure to find a job or to start a business. The thought of letting my Children down crushed me. I was letting myself down.

Often during such times of my feeling hopeless with no future I would ask myself the rhetorical question—why did I not commit suicide? Always came back the answer—I loved my Son and my Daughter and that I would never hurt them as I had been hurt by my own Father's suicide. It remained just a 'rhetorical' question and no more!

I remain 'haunted' by questions such as: what would I be like and what would my life be like if there had been a woman with whom I had shared love? I had certainly married the wrong woman—surely she must have felt that she had married the wrong man. Another question that 'haunted' me was: what would my life been like if I'd won the $3,000,000 in the New Jersey lottery at the end of 1986? Instead I missed out on winning that jackpot by just one digit on one number! I concluded that God had a very cruel and sadistic sense of humor.

While still out of work in 1992 I answered my Daughter's request for assistance in her decision to move from Tennessee to New Jersey. So, I flew out to TN, rented a moving truck with a car trailer, and the two of us packed the truck with all of her furniture and belongings. Despite the untimely financial expense for me, I responded as I knew I should, which was with support for my Daughter's decision to move and I assisted her.

It was quite a trip—an 'adventure'—I'd never driven a sixteen foot truck before, pulling a car trailer which made it even a tougher and more dangerous drive for me. Eleven hours together in the cab of the truck with much conversation to keep each awake—it turned out to be an enjoyable trip for both father and daughter.

I got to better understand and appreciate the young woman who was my Daughter. Perhaps she got a better view of her Father, who for all of my outward toughness and hardness, I actually was tender at heart. To each of their surprise I was showing some signs of becoming 'mellow', which is something that I never expected to happen. I was more surprised at that than was she.

One of the rather funny incidents that occurred during the trip was when I drove the truck with trailer into a motel driveway in Eastern Virginia only to discover, to my dismay that the driveway did not go around the motel. I got stuck and just could not get the truck with trailer backed up despite my best efforts. There were people who came out of their motel rooms to move their cars out of my way—fearful that I would hit their cars! I darn near turned over the car trailer.

Finally after an hour I gave up and accepted that I just could not get the truck backed up. I was walking down the driveway to go over to a diner to try to ask some truck driver to do me a favor and to back up the truck for me when I encountered a young County Trooper who asked ME what was the trouble. I explained my predicament to the trooper who in five minutes time had the truck with trailer backed up so that my Daughter and I could proceed on our trip to NJ.

My Daughter was quite surprised that her Dad, for the most part, remained 'cool' throughout the ordeal. Yes, there was some cussing by me—yet I actually could laugh at the situation in which I had found myself. I had never driven a truck with trailer before. Our trip had been adventurous! I can still see my Nephew looking out the window at the truck with trailer, and I can still hear him ask me in his amazement: "it is really big; how did you drive it all the way here?"

I had gone back a few months later for my Niece's wedding, which was yet another untimely expense. Even my Niece had asked me "if I was crazy", as my cash wedding gift had been quite generous especially since I was still out of work.

At my Niece's wedding reception both my Son and my Daughter had had a ball! My daughter had really partied hard and enjoyed the reception—perhaps she had partied too hard. Unknown to me others had remarked to my Brother-in-Law if I was bothered by her excessive partying? After all my reputation had preceded me and was well known by most everyone. Didn't my own Mother often state to my Children: "you know how your Dad is." I allowed the partying by my Daughter—never saying a word about it! That surprised everyone!

After I had returned home my Daughter wrote to me to thank me for "being cool about the wedding reception and everything"—about her partying! She further stated that: "she had been impressed by me."

It made me very happy to know that my Princess was safe in New Jersey with family surrounded by love and people who truly cared for her, which was something that she had not been getting from her Mother in Tennessee in 1993.

After my trip to NJ and my return home to NC I'd sunk even deeper into a feeling of hopelessness and despair. I did <u>not</u> envy the people in NJ who enjoyed success, love, happiness, and financial prosperity—I was happy for them. But having been in such a 'normal environment for a brief moment in time made me reflect on my own failures and sad aloneness; how my own dreams were destroyed; and how I seemed to be on the outside of 'life' merely looking in while not really partaking or enjoying life.

There was the issue with 'God' with which I struggled daily. I tried, really tried, to have faith in an all-loving and in an all-powerful God. When I accepted the downsizing from Xerox I had fully trusted in God with an expectation that as the door at Xerox had closed on me that God would open another door for me. I really tried hard to believe in God's promise to Jeremiah:

"For I know the plans I have for you, for good and not for evil, to prosper you and not harm you, to give you hope and a good future"

When I left Xerox I had been filled with faith really believing in and expecting a better future. I had trusted God to open a new and even a better door for me and to provide me with an opportunity to realize my dreams. Now towards the end of 1993 and after 18 months of unemployment my faith had given way to despair and hopelessness. I could see no good, no future, no opportunity, and worse yet, I could no longer see an all-loving or all-powerful God Who cared that I was hurting.

I often asked myself the question: "why does God not love me?" Hadn't I responded to his Daughter's plea for assistance and moved her from TN to NJ, as any loving father would do? Why then did God not respond to my own plea for help?

How did other men handle such an important spiritual question? Did other men become bitter and discouraged as I did? Did they lose their faith, as did I? Obviously men who commit suicide do so because they've lost faith in God and in any promise for a better tomorrow. Did my Father commit suicide because he has lost all faith in God? I remember attending Mass with my Father when I was still just a little boy. It seemed that whenever I looked up at my Dad while at Mass—my Father's eyes were always filled with tears. I had always wondered why? It seemed perhaps that my Father had lost the battle for faith?

It was a battle that I was fighting and losing—the struggle to have faith in a God Who seemed to have totally abandoned me. I suffered deep wounds in this battle to my heart, to my mind, to my soul, and even to my body. I had to ask the 'Fates'—was it my destiny to only suffer in this life? Would my life never have any meaning to it?

Finally in mid-year 1994 I accepted an offered job as a Branch Sales Manager for a copier company. It was a job back in 'Corporate America' working in an industry, which I had left when downsized from Xerox. Although I did not really like the job, in typical fashion I gave my 110% effort working really hard to make a go of it.

In the end and after 14 months on the job I became a victim of corporate 'politics' and my own attitudes. I refused to play the game of 'kiss ass', which appeared to be a requirement. And there were those who worked against me both publicly and behind my back. Eventually I lost the job and became unemployed once again. I did not really blame anyone for the loss of that job—after all I had decided not to play the corporate game. IF anyone was at fault—the fault lay with me for having lost that job!

Yet while working at that job I had made friends among the young sales representatives that I managed. I had become a mentor to many of them. I had even helped a few of them find better jobs. They had invited me to their weddings. A few remained in touch with me over the subsequent years.

Yet, the whole experience deeply hurt and discouraged me while leaving me to once again question God. Why did it seem that none of my prayers, needs, wants, or desires was being answered? I again felt helpless and hopeless; and so very, very alone. Deep sadness overwhelmed me.

The religious season of 'Lent' had ended and I was still attending Mass as I tried to fulfill a commitment to have faith in God. Even after my latest lost battle and heartbreak I was still committed to attending Mass and to reaching out to a God Who seemed to have continually abandoned me throughout all of my life.

For the past few nights I had prayed for 'the Angel of Death' to take me as I slept; to end my pain, heartbreak, and suffering. I suspected that I would indeed exist to be 100 years of age, alone, and sad. As the Country and Western song goes: "thank God for unanswered prayers." Yes!

The sun was shining; it was a warm day; I'd jogged and walked. Now I lay back on a lounge chair in the sun, drifting off to yet another dimension of time and space to that of the warrior. It was where I longed to exist always. I entered an imagined <u>daydream</u> again written in a second person narrative format as though I was seeing myself in a movie as some warrior:

He was a Branch Sales Manager and he was working in the field making sales calls with one of his young Sales Representatives, Denise, a pretty and sweet and young lady for whom he had become a mentor. They were in the parking garage of one of the downtown office buildings walking towards the elevator when he saw the two men slip out from between the parked cars.

Their sudden presence startled Denise, but he remained controlled, icy cool, sensing the danger before them. All of his warrior senses were alert. It was as if he'd suddenly been transformed into some other being, into a warrior who was about to enter battle and who was prepared for it.

"Got any spare money for us?" One of the men asked as his right hand reached into the pocket of his jacket. Both men were in their late twenties of age. The other man just looked at Denise in a lustful, threatening manner, which frightened her and made her draw closer to our warrior.

"No." Was all that our warrior answered the man. He stepped forward in the direction of the two would be assailants positioning himself between them and Denise. His eyes held both men in his vision, a seemingly blank stare. But it was like the eyes of a cobra, actually focused, and he was ready to strike.

"If you don't have any spare money then maybe we'll just have to take all of your money." One of the men laughed as he pulled a knife from his jacket and waved it at our warrior.

"No." Our warrior responded rather loudly and firmly.

"Hey, empty your damn pockets. I want your wallet, wrist watch, everything you got." The man with the knife waved in front of the face of our warrior who remained calm and controlled.

"Yeah, you too, little woman, we want all of your jewelry." The other man ordered Denise whose eyes filled with tears of fright.

"NO!" Our warrior said a little more loudly and emphatically. The look on his face, hardened ever so slightly. There was a certain warning that was barely perceptible in the tone of his voice. The two would be assailants missed the warning.

"Hey, man, don't you hear too good? I said give it over to us, both of you." The one with the knife took a threatening step forward.

"Please." Denise let out a low cry as she trembled in fear.

Both men turned their eyes towards her, leering at her lustfully and threatening as she continued to tremble in fear.

"Yeah, let's take her with us and have some fun with her. Ha! Ha!" The man with the knife said as he took a step towards Denise who was trembling behind our warrior. "Yeah, we can make her beg for it."

Quick as lightening like a rattlesnake striking its prey our warrior reached out to the assailant with the knife and grabbed the wrist of the hand holding the knife; twisted the arm; brought it over his shoulder with his back to the assailant; and pulled the arm down breaking it at the elbow. The man screamed in excruciating pain and dropped to his knees. He released the knife, which our warrior quickly picked up and held in his right hand in an attack mode used by the Marines.

The tactic of grabbing an assailant's knife wielding arm and twisting it over one's shoulder and breaking the arm was something that he had seen his physician demonstrate in a karate class that he taught—the doctor had a black belt in karate. Our warrior remembered how to defend himself against such an attack.

"Don't even breathe hard." Our warrior took a step towards the other assailant with knife in hand. "Take your partner and get out of here or else."

Our warrior let the "or else" just sort of hang out there as a warning to the two men. The one man helped the injured assailant who was writhing in pain from his severely broken arm, up to his feet and they both scrambled away from our warrior.

"It's okay, Denise, you're safe with me." He whispered as he held her close. She was safe. She would always be safe with him. He was her protector, her "Knight in Shining Armor." He loved her like a Daughter. He was like an 'old warrior' sworn to protect the 'young maiden.'

For a few imagined moments I was in that other dimension of time and space in which I was an old warrior protecting a young maiden. Was it all imagined? It had been just a daydream. Was it all real? No, it had been all imagined. Could my mind tell the difference? Could my conscious or subconscious mind tell the difference between a daydream and a real event?

Denise was real. My pure affection for her was real. She was, as I had even told her Mother, a "very special young lady." I was her mentor and protector.

Who was I? Who was the real man? How much of me and how much of my character and personality was drawn from my dream warrior world? Or, could it be that my true character and personality were revealed in my dream world? Wasn't I a 'warrior' in both worlds?

So very often I asked myself the rhetorical question: "Why did I not commit suicide?" So very often I had prayed for the "Angel of Death" to take me during the night. How else could the emotional and spiritual pain end? NO one wants to die! Don't they just want the pain to end? At times the pain was so unbearable that it made my existence a horror.

Yet I was a 'warrior.' The question of suicide was only 'rhetorical' and no more than that. As repeated previously herein, I was hard and I was tough, I had been the "G. Gordon Liddy of Xerox", recognized by others in the company for my toughness. I admired Liddy because of the man's quality of toughness.

In my deep depression—or, was it just a deep sadness—at the time and in my discouragement, I had momentarily lost sight of who and what I was. I was a warrior. I loved battle. I was at my best when I was challenged and when I was at 'war.' Or, so I believed, or, so I imagined, or, so was my reality?

My daydreams were all about being a warrior and a hero. I may live alone but I was not a 'loner.' I yearned for companionship, for friendship, and especially for love. The warrior persona that dominated my conscious mind and subconscious mind built protective walls around me that prevented others from fulfilling my needs for companionship, friendship, and love. Why was it that I seemed to keep most people at arms length distance away from me?

Each day I prayed for my "woman, lady, lover, and friend"—that one special woman with whom I yearned to share love and life and passion. Yet I was alone without love; alone behind walls I constructed around myself. In trying to protect myself from the hurt that I had suffered in my marriage, I was suffering the worst hurt of all—a life spent alone. There was no greater hurt!

Why was I the man, and the warrior that I was? How had I become so? When, at what age, had I become such a warrior? It is such a redundant question for which there seems to be no answer—why was I the man that I was? How and why does any man become the man that he becomes? Do other men ask why they think the way that they think? Do other men wonder why and how they became the men that they are? Is it all a matter of a man's destiny?

Was there something deep within my dark subconscious mind that had created me to be as I was? Did I suffer an injury so severe and so traumatic that it was buried deep in my subconscious mind and that my conscious mind could not remember or recover it? Again, could it just have been my destiny to be as I was?

Such questions trouble me greatly. Did other men ask these same questions of themselves? I could not recall any event from my childhood, other than the suicide of my Father with me in the house that stood out as the even that defined me? Was I just being a 'Taurus?'

I had always valued warriors and stories about their exploits. Ancient History had been a favorite subject of mine in grade school. As previously remarked, I loved reading the stories of the Greeks, of the Spartans, of Alexander the Great, and of Roman warriors. Didn't I often envision myself as being a 'gladiator?' Every such role in a movie that I watched, I identified with it.

It is such a redundant question that I continually asked of myself—why am I the man that I am? Why is any man the man that he is? Does a man 'choose' to be the man that he becomes? What 'forces' in the subconscious mind and the conscious mind create each man to be as he becomes? Are there personality 'genes' and character 'genes' that are inherited and which define a man? What are the factors that make a man as he is? Does a man have any choice in who and what he becomes? Is the man that a man is today merely the reincarnation of the man that he once upon another time was?

The suicide of my Father while I was still just a boy; my experiences in the Viet Nam War; my bitter and heartbreaking divorce—these were the most serious traumatic events in my life—did they shape me into the man that I am? Such events helped to shape me but wasn't I always as I am today? Perhaps my Father's suicide was the one event in my life that made me into the man that I am, yet it just seems that I was shaped and formed long before then.

Again, if 80 percent of a person's personality and character are formed by the age of 5 years, it just seems that there are all of these forces and factors shaping a person before a person is even old enough to recognize them and to be aware of their influences—and certainly before a person can really choose to be who he or she wants to be.

Vito Corleone from 'The Godfather' would again remind all of us that: "A man has but one destiny." Who or what determines that 'destiny?' Who or what determines who and what a man will be? Is it all in the 'stars' determined at the moment of birth? Again it bears repeating—didn't God tell Job that He knew him while Job was still in his mother's womb? What does that mean—that God formed Job to be who and what he was before he was even born? Does each man's 'destiny' come from God?

I was who and what I was. It was not within me to be any different from what and who I was. Could my ex-wife be any different from who and what she was? Were we both victims of forces and events, which influenced and shaped us, which controlled us, over which we had no control? Could neither help who and what we were? Can any person prevent who they become?

Do other men ask such questions of themselves? Do other men wonder and ask of themselves: "how did I get to become the man that I am?" Do other men wonder how did their lives play out as they have? Surely other men, as they reached retirement age, look back in reflection upon their lives and wonder about all of the could haves, would haves, and should haves? Don't other men ask such questions and wonder?

I asked too many questions. As the author of Ecclesiastes in the Bible stated:

"To those with much wisdom comes much sorrow.
It was better to be the happy fool"

Towards the end of 1995 I accepted an opportunity to be a Sales Manager for another company—that job lasted 30 months. They downsized the number of sales managers and I was a casualty. I worked for three other companies as a Sales Manager until I finally ran out of job opportunities near the end of 2003. By 2005 I finally signed up for Social Security retirement benefits at my then age of 64 and it seemed that my formal work career was over. I felt really 'old' and quite useless. Remember—'a man is what he does.'

What had I done with my 66 years of life? What was I going to do with the rest of my life? How the heck was I going to accept that I had never truly shared love with a good woman? How was I going to accept that I had not ever really achieved the success that I once thought that I was capable of achieving? How was I going to accept that love, happiness, success, and financial wealth had eluded me and would most probably never be enjoyed?

How does any man, especially war veterans who left friends and comrades behind, deal with such questions and with the reality of their lives? Just how do other men deal with their thoughts and feelings? How does any war veteran answer the question—"did I earn it?"—in regards to having survived a close brush with death in war while others died?

The radio was playing Frank Sinatra's song—"That's Life"—and the words of that song put a big smile on my face—a really big smile as I laughed out loud to myself. Whatever hand of cards that Life deals out to a man—he has to play the hand that is dealt to him—even if it is a losing hand. That's life! Ha! Ha!

"There is no wealth better than health of body"
—Sirach

Every day I think about Ron and the 44 officers and sailors who died in the Oriskany fire on 26 October 1966. Such a thought enables me to be very thankful for being alive and very thankful for my life. I had married; I had Children; I had Grandchildren; I had my health; I was still alive 40+ years after that tragic fire. How many of those who had died would gladly trade with me? How many would trade their early death to have lived 40+ more years despite the outcome of those years?

Would those who died complain if they had enjoyed 40+ more years—even if those years had been filled with adversity, disappointments, failures, heartbreak, unanswered prayers, hurt, and pain? Would those 44 who died in 1966 gladly change places with me to be alive in 2007? Most likely YES!

What would they give to hear a Grandchild say to them: "Pop-Pop, I love you?" Wow! And so I was very thankful to be alive; to have been spared from death in 1966; and to have led the life that I have had for these past 40+ years.

What are the thoughts and feelings of other men, especially of war veterans, and how do they handle them? Are there any answers for any of us? And what is the bottom line to it all? The bottom line is that:

"That's life"—and life is good!

My nine years old Granddaughter and most special Princess visited with me for a week in July 2007. We went to the local and to the state zoo; we went to the local minor league baseball team's games; she made brownies; and we had a wonderful week shared together. The memories of our time shared together would remain in my heart and mind until I die. I hoped that she would also treasure the memories of the time she shared with her 'Pop-Pop.' I love her dearly!

I dearly love my Son, Daughter, Daughter-in-law, Granddaughter, and three Grandsons as high as the sky and deep as the ocean. I am so very thankful to God that I had been so blessed with them. They put all of my life in proper perspective—that I have been so blessed to have them in my life. Family is what it was all about—the rest really didn't matter much. For all of my thoughts and complaints about 'unanswered prayers—well—it seems to me that God has been answering a lot of my prayers all along the way throughout my life. I no longer felt depressed. The sadness was still there and it would probably always be there. But there was also the joy felt in every moment shared with my little family of loved ones. And there was the laughter, as when one of my twin Grandsons spoke up one day and said: "Pop-Pop is a knucklehead." What cartoon did he get that from? Ha! Ha!

I drove my Granddaughter back on a Monday. During the five hours drive back alone I heard a few songs on the radio, which affected me adversely by causing me to be reminded of my aloneness. Suddenly I felt the hurt and pain from all of the failures, adversity, evil done to me, aloneness, and unanswered prayers that I had suffered. I was alone and I felt a cold aloneness as my eyes filled with tears.

All of the unanswered questions filled my mind. If I stood at the grave of Ron and asked the question: "Have I earned it?"—I wondered about the answer to that question. Ron died at age 23 in 1966. I was now age 66 in 2007. Had I lived a life that 'earned' me these past 40+ years of borrowed time? I had lived my life on my own terms. I did not lie or cheat; I was honest and ethical in all of my personal and business dealings; I had lived by a strict moral code of honor. But, had I really earned these past 40+ years since the tragic fire aboard the USS Oriskany in 1966 in the Viet Nam War? The question haunts me, as I did not really know the answer to it. How would Ron answer me? I sort of felt like someone of whom it could be spoken:

"He had played by the rules at the game of life, but he had not won"

What of all of the other survivors of the fire aboard the Oriskany who, were still alive—did they ask such a question of themselves? It is a redundant question—how do other men, especially veterans of war, deal with their thoughts and feelings about their lives? Do they ask themselves whether or not they had earned it? How do they look at their lives as they reach the 'September of their years?'

I picked up my sword and my shield and I escaped into that other dimension of time and space in which I existed as a warrior and as a hero. As I entered into that 'dream world' mine tears subsided. My life was what it was. I was what I was. I was 'The Dream Warrior'! I accepted my destiny. I understood and accepted the truth in the words of Don Vito Corleone of "The Godfather" which have been often repeated herein:

"A man has but one destiny"

While my nights were lonely and my days were sad, I recognized that Ron and all 44 fellow officers and sailors who died in the Oriskany fire on 26 October 1966 would gladly trade with me—to have been alive these past 40+ years as I has been no matter what.

So—as the song on the radio played—I too wanted to just celebrate being alive another day! And isn't it possible that the best was yet to be? There was always tomorrow and all that it could bring! In an instant a man's life can be changed. I looked forward to tomorrow. I still buy lotto tickets! Amen to that!

I am damn happy and thankful to be alive!

978-0-595-51712-1
0-595-51712-9

Lightning Source UK Ltd.
Milton Keynes UK
13 September 2010

159808UK00003B/105/P